Robert Massey

G000231308

From *Able* to

Remark-

^ **able** /ˈeɪbl/ adj

be **able to** h

ledge to do so

Help Your Students Become Expert Learners

Crown House Publishing Limited
www.crownhouse.co.uk

First published by
Crown House Publishing
Crown Buildings, Bancyfelin, Carmarthen, Wales, SA33 5ND, UK
www.crownhouse.co.uk

and

Crown House Publishing Company LLC
PO Box 2223, Williston, VT 05495, USA
www.crownhousepublishing.com

British Library of Cataloguing-in-Publication Data
A catalogue entry for this book is available from the British Library.

Print ISBN 978-178583435-6
Mobi ISBN 978-178583457-8
ePub ISBN 978-178583458-5
ePDF ISBN 978-178583459-2

LCCN 2019945820

Printed in the UK by
TJ International, Padstow, Cornwall

Foreword by David Didau

At the start of my career as a teacher I worked for some years as a gifted and talented co-ordinator. Back in the early 2000s, the government of the day decided that more ought to be done to challenge the intellectual development of more able children, and, in turn, schools were tasked with the identification and monitoring of the small percentage of students at the top of the ability curve. As this was my first promotion, I threw myself into this task with a will. I combed through the results of cognitive ability tests, cross-referenced with attainment data and teachers' reports from the pupils' primary schools and drew up a list of anointed individuals who were to receive a bespoke package of educational excellence. I organised visiting speakers on a range of mind-broadening topics, funnelled students into improving extracurricular activities and generally made sure that they, their parents and the other teachers in the school knew just how special they were.

It was years later that I began to suspect that these endeavours were, although well-intentioned, entirely wrong-headed. It's become clear to me now that educational attainment is based, in large part, on how knowledgeable you are; the more you know, the better it's possible to think. No one, no matter how clever they believe themselves to be, can think about something they know nothing about. And the more you know, the easier it is to learn even more about the world. Academic success is founded on a triumvirate of background knowledge, the good fortune of having been born with an above average working memory capacity, and the determination to work hard and practise, practise, practise.

School is a sorting machine designed to separate the academic wheat from the chaff. Children who are identified as able are treated as able. They're put into 'top sets' or academic streams and fed more challenging content at a rapid pace. Children who present as being less able are put into more 'nurturing' environments where they're given less challenging material at a much slower pace. All this ensures a self-fulfilling prophecy; if children were not more or less able at the start of the process, they most certainly are by the end. So why would anyone concerned with the attainment of the most able focus on those who have already got themselves noticed?

While we may not remember how or why we found ourselves on a particular academic path, our route through education was almost certainly the result of some sort of feedback. Most human beings enjoy doing what they're good at and avoid what they're bad at wherever possible. If we're fortunate enough to find it easy to turn letter combinations into sounds, we're also likely to enjoy doing so. The more you do anything the better you get at it. A small early difference in the ease with which we accomplish a task is very likely to turn into a large difference over time. The result is, some children become fluent decoders and quickly move from learning to read to reading to learn. Because they read, they fill their minds with information they find much harder to acquire independently and their minds take on the qualities of intellectual Velcro: school stuff sticks.

But those who struggle soon perceive the difference between themselves and those fortunate peers they perceive as being 'more able'. Somewhere along the line, many children seem to acquire the belief that hard work and effort are a sign of being thick. Children who feel themselves to be 'rubbish at school' are likely to search for any other area at which they can excel – and, for many, this leads them to practising less at those things rewarded by the education system and, in far too many cases, more at those things teachers consider undesirable or anti-social. Maybe they become brilliant skateboarders, maybe they're fantastic at playing computer games, possibly they're amazing at applying make-up, but the belief that they're not cut out for school will probably be proved correct day in, day out. Correspondingly these children can sometimes seem to have minds composed of intellectual Teflon.

This no doubt sounds unnecessarily brutal, and maybe it is, but it certainly isn't fate. There is another way. The trick – if we can call it that – is to assume that all children are capable of remarkable things and, crucially, to treat them as if this is true even – and *especially* – when they don't believe it themselves. Robert Massey's book is written with this very much in mind. *From Able to Remarkable* is a guide for those who want desperately to believe that school can make a difference, that the way teachers act and interact with young people matters, and that every child is (or can be) remarkable. Robert's conceptualisation of the 'expert learner' should be seen as a message of hope and optimism. Being remarkable doesn't have to be the preserve of the few and the fortunate. With careful guidance and support, every child can become more expert at learning – and this, in turn, is likely to lead to a more positive and successful experience of academic education. Of course, not every child can or will become the next Einstein or Mozart, but that hardly matters. The real message is this: we are all capable of so much more than we believe.

David Didau, Algajola

Acknowledgements

Family first. Tom, Anton, Molly, Beth and Felix: this book is about you and for you. You have all been on your own remarkable learning journeys, and one of the joys of parenthood is in observing and sharing what each stage involves, and will continue to involve, for each of you. Paul and Maggie Greensmith have offered me wisdom and practical support as retired former teachers of distinction, as well as lending truth to the maxim that teaching runs in families. This book is dedicated with love to my wife, Annie, herself an outstanding teacher, coach and role model.

My own learning journey started in Luton thanks to two men who lived in entirely separate compartments of my young mind. Roy Meek, choirmaster and church organist extraordinaire, led by patient and kind example. Michael Miller at Challney Boys' High School was *that* teacher for me – the one who opened every door and made learning an essential requirement of life. I've written a little about him in this book but nothing like enough. A mutual love of music meant that these two polymaths knew each other in real life, of course. I hope they know the impact they have had on so many young people.

As the first person in my family to go to university, the conventional choice of a history degree took a twist as I was introduced to medieval attitudes, beliefs and events under the inspirational Christopher Allmand. Christopher's integrity, kindness and generosity as a teacher and thesis supervisor have been lifelong legacies of my years in Liverpool, not to mention a model of good practice in their own right. At Bancroft's, another fine teacher, Chris Taylor, took a rookie under his wing and showed me on a daily basis how much was to be gained from a hugely committed and dedicated classroom life: the same investment returned but with added interest. At Bristol Grammar School, I have been allowed the freedom to practise a lot of what I preach in this book, and I am grateful to every colleague, past and present, who has been part of this. If I name and thank Niki Gibbs, Paula Lobo, Andy Nalty, Mike Ransome, Richard Smith, Dan Stone and Colin Wadey, that is not to say that others have not contributed too.

Bristol schools have allowed me access to some of their great ideas and practices. This has included building meaningful networks and working partnerships, which are set to continue in exciting ways in the coming years. Two utterly inspirational primary heads, Inger O'Callaghan at Glenfrome School and Adam Barber at Henleaze Junior School, generously shared their time and expertise with me. Further afield, I have benefited from conversations with Mark Anderson, Alex Quigley and Nick Dennis. Watching Nick conduct the first

TeachMeet I ever attended at the wonderful Schools' History Project annual conference in Leeds some years ago was a turning point.

Without teachers sharing ideas, resources and opinions via blogs, tweets and teaching and learning conferences, books such as this would never be possible. I have profited over the years from hearing speakers as diverse as Daisy Christodoulou, Christine Counsell, David Didau, Tom Sherrington and John Tomsett: their knowledge and insight has been entirely my gain.

At Crown House Publishing, Caroline Lenton had the initial faith, which David Bowman and his team have exemplified since; my thanks to them all. My copy-editor, Emma Tuck, has brought clarity to confusion. Thank you to Russell Earnshaw for inimitable inspiration. Lastly, very special thanks to Nazuna Aida, once a high-attaining pupil at my school and now a remarkable illustrator of ideas. Naz, you have brought the text to life.

Contents

He paid the greatest attention to the liberal arts; and he had great respect for men who taught them, bestowing high honours upon them. When he was learning the rules of grammar he received tuition from Peter the Deacon of Pisa, who by then was an old man, but for all other subjects he was taught by Alcuin, surnamed Albinus, another Deacon, a man of the Saxon race who came from Britain and was the most learned man anywhere to be found. Under him the Emperor spent much time and effort in studying rhetoric, dialectic and especially astrology. He applied himself to mathematics and traced the course of the stars with great attention and care. He also tried to learn to write. With this object in view he used to keep writing-tablets and notebooks under the pillows on his bed, so that he could try his hand at forming letters during his leisure moments; but although he tried very hard, he had begun too late in life and he made little progress.

Einhard and Notker, *Two Lives of Charlemagne* (1969)

Introduction

Starting Our Learning Journey

> When teachers say to me, 'My job is to help kids reach their potential,' ... I say, 'No, it's not. Your job is to help them exceed their potential.'
>
> John Hattie, 'Visible Learning, Part 2: Effective Methods' (2011)

What do your remarkable students look like? You may be thinking of adjectives such as resilient, creative, intelligent, interesting, interested, compassionate and more. We might add to the mix terms such as adventurous and intuitive – perhaps the very qualities enshrined on your school or college's website as characterising your student body.

High attaining academically, these model students may also be excellent at drama, hit the high notes musically or play sport to a very good level, as individual players or as part of a school team. They will certainly be admirably adept time managers, able to juggle a raft of commitments and extra responsibilities, maybe on a school council or as prefects, all without seemingly missing a beat.

What has made them what they are? Were they born this way, or did their abundant capabilities emerge at primary school before they came to you? What has your school or college really done to help generate excellence in learning among these students? Such questions may make you feel uneasy, as they do me, prompting you to reflect on what is often labelled as 'gifted and talented provision' in your school. Perhaps, like me, you have been on external continuing professional development (CPD) courses or had some in-house training on this aspect of educational policy. And yet ... shouldn't we be producing more students like Emma, who went off to medical school, or Majid, who is now reading English at Oxford? We might think, 'Those two were great when I taught them lower down the school, and they seemed to have it even then – that desire to do well and a bit of confidence. Yes, they were a pleasure to teach, but when I come to think about it, they weren't the only ones in that year ...'

This book is designed to help. We need to change the way we think about producing remarkable students in our schools. When we do, the outcomes will be impressive in their own right and we will have irresistible impacts on every child, and not just the high-attaining ones. By making room at the top available to everyone, we make access to the top possible for all. This is not a book about the education of an elite; rather, it signposts a route to the top for every learner on their individual learning journey. By getting this approach right much else will fall into place. Wholesale changes to what you already do are not needed, spending on expensive new software 'solutions' is certainly not needed and the search for the legendary philosophers' stone, in the form of a particular magic teaching or learning technique, can be abandoned before it wastes your or anyone else's time.

This book offers five big ideas regarding provision for high-attaining pupils:

1. All students can and should become expert learners. There is no separate category labelled 'gifted and talented provision'.

2. Teachers make a difference to the learning of high-attaining pupils: *adults teach, students learn, students lead*.

3. Teaching to the top (and learning to the top) will make a difference because it will help to unlock the latent potential of every child in our classrooms.

4. The learning journey for all our students is lifelong and is undertaken for its own sake – for the love of learning, not the passing of exams.

5. Our expert learners will become remarkable students.

1. Expert learners

Here is an extract from my own school's (Bristol Grammar School) current mission statement:

> We aim high … and are proud to do so, inspiring a love of learning, fostering intellectual independence, and promoting self-confidence and a sense of adventure amongst our young. We set our sights on excellence in everything we do.

If you look at your school website, curriculum documentation or school enhancement framework you will probably find similar statements championing high aspirations and achievements, outstanding results and everybody's favourite, the growth mindset. There is nothing wrong with this. Indeed, it would be surprising and worrying were this not the case:

> Pupils at Acacia Avenue Academy do OK. The ones with high IQs we leave pretty much to themselves and they get the great results we all need. Phew! Middling ones who are polite and well behaved make reasonably good progress and some of them even get to university. Weaker students we support

well and get nearly all of them their core grade 4 passes so they can scramble their way into college and we don't get hammered by Ofsted. Standards are high at Acacia!

I doubt that many of us would send our child to a school like this in Year 7. If there is even a grain of truth in the caricature it is worrying. And Ofsted thinks there is (as we will discuss in Chapter 1): schools are failing on a large scale to stretch and challenge our high-attaining (or potentially high-attaining) students. It's not that as educational professionals we don't know what we need to do in order to improve student achievement. To a large degree we do. It's just that we don't seem to be doing it, or not sufficiently well or often enough to make a difference. It's what Dylan Wiliam (2018: 118), citing Stanford management professor Jeffrey Pfeffer, refers to as the 'knowing–doing gap'. This book aims to help fill that gap.

The book will reiterate some of what we know – in fact, quite a lot of what we already know and do as part of good practice – and aims to help teachers and schools kick on from there to start doing what works more consistently. A key premise is that we may be looking at our current Year 9s and missing their latent potential to be everything we see in that mission statement ideal student checklist. Likewise, there may be bright and eager Year 7s in our daily gaze whose dormant qualities as expert learners we are overlooking.

Forget easy labelling such as gifted and talented. Every pupil that you and I work with is potentially a teacher and a learner capable of excellence. If this journey is not worth taking, or at least attempting, then I don't know what education is for. Surely, it is worth doing for its own sake and for the greater good that will result. If we need more prosaic reasons, then Ofsted's *School Inspection Handbook* (2018: 60) states unequivocally: 'Inspectors will pay particular attention to whether the most able pupils are making progress towards attaining the highest standards and achieving as well as they should across the curriculum'. Quite rightly in my view, there is now an explicit reporting requirement concerning more able provision. The sense is that if provision for what Ofsted labels 'more able' pupils is satisfactory, then there is a good chance that other learning and teaching is likely to be achieving its aims. If not, then this is very much less likely.

2. Teachers make a difference

The second and most obvious proposition of this book is that we, as educators, have a large bearing and influence on the quality and quantity of the high-attaining students in our schools. It may be an alchemical process we don't fully understand, and it may well be that we disagree as individuals and institutions about precisely what proportion of influence and effect that we, as teachers, have on our charges and what may come from hereditary, family and other outside sources. Nevertheless, there is a correlation – if not a measurable, causal effect – between what we do (or don't do) and significant, lasting consequences for our students.

Despite the fact that we don't fully understand how we shape and influence young people towards successful outcomes, this is not to suggest that we should be leaving learning to chance. This would be like saying that med school high-attainer Emma just emerged because a 'bright student' always comes along eventually. Instead, this book puts teachers at the heart of a modelling process which is more akin to coaching than traditional pedagogy. Techniques for questioning, for feedback and for team activities model excellent processes and outcomes, which are then taken on by students, modified and improved according to context and then applied. *Teachers lead, students learn, students lead.* This simple mantra empowers students to become their own agents of change. They become responsible for their own learning journeys. They may even meet the accolade to be found on posters and websites in just about any school or college in the country: independent learner.

Our attitudes and actions as teacher-counsellors, teacher-supporters, teacher-motivators and teacher-role models help these journeys to happen and to continue towards successful outcomes. They are not the preserve of first-class ticket holders only. This is coach-class travel at an affordable price for everyone.

3. Teaching to the top

Every teacher has a desk full of anecdotes about that dreadful Year 8 boy who later became a prefect and went on to read engineering at Cambridge, for example. Stories don't make evidence but experience still counts for something. How dare we limit anyone's potential? All our students have abilities and remarkabilities. Perhaps we just haven't found them yet or they haven't shown them yet. If our lessons, games practice, chess clubs and school musicals are replete, and I mean absolutely replete, with opportunities for these abilities to emerge, then that is a fully fledged, live action high-attainer programme in action. If every sequence of maths lessons contains some spark and 'I never thought of that' moments, if year group assemblies leave staff and students feeling positive about the day ahead, if the geography department really sit down and plan how to turn 'routine' GCSE fieldwork into something memorable because of the learning and engagement it brings, then remarkable things will happen. As Andy Tharby (2017b) tellingly puts it: 'if we are to encourage more and more students to aim for the very top, then we must all play our part in the wider school culture – however immeasurable these actions may be'.

An academic culture needs to seep into every crack of conversation, meet-and-greet, lesson and assembly. Andy Tharby's school, in a coastal town taking in pupils from a wide range of backgrounds, is not afraid to tap into and shape peer and whole-school culture. I believe that modelling teaching to the top leads, via encouragement and repetition, to the students themselves setting high expectations for their own work and progress. If teachers lead to the top, students will learn to the top and then lead those around them in the same direction. Learning to the top then becomes a natural and embedded process because the students are becoming self-actualised, self-monitoring and self-aware learners who are capable of reaching remarkable heights. Scaffolding and support will be needed along the way as part of the rollercoaster journey that classroom learning represents, but that is something that we, as teachers, are already adept at providing.

Generalising hugely, but not totally inaccurately, in much of our educational provision in recent years we have made advances in our professional skill and understanding of supporting students with learning needs and those at the lower end of the ability spectrum. We are perhaps happiest teaching to the middle or just above the middle of the ability range of the class before us, catering best for the majority (as is reasonable) and occasionally remembering to set some stretch and challenge by way of a worksheet or extra reading for the bright ones. We worry about aiming too high in our own practice and leaving too many floundering in our wake. This is understandable professional caution, and no teacher or institution should be judged harshly for getting a lot right for a lot of pupils a lot of the time.

However, a different approach would benefit all learners. Tom Sherrington's influential 2012 blog post 'Gifted and Talented Provision: A Total Philosophy', was part of my own learning journey in terms of opening up the possibility that setting the bar high for all learners is both appropriate and practical. We are doing no student any favours by excessively simplifying, stripping away and reducing meaningful content to a bare minimum. Subsequently reading no-holds-barred Ofsted reports from 2013 and 2015, now reinforced by Rebecca Montacute's Sutton Trust report, *Potential for Success* (2018), has bolstered my thinking: a new approach is not just desirable but absolutely necessary. We are failing many students in our classrooms by not offering them the challenges they need and deserve. We are underestimating what they are capable of, in secondary schools in particular, by failing to build on the progress pupils make at Key Stages 1 and 2. This is a disconnect with significant social implications: the attainment or excellence gap whereby high-attaining children from disadvantaged backgrounds underperform in comparison to their peers is not being addressed. Learning to the top, based on modelling by teaching to the top, can help to address the issue squarely.

Allow me to clarify. Schools have been working hard for years to close the attainment gap between pupil premium students and non-pupil premium students. Likewise, schools have historically concentrated on their GCSE C/D borderline pupils (now levels 4/3) with considerable success. But have schools forgotten to focus on the need to raise standards for all, especially high-attaining pupils? Are teachers and schools afraid to 'push the top end' for fear of actually widening the attainment gap? If so, this may not be the right approach. It would be better to raise expectations for all and to bring all pupils to the summit.

4. Lifelong learning

This book unashamedly champions lifelong learning for learning's sake. Regardless of where individuals start from we can end up in unexpected and glorious places, having got there with the help not only of schools and teachers but also employers, public libraries, universities and many others. An unexpected and glorious place for me when I was starting my own learning journey as a child was Luton Central Library. It was new and big and exciting. I learned the layout, recognised the librarians and, even then, I think I understood something of what it represented and what the people who had built it wanted. I loved it and it really mattered to me. We had no books at home (where the word book meant magazine). Now, I had proper books.

Our journeys should be entirely self-justifying. Art for art's sake? Absolutely. Learning for its own merits and wider cultural value? In an altruistic society we should expect nothing less. We may need thousands of engineers if our future world is not to fall apart, quite literally, but we also need philosophers, dancers, authors and artists to interpret and reimagine those worlds, crumbling or creatively dynamic as they may turn out to be. We are not so well endowed with riches that we can afford to throw away the potential and capacities of any pupil in our care, because who knows what and how that child will contribute to the future? We can only be certain that they will offer something, so let's help to make it the best it can be.

That great educational success story of the twentieth century, the Open University, encapsulates this ideal perfectly (its significance is discussed in Chapter 10). Lifelong learning doesn't have to be this literal, of course, but anything we can do to foster critical, evidence-based thinking in our schools, alongside the acquisition of culturally enriching knowledge and then more knowledge, has to be worthwhile.

5. Able to remarkable

'It's not as if we never produce really bright kids, is it? Dr Emma came in the other day to say hello. She told me that Yolanda from her year group is now at university after taking a year out. Just goes to show!' What does it go to show, exactly? That the school offered an impressive programme of aspiration, stretch and challenge to the one and not the other? Yolanda's remarkable learning journey reminds us that students develop at different rates, both in terms of their academic attainment and their motivation to succeed. It also tells us that if we get the philosophy right of seeing all students as potentially remarkable and of viewing learning as a process, not an outcome, then we stand more of a chance of seeing Anna's fine achievement as normal rather than exceptional. Not to mention the equally meritorious successes of Maya retaking her maths GCSE or Tom's resolute adoption of coping strategies so that his mental health issues do not prevent him even thinking about a higher education course.

The great majority of activities and strategies included in this book are appropriate to all pupils and are not reserved for top sets or high prior attainers. It is hardly my job to tell you what suits your pupils. All I ask is that you keep an open mind as you discuss the approach and strategies in your department or school and consider whether they might work for you. I am taking as an absolute and irrefutable given that you, like every other teacher I have ever met or known, want nothing but the best for your students.

High-attainer provision has to compete for attention with many other major issues facing schools and education, including behaviour management, monitoring pupil premium provision and the attainment/excellence gap, to name but a few. Business seen as more relevant or more urgent trumps it on CPD days and in regular departmental meetings. An elite of high-attaining students can surely look after themselves for another week or term?

However, 'what aboutism' is never a strong argument to distract attention away from a central dilemma. The fact that education in the 2020s will face a number of key challenges and problems does not preclude us from asking some tough questions about why the purple prose of our school prospectuses and the anodyne adjectives of our mission statements are not grounded in the everyday reality of setting the bar high for every pupil.

Obstacles to overcome

However, there are significant obstacles in the way of this learning journey.

Firstly, if some official baseline data is to be believed, we are at a very low starting point. 'Failing', 'mediocre' and 'depressing' are not the adjectives we might expect to read about the education of high-attaining pupils in the twenty-first century, but these damning descriptions are taken from recent Ofsted documents on the state of more able provision in English schools. In particular, a report published in 2013, and a follow-up one in 2015, raise serious misgivings about the willingness and ability of some schools to challenge the underperformance of this cohort of children.

I'm going to pick out a few of the main findings of the 2013 report *The Most Able Students: Are They Doing As Well As They Should in Our Non-Selective Secondary Schools?* 'Most able' was defined here (and in the follow-up report) as referring to Year 7 students who had achieved level 5 or above in English and/or maths by the end of Key Stage 2. Some 65% of pupils achieving level 5 in English and maths at primary school did not reach an A* or A grade in both subjects at GCSE and 27% of them did not reach a B grade. In 20% of 1,649 non-selective 11–18 schools, not one student in 2012 achieved A level grades of AAB (Ofsted 2013: 4).

Such was the gravity of the findings that Sir Michael Wilshaw, then chief inspector of schools, felt that they challenged the very principles of comprehensive education:

> Too many non-selective schools are failing to nurture scholastic excellence. While the best of these schools provide excellent opportunities, many of our most able students receive mediocre provision. Put simply, they are not doing well enough because their secondary schools fail to challenge and support them sufficiently from the beginning. (Ofsted 2013: 5)

The report's key findings included:

- Schools do not routinely give the same attention to the most able as they do to low-attaining students.

- Teaching is insufficiently focused on the most able at Key Stage 3: too much work is repetitive and undemanding. Parents and teachers too readily accept underperformance.

- More able children receiving pupil premium funding lag behind their peers and are less likely either to be entered for the English Baccalaureate or achieve it.

- Able pupils who qualify for free school meals are particularly overlooked.

- University entrance is not a sufficient focus for many schools.

From over 2,300 lesson observation forms, the most able students in only a fifth of these lessons were supported well or better. In a few schools, the teachers didn't even know who the most able students were.

In 2015, Ofsted published *The Most Able Students: An Update on Progress Since June 2013*. Unsurprisingly, the picture had not improved in such a short time. Inspectors reported 'too much complacency' in many of the schools they visited, a 'glass ceiling' that too few leaders were ambitious enough for their students to smash, and a lack of prioritising for more able students. Unchallenging teaching was too often accompanied by low-level disruption, and there was a failure to provide more able students with the information and guidance to prepare for higher education, especially those from a disadvantaged background. In a monthly commentary in June 2016, Sir Michael Wilshaw was so cross about schools that were failing to meet their responsibilities to 'thousands of our most able pupils' that he proposed the return of national testing at Key Stage 3 and even sanctions, such as refusing to allow such schools to become academies.

Hugely important among Ofsted's findings is that disadvantaged pupils of high ability are consistently failing to make the progress they should from their starting points. This is an urgent issue of social mobility which we cannot ignore. The excellence gap must be tackled.

To add to this gloomy picture, a recent survey of the UK landscape for the education of the most able children by two respected former teachers and current experts in the field, Martin Stephen and Ian Warwick (2015: 6), offers a stark conclusion: 'The first [conclusion] is that provision for the education of the most able children in the UK is in major crisis, and declining to the level where if it were a species of animal it would be deemed close to extinction.' They characterise the UK as 'something of a desert for the teaching of gifted and talented children' (2015: 29–30), with viable schemes starved of funding and teachers given little training or the means to develop clear careers in this area.

Furthermore, we can't even agree on our terminology. Are our best students gifted and talented, outstanding, able, more able, high starters or just bright? And do labels matter anyway? It gets worse: we confuse ability and attainment. Oh, and IQ and intelligence. Whatever label a school or college applies, there is a natural tendency to treat high-attaining students as if they somehow just look after themselves emotionally. This is not the case. Many will have well-being issues which require and deserve as much care and attention as those facing other pupils.

Where to start? Heaven knows, we teachers beat ourselves up about everything we cannot do and would like to do, and now there are distinguished commentators telling hard-pressed, under-resourced schools that there is something else that we are getting very wrong indeed. There are 101 sound, structural reasons why provision for what Ofsted terms our more able students is not what it should be, but it is not the purpose of this book to start blaming schools and teachers for everything that has hitherto gone wrong.

Getting the approach right

If we are to address meaningfully the challenges of educating our high-attaining students, let's put the issue, and the students themselves, centre stage. Treating such provision as a fringe benefit for a lucky few is entirely the wrong approach to take.

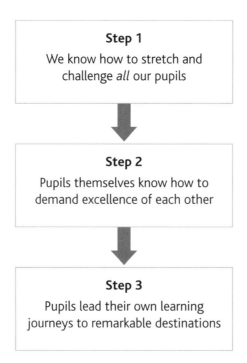

Step 1

We know how to stretch and challenge *all* our pupils

Step 2

Pupils themselves know how to demand excellence of each other

Step 3

Pupils lead their own learning journeys to remarkable destinations

If we know at step 1 how to stretch and challenge all our students every day, in every lesson or every sequence of lessons, then we go a long way to moving them all, and not just the elite few, from able to remarkable. Better still, if all our students themselves know how to demand excellence of each other (step 2), then we are even closer to getting the approach right. Something amorphous called 'good teaching' or 'effective teaching' will always be subjective and hard to pin down. But if we focus instead on how well teaching enables students to make good, effective and sustained progress, and then to behave as expert learners and as exemplars for those around them, we are more likely to have something worthwhile to measure and assess. *Adults lead, students learn, students lead.*

Of course, some students will always start with more intelligence than others (we will look at the contentious issue of intelligence in more detail in Chapter 1). Some will secure better exam results than others. Some will have stronger language, spatial or movement skills helping them to audition for and secure leading roles in the school play. Some will score more points at basketball than others because they have more fast-twitch muscles and superior gross motor coordination. This is a fact of life that no amount of positive thinking or equality of provision can deny.

Some students will simply be outstanding achievers in everything they do at school. But it is not for us as teachers, parents and educators to put caps and limits on any student. Putting a label on one child and not on another risks doing precisely that – unless our schools implement policies and practices which mean that, in effect, such labels are just a convenient, temporary shorthand and not a guarantee of anything.

I'm ready to start this learning journey – give me solutions, not problems!

Reassuringly, there is plenty to suggest that if we accept and address some of these issues, the steps we can put in place to modify and improve our daily practice are modest, attainable and will produce results. To nourish us on our way we can draw on the research evidence of, for example, Sarah-Jayne Blakemore, Dylan Wiliam and Daniel Willingham and access the websites and recommended further reading of the Education Endowment Foundation (https://educationendowmentfoundation.org.uk) and the Centre for Evaluation and Monitoring at Durham University led by Rob Coe (www.cem.org). Alongside this, we can implement the countless good practices currently adopted by many schools across the country. There is no need to reinvent the process of making fire because already in many schools the logs are glowing, the results are warming, and schools and teachers are happy to share their firesides. TeachMeets are integral to this. Even that once unwelcome visitor to the hearth, Ofsted, is happy to offer examples of observed good practice and pupil achievements, and surely deserves to warm its hands with us and contribute to a very necessary dialogue.

Meet your five expert learners

YOLANDA

TOM

MAYA

ANNA

ASIF

Anna and Tom sit in the middle of the ability rankings when they join your school in Year 7, although Tom's difficult home life has already been flagged up as a pastoral concern. Slightly below them in attainment sits Maya, who is thought to have plenty of potential by her feeder school but is lacking in motivation. Asif is a high attainer with sufficiently strong SATs scores in English and maths for him to join your high-attainer programme. You are aware from a primary school visit that Yolanda is another pupil of great potential.

Your students are not 'typical', and nor are mine. They have one shot at secondary education, so they and their parents/carers would like your school to do your best by them, offering as much stretch and challenge in as many areas of the curriculum as possible. As

Christine Counsell recently reminded us, the origin of the word 'curriculum' lies in the Latin verb 'currere', to run; she brilliantly defines curriculum as 'content structured *as narrative over time*' (Counsell 2018; original emphasis). Your runners and my runners need to finish, but they're not in a race – still less one which only rewards the first over the line. The aim is for each of them to achieve the best of which they are capable, whether they leave the starting line with prior training and genetic advantages or little experience of, or appetite for, running. Nor does the finishing line represent GCSEs or BTECs: it recedes as learning becomes lifelong. The narrative of the run will embrace ebbs and flows, ups and downs because it is more cross-country than track: runners can be pacemakers for others and help each other. The progress of our five expert learners will not be linear. What we may term their 'interim outcomes' as they hit one checkpoint – namely, the exam results they achieve and what they do upon leaving school at 16 or 18 – may be surprising.

This curriculum matters because its success or failure in supporting all our learners can be measured both *across* time among the peers and contemporaries of our five expert learners as they experience it from week to week, but also *over* time as students continue on their lifelong journeys. The significance of a curriculum which builds understanding via knowledge and skills in both dimensions can hardly be overstated.

What we will never find on our journey, of course, is a magic bullet or simple answer. Brain Gym won't do it. Yes, I sat through those sessions too. I was there for key skills and have the blister from rewriting every scheme of work. Finding every student's unique learning style won't address it – yikes, no. There are still posters of Edward de Bono's Six Thinking Hats on the walls of a department at my school. Those books were a cult back in the 1970s and must have sold millions. If the posters are just being used in light-hearted fashion to stimulate creativity in a lesson, then fair enough. But if any teacher can demonstrate that any of these methods produces a verifiable positive difference in learner outcomes, then I raise all of my thinking hats to them and will spend my next CPD session under an energy pyramid, stroking my black cat and reading my horoscope. Growth mindset has been seized upon by some with a fervour matched only by its detractors' gleeful criticisms. Even Carol Dweck herself has reservations regarding teachers who have adopted ideas that she never intended to apply in schools, and about which she professes little expertise.

As teachers we are as vulnerable as Year 7s to the new fidget spinner fad of the staffroom. What will it be this time: exit tickets? Pose-pause-pounce-bounce questioning? Visual, auditory and kinaesthetic learning styles (VAK)? Feedback? (It's got to be feedback – it always is!) The twin volcanoes of Twitter and educational research emit a lava flow of all-consuming intensity, so surely we can identify some riches among the fire and rubble? All these trends and fads can have the effect of leaving us jaded and judgemental, sticking to what we know for our bright ones. After all, it works for us, doesn't it – at least for some of our students, some of the time?

This can lead to what seems to be a logical position – namely, looking to other countries to see what works there and to recommend its introduction here. Every year we hear siren calls from commentators and journalists to look to the educational equivalent of the World Cup, PISA rankings, and to follow their lead to Scandinavia or South-East Asia. Whatever we are doing is flawed, and we can surely learn from these clever lands?

Forget Finland. With all due respect to Finnish educationalists, and the admirable education systems of other countries, what works for them will not necessarily work for us. Their achievements reflect structural measures introduced a generation or so ago, perhaps longer, because lasting change in education takes decades not months. Holiday anecdote is no match for peer-reviewed educational research worthy of the name. If we are to address the low starting points acknowledged by Ofsted and others, then solutions must be found in Teignmouth and Tynemouth, not TripAdvisor.

Read 'Rotherham' (Ryan 2018). Will Ryan's essay describes his recent journey to one of the country's most disadvantaged towns to trace the legacy of a man called Sir Alec Clegg, chief education officer for the West Riding until 1974. Clegg championed an 'ethic of excellence' in Rotherham's primary schools which was rooted in the local environment and in a sense of awe and wonder. At Thornhill and Ferham, Meadowview and Canklow, Ryan finds evidence of success in so many areas – from pupil values and sports to music and art to head teacher leadership and reducing teacher workload – all achieved against a backdrop of one of the most deprived communities in the country. His anecdotal evidence is corroborated by Ofsted. Solutions and inspirations may be closer than we think.

This book aims to offer a pathway for our learning journey through the gorse bushes of gifted, the underpasses of underachievement and the roadblocks to remarkable. Can we produce more students who are not just able but remarkable? Not just high-attaining but the highest attaining possible? Not just very good students but expert learners? I believe not only that we can but we must. On the one hand, we have to be aware of the demands of the society in which we live for more engineers, computer coders, nurses, entrepreneurs and app designers. If there is a chance for today's schools to produce another J. K. Rowling, Mary Beard or Tim Hadfield, let's not waste any more time. If that utilitarian motive is not sufficient – and it really isn't because we can't have much of a clue about the future needs of society and tend to get it horribly wrong when we try – then we can legitimately argue that helping to get the very best out of all our students is surely worth the effort as an aim in its own right, whatever the outcomes. That is what most of us came into teaching to achieve. Like politicians, we want to make a difference; unlike many of them, we really mean it. Learning matters for its own sake, not for Ofsted and not for an academy leadership team.

The message of this book should be an obvious and reassuring one: if something works with high-attaining pupils then it will work with all pupils. You do not need to find horcruxes amid the deathly hallows of learning and teaching before you can destroy the Voldemort of underachievement. No box of delights, no glowing magic key, no wizardry is needed. If you have robust, triangulated evidence that what you are doing currently offers best practice for your classes, then those good habits and practices will work for your brightest pupils. Conversely, there is no amount of self-delusion that a scheme of work currently aimed at somewhere in the middle of an attainment range will interest and stimulate those pupils – still less their high-attaining peers – to ask big, interesting questions or to make an unexpected connection. You are a teacher, not a magus. A trained and experienced professional, not a charlatan. Your pupils are typical, not geniuses. Spoiler alert: geniuses don't exist.

Here is my approach:

1. Make every lesson as stimulating and interesting as possible for as many students as possible as often as it can possibly be achieved in a sequence of lessons. Teach to the top – scaffold and support all students as necessary. Model these attitudes and activities so they become second nature to students who can then carry on the modelling themselves. Effective curriculum mapping is essential both within and between subjects to avoid repetition of content and approaches.

2. Treat all pupils as if they are capable of high attainment from the minute they walk into your classroom. Offer them all, without exception, opportunities to thrive and excel in drama, music, design technology, chess, Raspberry Pi and whatever the pupils themselves can offer each other and whatever your staff can offer. The ones who are currently high-attaining students may be among the first to take advantage, but they will not be the last once the word gets around: you will benefit from a changing cohort of interested and interesting pupils. Set the bar high and don't let it clatter to the ground when it's knocked off – just put it back.

3. Offer the best enrichment programme, personal, social, health and economic (PSHE) programme and extra-curricular opportunities you can, ideally with student input into what is created and how it is delivered and offered. Complementary curriculum design which recognises tangents and crossovers is surely, at least in part, the province of experts – namely, the students who experience it every day and can identify and isolate the fertile and the fallow.

Retrace your steps for a moment

Please go back to the list of qualities you noted for your outstanding students at the start of this chapter – you might have thought of a few more. Now think of a student or a class which you are convinced does not at first sight share these attributes. Are you sure? Have you observed them as part of a stage crew, playing basketball or tackling a sonnet? Have you done a 'pupil pursuit' and observed that student/class in the round during a school day (let alone a week)?

Perhaps I am guilty of motherhood and apple pie naivety, but so often when we literally move outside our classroom and look at the same pupils elsewhere, we see evidence of qualities and abilities not apparent when they are with us, for any one of a thousand reasons. But this does not mean that those attributes are not there in some part of a busy school week or outside school time.

My argument is that these remarkabilities are there, latent and dormant, in many more students than we might at first acknowledge. Anna and Asif may be unaware of what they can do or may be unwilling to acknowledge it – again, for many different reasons. Yolanda may be further along the route as a high prior attainer, with clear academic successes behind her at Key Stage 2 , but she too has not yet reached her destination. It's our job to bring these qualities to the surface within *all* our learners for the benefit of the whole school community. Maya and Tom know all about resilience and determination because they've been attending Scouts and they've both played football matches after school. But Tom's home life has been challenging of late and Maya has been in with a group of girls who have never seen the point of trying too hard in lessons. Helping all these students to create mental models of success for themselves will be part of their learning journeys. This will be made easier because they have shown the ability to do it already. We can help them to apply the deliberate, purposeful practice of hockey to history or from Scouts to science to encourage them to make themselves into remarkable lifelong learners.

Don't take my word for it:

> Dismantling students' own modest perceptions of what they can attain seems to me one of the most important priorities for classroom teachers. If we can set the level of challenge at a high level early in our students' secondary career, the better equipped they will be to tackle the increasing demands of GCSE and A Level. (Tomsett 2016)

This quotation from a characteristically personal and engaging blog post by teacher and head teacher John Tomsett strikes the key note. Teaching *Macbeth* to a Year 7 class of thirty, none of whom has ever learned Shakespeare previously? Of course it's possible.

Writing paragraphs of literary criticism using a point-evidence-analysis model? Yes we can, because Sir modelled it for us. Tomsett's approach created challenges for some learners who found the work hard, but he turned this to collective advantage by encouraging creative outcomes in the form of a sketch or a story on a class blog. Completing a full circle of benefits, parents heard some of their children's literary analysis at a subsequent parents' evening. This approach to mixed-ability teaching is unashamedly demanding and complex, but ultimately it is much more respectful of potential than many curriculum models based on setting and prior assessment data. Great material, a humane and flexible approach, uncompromisingly high standards and clear goals led to measurable progress and worthwhile outcomes.

Alongside the gauntlet thrown down by Tomsett to unpack students' own, often poor and limited, perceptions of themselves as potential learners comes another glove from me to make the pair. Some of the biggest obstacles to raising student attainment come from teachers, unwittingly and unconsciously. We don't provide sufficient challenge to our classes sufficiently often. We mistake noisy group work (or less often its opposite – a calm and quiet classroom) for purposeful activity. We cover a scheme of work and there is lots of green ink on books for the next work scrutiny. These and many other poor proxies for learning and student progress are the tripwires I negotiate every day, dodging a few and falling over others.

If, on a national scale, we are seriously failing to educate our high-attaining pupils in the numbers and to the standards that we should be – and as evidence suggests we are – then we, as teachers, the adults in the rooms, need to think carefully about why that is. For therein lies at least part of the solution. In subsequent chapters, I will be discussing activities designed to encourage students to think hard by leading them, or better still getting them to take themselves, into their 'struggle zones'.

Elitism

Spend time discussing excellence or scholarship in an educational context today and terms such as 'elitism', 'privilege' and 'posh' will soon emerge. Excellence = elitism. Scholarship = social superiority. The best = the least deserving. Independent schools such as my own are accused of all this and more, including gaming the system by choosing IGCSEs over GCSEs. Certainly, many independent schools have taken clear advantage of their freedom from national mandatory restrictions to maximise their chances of securing the results-driven outcomes which are among their benchmarks for success.

However, if public schools believe that dominating the top positions of national league tables makes them excellent, I would beg to differ. Exam results alone are a poor proxy for excellence; value-added scores are just one indicator to the contrary. Many independent schools already offer bursary support, but in my opinion they should be legally obliged by the terms of their charitable status to take in (at steeply subsidised rates) a much larger quota of students from economically and socially challenged backgrounds.

Where such schools have good claim to be offering excellence is in extra-curricular provision. Weekend sport, drama, music, lunchtime clubs and residential overseas tours are norms, not exceptions. High-attaining local pupils from families which could ordinarily provide few, if any, such chances are unquestionably as deserving of such opportunities as their more fortunate peers.

Countering charges of elitism requires schools in affluent neighbourhoods to accept the responsibility to lead pupils into an awareness of how other people live, work and are taught – in some cases, just a few streets away. Enrichment activities and PSHE and well-being programmes should be as carefully planned and as excellent in their outcomes and in the responses they generate as subject lessons. A school which has not looked long and hard at where it sits in a local and global context needs to do so if it is to deserve to be called excellent.

As a teacher in a large independent school, I realise that I am in no position to get preachy about elitism. I fully understand how privileged I am to work in such a stimulating environment where pupils want to learn and the first response to any planned activity or enrichment is always a positive one. I value it all the more because it does not resemble my own background and experience at school.

My former primary school in the centre of Luton no longer functions as a school – its Victorian buildings replaced by more modern provision nearby. Dunstable Road Junior School is now a Sikh temple, and it is a hugely uplifting (if slightly unnerving) experience to visit today and be greeted by friendly worshippers in what I vaguely recall as the school hall and classrooms. Luton abolished the 11+ early, and my subsequent move to the local comprehensive, Challney High School for Boys, offered wonderful, if somewhat patchy, opportunities to an eager learner such as myself.

We had Latin and Spanish but poor provision in the sciences and maths. Mr Miller is my all-time teacher hero. Old school, strict, hugely knowledgeable and inspiring, he was the librarian, a linguist and the conductor of musical ensembles. A typical first year (Year 7) French lesson would comprise French for ten minutes and then one of many possible diversions: he might respond to an innocent yet artfully planted question by reading to us a self-penned Mr Jolly story, or he might go off on one about Latin verb endings, or berate us for not reading enough fiction of the right kind. It was an unconventional learning journey but a simply magnificent one. Sandwiched between the M1 motorway and a Whitbread brewery (the school motto was the insanely appropriate 'cheerfulness and industry'), Challney offered some of the very best of the comprehensive system.

My dad worked in a car factory and my mum in the same factory's canteen. If this was educational disadvantage, I wasn't aware of it at the time. Later, I was the first in my family to go to university, and only went because there were no tuition fees and full grants were available. I am a classic product of a society which valued education and learning for its own sake. Mr Miller knew what excellence was and demanded that we all absorb it and aspire to it. The only time I went abroad as a boy was on the school trips he led. My own children have benefited in their maintained sector schools from similar excellent provision and teaching to the top.

This book's learning journey

In the first chapter, I set out some of the common problems besetting gifted and talented education, from definitions to roles. If schools and colleges have the appropriate terminology in place for their contexts, then they are ready to begin the journey proper. This learning journey begins with some stretch and challenge of its own.

Chapter 2 dares to ask students to construct an ideal lesson. It's a brilliant thought experiment in its own right, and one which puts trusting students at the heart of this book. Students want to learn and they want to learn more, more imaginatively, than we are often prepared to consider. That challenges me, for sure. They also don't like wasting time because they are often much better time managers than we give them credit for. Therefore, Chapter 3 looks at recent work on deliberate, purposeful practice and champions this approach as a more credible, evidence-backed alternative to a lot of what passes for 'gifted' interventions.

Learners can learn to be expert, as Chapter 4 outlines, by improving their abilities to receive, respond to and then deliver feedback and reflection on their own work and the work of others. In Chapter 5, collaborative learning offers some immediate stretch and challenge to our own perceptions of high-attaining students by asking them, and us, to be creative about using team learning both in our lessons and outside them. I've also included here some examples of what Ofsted has praised in recent inspections.

Chapter 6 looks at questioning strategies suitable for all pupils. The focus in this chapter is on practical classroom methods to make questioning, self-review and greater student ownership of questioning within lessons integral to what we do.

Then the journey resumes full tilt on the learning rollercoaster of Chapter 7, where I argue that progress for all students is often uneven and frightening but that with careful scaffolding and support the ride to the top can be exhilarating. The neglected topic of the well-being of high-attaining students is the theme of Chapter 8, which aims to bring previous chapters together.

In Chapter 9, I ask the question, 'What does the remarkable student look like?', addressing whole-school provision for our renaissance scholars and offering advice to make sure that we are getting the approach right. Finally, Chapter 10 offers some robust stretch and challenge of its own to educational leaders in a section which aims to open up debate about what excellence in education might look like.

This book necessarily touches on a good many issues relating to learning and teaching, but, inevitably, it cannot do anything like justice to many of them. I've tried to write about what I know and leave to others far more expert the many areas of which I am ignorant. This book is written by a practising teacher for practising teachers. I have been a history teacher for twenty-eight years, including fifteen as a head of department. In recent years, my interests have broadened to encompass the education of high-attaining students. For the last six years, my role in school has been as director of scholars. As part of that change of role and focus I have joined the large and hugely stimulating company of teachers sharing ideas on Twitter. I organised Pedagoo South West in 2014 with Mark Anderson and Rachel Jones and have presented at plenty of TeachMeets and internal learning and teaching days.

This book is informed by evidence and reading, but it makes no claim to offering a definitive and authoritative overview of a neglected area of educational provision. The neglect is surprising, which is why I wrote the book. Teachers are magpies, but I offer here my own approaches and ideas to discuss in your college or school. Where I have borrowed from others I have said so. If this book offers useful guidance and practical strategies to help colleagues then it will have fulfilled its modest aims. Suggestions for further reading are included in the bibliography.

Part I:

Starting Our
Learning Journey

Chapter 1

What's in a Name?

From Able to Remarkable

We can maximize the intelligence of all students by ensuring that all students are exposed to maximally challenging environments from as early as possible for as long as possible.

Dylan Wiliam, 'Measuring "Intelligence": What Can We Learn and How Can We Move Forward?' (2005)

Key themes

- Teaching to the top means getting the approach to provision for high-attaining students right, and that begins at whole-school level with a common currency of agreed and appropriate names and labels.

- Whatever names and labels are chosen as appropriate for a particular college or school, everyone in the school community needs to know and understand what they mean.

- A rich and stimulating school environment will make more of its pupils more intelligent, remarkably.

- Expert learners are made, not born. Excellence in classrooms should be the outcome for the many, not the few.

All kinds of names and labels are attached to more able provision, and it is no one's job to tell a particular school or teacher what is right or wrong about any given appellation, provided that its implications have been considered and the context is appropriate. Certainly, public bodies such as Ofsted and universities are entirely relaxed about what schools and colleges consider suitable for their needs, and this includes nomenclature. If your school or college has thought about your terminology and it forms part of a coherent approach and policy, you can safely treat comments from an outside source as friendly advice and an alternative perspective rather than instruction from on high.

For me, 'excellence' is the most relevant and overarching term to apply. If 'gifted and talented' has any redeeming merits as a label it is because it implies an association between a pupil and excellence in one or more areas. But other terms make the same connection without connotations of preordained, deterministic advantage, which is why they are much to be preferred. What matters is that pupils are being stretched and challenged. Not just some – the scholars or the high prior attainers. Everyone, all the time.

Excellence for the many, not the few

Ruth Powley is a deputy head at a secondary school in Cheshire. At a talk I attended in 2013, she made the excellent point that students sometimes self-limit their expectations and abilities in order to fit a 'life script'. This certainly throws into question the '5% gifted and talented' model some schools use. Ruth advocated a school ambition plan and an aspiration programme for students and parents with guest speakers, university visits and financial advice about higher education. I would endorse this. My own counsel would be to include students and parents in establishing and reviewing a high-attainer programme.

What does this wider community regard as student excellence in music, maths or electronics? How would pupils label their peers, and why? Do parents understand your current system in the same way that teachers do? Some student voice work or SurveyMonkey evidence may well throw up interesting insights about what your community wants from a programme for high-attaining students. What methods are currently being used in your school to differentiate high-attaining pupils, and do the pupils think they are working?

The same point applies, of course, to learning support students. In my school, the assistant head of learning support sees every learning support student once a term expressly to complete a questionnaire about whether the reality of lessons matches the fine words of the departmental policy. The results for each year group are then distributed to heads of subject. This is evidence from the chalkface to triangulate against book scrutinies and learning walks, among other information. What would be the result in your school of a similar survey among your high-attaining pupils? Learning support students need access to high attainment too.

When I started thinking about this subject, my initial view was that labels mattered little. Provided that the approach was right, talking about Asif and Yolanda as 'high ability' or 'bright' or whatever was fine because the school setting contextualised the label, and a good fit was almost always assured between expectations and outcomes. But then I realised that what we call things in schools does matter. At a whole-school level labels set tones. They give evidence of those elusive concepts – the ethos and culture of a school. If a head is keen to re-examine or change the culture of a school, she can gain a quick and easy win by looking at why things are called what they are, from classrooms themselves to groups of students to areas of school life. In my school, I've advocated the use of 'enrichment' to replace 'activities'. If we value what staff and students are sharing as more than just doing something together at the same time (activities) but see it as deepening and making more valuable that shared time together, let's choose a name for it that reflects what we aspire to (enrichment). By itself a new name may be seen as mere window dressing, but if it foreshadows and accompanies a changing attitude and approach to an area of school life then it is justified as being more than cosmetic.

Labels stick to us

Labelling pupil groups is more problematic. Do we tell pupils their labels? What happens when one boy works out that he is in the middle set or, far worse, bottom set? Is he branded for his whole school career? The setting may legitimately be based on Key Stage 2 outcomes, but once in a set, do the expectations of the teacher and the pace of learning mean they stay there for the duration of their school career? How can their learning trajectory change? What kind of learning journey are they on if they have no parental support or a limited interest in, and familiarity with, school structures?

Some teachers with pastoral roles say that tackling inflated or unnecessarily deflated student self-esteem is one of the biggest challenges they face. Having a programme, or even just a designated level, for high ability students leads to inevitable questions about the rest – necessarily constituting a majority of the school. Ideally, therefore, labels will be as neutral and evidence informed as possible in accordance with professional standards and the culture of the school. This is another reason to prefer, for example, 'high attainers'.

My wife teaches in an academy chain which uses HPA, MPA and LPA (high, middle and low prior attainers). I like this and can see few difficulties in explaining to a governor, parent or pupil what this means and why a particular label applies to Anna or Maya right now. The terms are benchmarked to data and not end capped. If students can move from red to amber to green without waiting a term (or worse, a full academic year); if the terms are light-touch, professional guidance rather than dead weights in marble attached to a girl for her entire school career; and if they are subject to challenge and review (what else is data for?) rather than fixed in a folder on a deputy head's shelf (not desk), that's fine.

There is another reason why we can't just follow the nursery rhyme and say that 'names will never hurt us'. Remember my story from John Tomsett in the Introduction about teaching Shakespeare to a mixed-ability Year 7 set to a very high level? My view is that when a teacher takes a class for a period of time without knowledge of prior attainment or target grades, but just teaches them with high expectations and no sense of whether they are of middle ability, for example, the outcomes improve. This may be anecdotal and unscientific, at best correlation rather than causation, but it is something to ponder. Consciously and unconsciously we may all be much more deeply and subtly influenced by descriptors than we would like to think. An argument from this is not to have special programmes at all for high attainers and perhaps to not even set at all, but to offer a genuinely comprehensive education in every classroom. That would be excellent. The following table sets out some of the issues surrounding the labelling of high-attaining students.

Label	Positives	Negatives	Comments
Gifted	A familiar term, especially in the United States. We know that it somehow equates to being clever. There is merit in keeping to names and meanings which we all recognise.	It implies an innate ability and perhaps a genetic advantage (e.g. 'a gifted linguist', 'a mathematics student of rare gifts'). It is confused with 'talented'.	The term traditionally identifies a student having abilities in more than one academic subject. It is an older term which does not reflect research in behavioural psychology. What room does 'gifted' leave for attainment? What account does it take of effort, motivation or the adept cultivation of effective study habits? While it may be a useful shorthand in education circles, it should be abandoned.

Label	Positives	Negatives	Comments
Talented	As with 'gifted', there is an implication of excellence.	As with 'gifted'.	The term traditionally identifies a student having skills in a broad area – for example, sport or art. Again, the term implies innate abilities which pupils either have or don't have: 'She's really talented in the creative arts.' Deliberate, purposeful practice always underpins any so-called talent. The term should be abandoned.
Outstanding	In common use, so widely recognised and applied.	Outstanding by comparison with whom? In one subject or all?	Qualifiers such as 'outstanding' convey a common-sense meaning and therefore have a place in the busy world of schools. If used more narrowly to identify a cohort of high-attaining pupils, however, they should be benchmarked: outstanding in relation to what level or target or cohort of pupils?

Label	Positives	Negatives	Comments
Able/more able	In common use, so widely recognised and applied. These terms are commonly used by official bodies (e.g. Ofsted, Department for Education).	These are comparative terms which beg many questions: are these synonyms for 'bright' students or do they refer to particular, defined cohorts?	As with terms such as 'outstanding' there is a case for being relaxed about the everyday use and meaning of 'able' and 'more able'. However, there is confusion between ability and attainment – see discussion on page 37. 'More able' than which pupils, and at what data point?
High achievers	In common use, so widely recognised and applied.	'High' in relation to what? What achievements are being measured, and why?	'Achievement' is a useful overarching term which includes, for example, academic attainment but can also incorporate musical or sporting accomplishments, among many others. Careful definition is needed of how these pupils' performances are being measured in relation to their cohort. Are outcomes being end capped because the achievement has already happened?

Label	Positives	Negatives	Comments
High attainers	A precise term which readily lends itself to definition by referring to statistical outcomes from an identified cohort of students.	'High' in relation to what – a past target, current performance or future expectations? What attainments are being measured, and why?	'Attainment' is a helpful term which focuses on reaching or exceeding an academic target; it fits nicely within the wider label of achievement. This term will suit some schools. But … attainment is not the same as ability. High attainment may be unevenly distributed – for example, to girls at GCSE or to higher socio-economic groups.
High prior attainers (HPAs)/ high-attaining pupils (HAPs)	As above. It keeps attainment under review and acknowledges that changes can happen in the future.	As above, but it allows students who have made progress to join the cohort.	High current attainers (HCAs) is another variation used by some schools. These terms are data supported and will suit many schools.

Label	Positives	Negatives	Comments
High starters	This term attempts to move away from ideas of fixed or innate ability by acknowledging that even the more able students in a cohort can make progress, with no limits.	Is the term sufficiently well-known and understood to be meaningful?	This term is gaining in popularity. It has the great merit of not seeming to cap progress, unlike 'high achievers'. It posits a promising beginning and not an end. But ... does it risk being seen as a synonym for 'gifted' – that is, these pupils start from a higher position than their peers. But what? Higher IQ? Higher capacity? What is the starting point, and how high is it?
Scholar	This word emphasises academic ability but can be refined (e.g. drama scholar, sports scholar). It has strong associations with high attainment.	This bears 'public school' or 'posh' implications. It has unavoidable associations with exclusivity.	Ofsted now embraces the term 'scholar' and unashamedly refers to 'scholarship' in inspection reports. This term works in the context of my own school but may well not work everywhere.

For the purposes of this book, I will use 'high attaining' as a suitable descriptor for students performing at a significantly higher level than their peers. This term has the benefit of precision because it can be referenced to a set of data. Where it seems contrived and inflexible to stick to a single term, I will use the common sense labels 'more able' or 'highly able' still deployed by official bodies such as Ofsted, although that usage may change in future. Rebecca Montacute (2018) defines highly able students as those with high attainment but also the potential for high attainment, and I like this inclusive approach. These terms are all freer, in my view, from associations with terms such as 'gifted' which are redolent of predetermined, genetically advantaged skills which are less susceptible to development, challenge and further growth.

Criticisms of gifted and talented schemes

This is by no means the end of the argument regarding gifted and talented programmes, however, regardless of labelling. Detractors accuse them of being socially and educationally divisive and damaging to the majority who are not selected for such schemes (Quigley 2016). Selective schemes have been found by the Sutton Trust to include few students receiving free school meals and are charged with widening social inequality (Smithers and Robinson 2012). Meanwhile, those fortunate enough to be chosen for such programmes bask in the glory and extra attention and do well – perhaps as they would have done anyway. The net result is a heavily imbalanced negative outcome.

Where such programmes and outcomes are found to exist they are clearly not working and should be scrapped. Nothing justifies the maintenance and worsening of the attainment/ excellence gap which currently sees thousands of high-attaining students from disadvantaged backgrounds doing proportionately worse than their peers. A school which feels the need to invent a club with badges and brooches for its most polite and well-behaved high-attaining students with the neatest uniform and winning smiles should ask itself some tough questions.

But this does not equate to a fatal criticism of programmes to support and stretch high-attaining students in themselves. Poor examples should not drive general practice. This need not be a binary question of very high attainment for a few and a reduced or middling package for the many; recent Ofsted evidence (2013, 2015) (summarised on pages 8–9) and Sutton Trust research (Montacute 2018) (summarised on page 244) has consistently revealed too little focus on high-attaining pupils and their outcomes, not too much. It would be hard to overstate the seriousness of the findings of recent inspection evidence about a lack of progress in core subjects from Key Stage 3 to Key Stage 5.

The Sutton Trust aims to help improve social mobility. In 2011, it set up the Education Endowment Foundation (EEF) to commission and fund research into which learning and teaching strategies can best help to close the attainment/excellence gap. EEF reports are already making a valuable contribution to educational practice by subjecting practices to rigorous quality control and evaluation. Interestingly, a Scholars Programme is offered by the educational charity, the Brilliant Club, to place postgraduates in state schools to deliver university-style tutorials to high-attaining pupils and take students into universities. Pupils as young as Year 6 take part in activities 'designed to emulate the learning that students experience at highly selective universities' (https://thebrilliantclub.org). Their work is similarly subject to scrutiny and it is very much to be hoped that this initiative is assessed as making a difference to young learners' expectations and life chances. It surely offers a valuable bridge to higher education for those who might not otherwise have considered it.

Contrariwise, teaching to the top and a common understanding of what the top actually looks like in daily classroom practice helps to drive up attainment for all, not just the few. Inflexible, bolted-on gifted and talented programmes certainly won't have much effect, but an approach for identifying, nurturing and modelling excellence using high-attaining pupils as models and expert learners can have a snowball effect to the mutual benefit of every learner. One size does not fit all. If a specialist programme is inappropriate for your context, don't bring one in for its own sake or for some perceived benefits. Your school or college will benefit from the thinking and discussion process with students and parents centre stage, from the formulation of the policies and, more importantly, from the daily practices which will ensure that all students – of whatever background and apparent ability – are being stretched and challenged in every single lesson or sequence of lessons.

How should you identify your high-attaining students?

All schools are awash with data, and important among it will be Key Stage 2 SATs and other results from primary schools, which constitute valuable evidence of prior attainment. If it can be supplemented by additional, qualitative information from feeder schools obtained via liaison visits, so much the better in terms of obtaining a rounded picture of that most elusive of qualities – pupil potential. Some schools then administer their own internal pencil and paper tests or use commercial packages from, for example, the Centre for Evaluation and Monitoring (including MiDYIS, YELLIS and Alis) in a sequence of stages to gain further evidence of where pupils sit in relation to each other. UK Maths Challenge data can also be useful, as can evidence of success in a local, county or national sport or chess tournament.

Whatever method or combination of methods a school uses, the key idea is to keep the identification of high-attaining pupils as open and flexible as possible. It may seem fair to identify as high starters the top twenty in each year group, based on performance in a series of verbal and non-verbal reasoning tests. But taking these tests is not a level playing field: pupils can improve with coaching and practice. The question then is what role is given to teacher insight and experience about the performance of these pupils and their peers during the year? Are these places fixed and immutable or open to review? Students' learning journeys are so varied and inconsistent that it seems unfair to exclude a student who has made outstanding progress during the year, who then wonders just what it is they have to do to join the programme. Nomination to, and continued membership of, a particular high-attainer programme should be a transparent process for a school community. This is not as easy to achieve as it is simple to state because many kinds of misconceptions can readily arise, but it should be an aim nonetheless.

The G&T coordinator

Many schools have a 'G&T coordinator' – a role I currently hold myself. The context and circumstances of each school and college are different, so it is not for me to lay down rules about how this should work in practice, but I would make the following observations for discussion in your institution.

The person responsible (ideally more than one) for provision for high-attaining pupils should themselves be a member of a senior leadership team (SLT), or at least should report directly and regularly to a school leader (typically a deputy head academic). After all, best practice and provision for high-attaining pupils is best policy and practice for every pupil in the school. A 2007 case study of provision in twelve London schools for 'able, gifted and talented' pupils found that 'best practice for able pupils is best practice for all pupils' (Wallace 2007: 2).

Many schools delegate responsibility for guiding and monitoring provision to a member of each department. This seems to make sense, in that how successfully a whole-school initiative works for high-attaining pupils in biology might be very different from the context in the PE department. What often happens in practice, however, is that a focus on high-attainer provision is lost among the plethora of demands on the time and energy of a colleague on a full teaching timetable. The result is a token commitment which is acknowledged in policy documents for compliance purposes but seldom makes a genuine difference to departmental provision, let alone whole-school practice.

It is better to devolve responsibility for all learning and teaching within departments to the head of subject. He or she is typically better placed, thanks to work scrutiny and appraisal, to monitor what is going on and how it can be improved, sharing good practice via department meetings. The head of subject knows what is happening at a nuts-and-bolts level in books, folders and classrooms. She is best placed to navigate the sensitivities of scrutinising books and the etiquette of entering classrooms to see challenging questioning in action. She can follow up on feedback to and by high attainers and discuss effective pupil debating at the next department or faculty meeting. At that meeting, of course, item 1 is always learning based. I endorse Montacute's (2018) recommendation that a group of teachers are trained to implement and monitor provision for high attainers. This will help to ensure that good practice is learned and shared within a school or across a multi-academy trust and that, for example, pupil premium funding is used effectively to support high-attaining pupils from disadvantaged backgrounds.

If schools follow this suggestion, it has the benefit of placing the G&T leads at the heart of learning and teaching. I think that is exactly where they want to be and should be.

They need to work with every head of subject to monitor provision and share what works between departments, insofar as it is practicable. The evidence gained is gold dust in terms of supporting the SLT in their moves to improve outcomes. If pupils are being challenged in every lesson or sequence of lessons, and if the G&T lead has chapter and verse evidence of this in at least some areas of school, then their role is being fulfilled.

A quick word in this context on those much maligned teachers: the SLT. Senior leaders need a flow of information about any obstacles to high-attainer learning – for example, a behaviour management issue. What is sometimes disingenuously termed 'low-level disruption' can adversely affect a teacher's choice of activities to the detriment of all learners, not just high attainers. SLTs and academy leadership teams (ALTs) need to be alert to behaviour problems, but they have more of a chance of picking up on it from heads of subject with high-attainer provision as part of their remit or from a group of teachers trained to monitor high-attainer outcomes than from a single G&T lead. It follows logically from this that if every single SLT meeting doesn't include discussion of learning and teaching, then it is not fulfilling its core purpose.

My advice is for G&T coordinators to embed themselves first and foremost in lessons across the curriculum and to gather evidence from a range of subjects and teachers. Only when this is underway should the focus move towards the many other pleasurable aspects of the role, such as lunchtime clubs or after-school activities. Visits to local sites of interest, university days and cultural opportunities, such as a play or film, are all used brilliantly in many schools as enrichment for more able students. Among the many benefits of such visits are the boost they can give to the self-esteem or the often neglected well-being of these pupils. It is very much up to individual institutions to decide who should benefit from such opportunities and why. The point I am making here is that any high-attainer programme is open to well-merited criticism if the primary concern of the staff who run it is anything other than monitoring and modelling a diverse range of stretch and challenge activities within routine lessons. Enrichment within the curriculum can then, and only then, be set beside extra-curricular or co-curricular visits to create a holistic framework for success.

Bristol Grammar School Scholars' Programme

At Bristol Grammar School we have a Scholars' Programme from Year 7 to 13 which covers all academic subjects but also art, dance, drama, music and sport. Most pupils enter it following an entrance test in Year 6 and then an interview with the headmaster and myself.

Those who come for interview have high prior attainment in verbal and non-verbal reasoning and in English, but what we are looking for in conversation is 'spark'. Is there a curiosity, a sense of adventure and evidence of potential? We are acutely aware of the pressures both of the process and the role, so we consider carefully the likely well-being of a young pupil as a Scholar. Will they be comfortable in the role? Not all pupils mature intellectually and socially at the same rates, so our Scholars' Programme remains open, and each year we look at data and make additions all the way through to Year 11. In the sixth form, students apply to be a Scholar in one subject only, which is likely to be one they intend to study in whole or in part at university.

All Scholars benefit from a programme of enrichment: I take them to a play, the opera or a basketball game and strongly encourage them to attend school concerts and visiting speaker events. Bristol has a Festival of Ideas, art galleries and cultural centres, so Scholars have no excuse not to take advantage of a range of opportunities on their doorstep. We expect Scholars to be 'beacons' on the games field, when enjoying a cookery enrichment session and in lessons.

The Scholars' Programme is not for everyone. We monitor academic progress and well-being, and when a student is unhappy or underperforming then conversations begin in order to arrive at the best solution for the student, parents and school. Sometimes students leave the scheme. Sometimes pupils who merit inclusion in many ways don't quite make it, which can be difficult. Our Scholars' Programme is very much a work in progress.

There are no events which are 'Scholar only' – for example, a science, technology, engineering and mathematics (STEM) event aimed at girls in Year 9 will be offered to the best female scientists of that year group regardless of whether they are Scholars.

There is another important, and arguably more important, strand to my role: I visit lessons and talk to heads of subject about what works for them in offering stretch and challenge in lessons. I offer CPD sessions at a whole-school level and share strategies which aim to improve learning and teaching appropriate to high-attaining pupils across the school, including our junior school. I'm trying to embed myself in the culture of learning and teaching in the school and to offer insight and information into how it is or isn't working.

Ability and attainment

Ability and attainment are not synonymous. Ofsted consistently and persistently uses 'most able', even though, as educational analyst Tim Dracup points out, this can be taken to mean almost half of a Year 7 cohort and as a definition it is actually based on prior attainment. I'm indebted to Dracup (2015, 2016) for his observations on this subject. *Attainment* is defined in the finest single-volume dictionary in the English language, Chambers, as 'achievement, especially after some effort'. Attainment is often represented in schools as a standard distribution, the so-called bell curve, with results clustered around the mean. When the new GCSE grading system was introduced, one of the justifications was that it would more finely distinguish very high levels of attainment than the old A* by offering new attainment levels of 9 and 8, and so stretching the curve. Attainment is often used to indicate what a student can do now or very recently (according to the latest data drop); alternatively, it is often labelled 'prior attainment' and will be related to primary school data such as a Key Stage 2 SATs score.

Ability is defined as 'the power, skill or knowledge to do something'. It therefore refers to a broad spectrum of characteristics or potential characteristics. When considering pupil ability, schools may have access to prior attainment data and teacher-based reports and, like some universities, may try to interview students who perform above a certain threshold so that decisions are based on correlated evidence. Cognitive Abilities Test (CAT) scores or verbal and non-verbal reasoning paper outcomes are valuable, but can be improved by training, and training can lead to gaming. The ability to pass a test does not necessarily predict suitability for a particular educational experience.

So, trying to assess ability is often educated guesswork. It can be unfair and plain wrong. Attainment is not infallible either. High prior attainers can suffer dips in outcome and middle attainers can beat them as their knowledge and understanding increase. However, this is not to say that every student in our care can become a high attainer. Tim Dracup (2017) cites international data from PISA and TIMMS to argue that even in countries where students' performance in standardised tests outstrips that of England and Wales, they struggle to broaden the numbers of students attaining such results.

High ability is widely spread across a population but high attainment is not. If we want a truly excellent education system, we should be increasing the proportion of students attaining at the highest level in international comparisons and in our own public examinations (what Dracup calls the 'smart fraction'), while at the same time closing the excellence gap so that those from disadvantaged backgrounds are helped to catch up more quickly than their advantaged peers.

Gene machines?

It would be remiss not to acknowledge the nature vs. nurture debate and its implications for stretch and challenge within the classroom. So far I've argued against the use of terms such as 'gifted' because they imply successful outcomes solely or very largely caused by the genetic advantages of, for example, greater processing power and verbal reasoning capacity. But as every teacher knows, some pupils are more intelligent than others: they can do more with what they know and do more with it faster than others. Learning to read and acquire vocabulary, learning maths and learning languages happens more easily and can be taken by such pupils to a higher level. Intelligence is strongly influenced by our genes, and the genes of some pupils give them more potential than others. However hard we work as teachers and whatever classroom methods we use, we can't make every pupil equally intelligent. But, here's the rub: far from shrugging our shoulders and giving up on nature, this understanding empowers us.

Nature gives us a neat bell curve or standard distribution of intelligence. If schools reproduce that bell curve year after year then we as teachers are not doing our jobs. We can smash the bell curve. We should smash it. Schools are ideal environments in which children can improve their intelligence. David Didau's *Making Kids Cleverer* (2019) makes a persuasive case for precisely this – schools make pupils smarter. Counterintuitively, schools increase the influence of our genetic inheritance because our genes interact with the environment: genetic potential needs the stimulus of an exciting school to be unlocked and released: 'The more egalitarian the society, the more genetic influences will matter' (Didau 2019: 93).

Following the work of Raymond Cattell (1971), Didau distinguishes fluid intelligence, which is what I'm calling processing power and is pretty much fixed, from crystallised intelligence, which is malleable and which avowedly can be augmented in a stimulating school environment that provides a knowledge-rich curriculum. Didau unpacks the myth that our intelligence can't be increased: we are the products of our genes and our environments and the relationship between them. Our pupils, all of them, have plastic intelligences and huge potential. Whatever their starting points, teachers can start them on a learning journey towards being more able and on to remarkable – a journey which they take on and lead themselves. Nothing in their genes can get in the way.

Practice using scales

One helpful way to think about this issue is to consider old fashioned weighing scales. Sometimes it is suggested that the educational scales are unfairly weighted. Asif's maths intelligence is greater than Yolanda's in terms of the areas of the subject he can tackle with proficiency, the difficulty of the problems he can solve (often at speed) and the amount of time he has already spent as a high attainer in maths. He has greater processing power and facility in non-verbal reasoning, and this is a type of intelligence which will give him consistently better outcomes in maths. The scales weigh heavily in his favour, and Yolanda, or her teacher or her parents, may feel that she will never be able to restore equilibrium for all the grit or growth mindset she displays.

However, everything we now understand about purposeful, deliberate practice and the construction and retention of mental models of success (to be discussed in Chapter 3) surely takes us a long way from either accepting 'genius' on the one hand or 'just try your best' on the other. Realistically, the scales may never fully balance, but they certainly won't if we do nothing or don't try anything new. Schools can help to change the readings on the scales to the benefit of every student.

So, let's apply some counterweights and see what happens. Yolanda can harness the explanatory modelling power of her teacher. She and her peers can challenge Asif through questioning and feedback to provide a gallery critique of his solution strategies. Now let's add to the scales some self-testing memory strategies and revision techniques based on retrieval practice and spaced learning. Asif watches as the scales realign over a number of weeks and reach a tipping point. For all that he is very good at equations by dint of his processing power, he is not yet an expert learner in maths. They are not the same thing.

By improving her knowledge about how to learn and by gaining an insight into the motivation she gains in every lesson, Yolanda is on a learning journey during which her genetic make-up is stimulated by the classroom environment. She is, perhaps in a self-aware fashion, becoming an expert learner. By channelling her knowledge and its application, Yolanda uses her malleable intelligence to secure the best maths outcome of which she is capable. The proportionate change in the scale of Yolanda's achievement is greater than Asif's. She can become a very high attainer indeed, on any measurable scale. As Daniel Willingham (2009: ch. 10) puts it, the key cognitive principle is that children do indeed differ in intelligence, but intelligence can be changed through hard work (among other things). We may not be able to make every pupil equal in intelligence, but we can go a long way to closing the gap.

Intelligence matters in the classroom

The Chambers Dictionary definition of intelligence is 'intellectual skill or knowledge'. Personally, I find it hard to distinguish knowledge from intelligence, but that's just my own observation as a teacher rather than something empirical. Why can't Yolanda just transfer to maths the pretty good set of generic skills she already seems to show in science lessons – formulating a hypothesis, predicting an outcome, testing, checking, repeating? This could work, but learning a generic skill without a specific body of knowledge won't.

André Tricot and John Sweller (2014) argue that intellectual skills derive largely from domain-specific knowledge. Helping students like Yolanda to acquire the domain-specific, mathematical knowledge she needs in order to solve geometrical problems is complex and difficult, as she has found out. It is about more than knowing the rules of Pythagoras' theorem, because there are simply so many cases to which it can be applied and she can't learn to recognise all of them overnight. To Asif it may be simple and obvious – or so it may seem. It would be easy to explain this away as 'Asif's just good at maths'. We are very adept as a society at explaining to ourselves Einstein's 'genius' or our own complete inability to learn foreign languages. This familiar and comforting reasoning is not more than self-deception on a grand scale. There are better and more powerful explanations. Tricot and Sweller (2014: 21) suggest that 'Knowledge held in long-term memory dramatically changes performance'. It is this which explains why a chess grandmaster will always remember more mid-game positions than a novice. It is because of the grandmaster's experience and what they have stored in their long-term memories, not because of a generic problem-solving ability. (We will break down 'experience' further when discussing Anders Ericsson's work on deliberate, purposeful practice in Chapter 3.)

Perhaps Asif has had many more chances to work through geometry problems in the past than his classroom peers, and he has motivated himself to practise with the mental model of success that is readily constructed from the warm, comforting glow of teacher and parental approval afforded to children who are 'good at maths'. As so often in anything to do with intelligence, genetics and IQ, appearances are deceptive. If this perception locks out much of the rest of the class, suffering from working memory overload as they furiously multiply the sides of a triangle without getting the point, as it were, it does them all a disservice and compounds easy labelling and, dare one say it, attainment setting.

Once Yolanda, her classroom peers and her teacher understand the need to acquire domain-specific knowledge, and have learnt how to store it carefully in their long-term memories from which it can be accessed with the efficiency of a retrieval robot in an online shopping warehouse coping with the Christmas rush, it will be a powerful and transformative mechanism. Praising effort (not ability) and improving students' (and perhaps even teachers') self-image about intelligence in an honest way will make a genuine long-term difference. The last word goes to Tricot and Sweller (2014: 11): 'The accumulation of knowledge in long-term memory during schooling provides an obvious candidate for the role of the major factor in the development of intelligence.'

Schools make pupils more intelligent

It is not just nature vs. nurture then. As pupils experience more schooling, and therefore more environmental influences, the impact of genetic factors increases rather than diminishes. Genetic variation is multiplied and magnified as genes interact with each other and the environment. Schools can make pupils more intelligent.

To return to the quotation from Dylan Wiliam at the top of this chapter, his argument is that if we want the best academic achievements from all students, we need to reduce the variability of environmental factors and increase the total heritability of intelligence by exposing every student in our schools to a stimulating environment. If, at the same time, we foster a sense that ability is not fixed but is incremental and that schools can improve students' intelligence, especially by improving their long-term memories, then we increase our own understanding as teachers of what research-informed practice looks like in the classroom. It really is all still to play for at any time in a child's education. We must expose pupils to the kinds of challenging classroom environments that I am trying to outline.

Asif and Yolanda's respective mathematical abilities fit within a distribution across a population, and we cannot know how much of their personal make-up comes from their genes or upbringing. But even if Asif has higher processing scores, the approaches and strategies I am suggesting in this book will enable Yolanda to match him.

Cleverer Yolanda

If Yolanda wants to make herself cleverer in a maths lesson, she needs to:

- Practise techniques to transfer knowledge into her long-term memory from which she can retrieve it rapidly and efficiently.

- Avoid overloading her working memory, which could happen even in a single lesson.

- Harness the skills of the expert learners around her and the modelling by her teacher (or by those expert learners) of how to select and deploy knowledge.

- Understand that she can become more intelligent and move from being a middle attainer to a high attainer by dint of purposeful practice, regardless of her genetic inheritance.

Attainment grouping: smash the setting

It isn't only the bell curve which needs smashing. Ability or attainment grouping deserves to come under very close scrutiny. In reality, in too many schools, Yolanda may never become cleverer because she'll not only be in a lower set than Asif but she is likely to remain there and may never have the chance to be taught to the top or learn to the top. Schools institutionalise setting and cap potential.

The research evidence is indicative rather than conclusive. According to the EEF (2018b), setting and streaming has a very small negative impact for low- and mid-range attaining learners, and a very small positive impact for higher attaining pupils. Two studies on setting and mixed attainment practices looked at whether some of the potentially negative aspects of setting could be addressed and attainment improved (Education Endowment Foundation 2018a; Francis et al. 2018), but each study found it difficult to recruit or retain schools and teachers. In this challenging area of educational research and practice, it is unreasonable to expect schools to make wholesale changes to such a core area of curriculum and timetable planning, such as moving from setting to attainment grouping, without appropriate training, planning and consideration for the implications for teacher workload.

In recognition of this fact, Becky Francis and her team at the University College London Institute of Education offer schools a set of 'dos and don'ts' as a statement of best practice for immediate consideration (Francis et al. 2018). Common to the list for setting and attainment grouping is the following advice: do have high expectations for all pupils, don't teach mixed attainment groups to the middle, and don't offer low sets a 'dumbed down' curriculum and/or teachers with the least subject expertise. If your school uses setting, ensure that attainment is the only criterion and that pupils are retested sufficiently frequently for them to be able to move sets. With mixed attainment groups, regular changes to seating plans are advised and an over-reliance on high attainers explaining material to other students is cautioned against.

In this crunch area of school life, the research evidence is not yet sufficiently persuasive to demand the end of setting per se. It is difficult to construct a study which will control for teacher quality and have the school and teacher participation rates and longevity of findings necessary to produce definitive results. In the meantime, the 'best practice' UCL checklist is a good place to start, with its emphasis on teaching to the top, high expectations for all and regular review of student groupings. Certainly, setting certainly should not be a self-fulfilling prophecy. Mixed attainment grouping has been implemented in the maths department at Huntington School in York, accompanied by training time for teachers and good communication, and the outcomes have apparently been pleasing (Taylor 2019). This is a classic area for schools to discuss in networks of schools.

There is an interesting corollary to all this. One intellectual justification often used for attainment grouping is that schools and teachers can successfully identify who goes in set 1 and who goes in sets 2 and 3. Well, up to a point, Lord Copper. Dylan Wiliam (2001) estimates that when tests are used to select children in this way, only half the pupils end up in the 'right' set. Furthermore, according to research by Wiliam and Bartholomew (2004: 7), 'in terms of mathematics attainment, it doesn't really matter very much which school you go to. However, it matters very much which set you get put into.' Parents fretting about getting their child into the 'right' local school might be better advised to pay closer attention to teacher quality, teacher expectations and attainment grouping practices within particular departments of the schools in question.

The EEF's *Best Practice in Grouping Students* study (2018a) found that around one third of pupils were in a different group to the one predicted just by looking at Key Stage 2 attainment. There was also stereotyping by race and gender (Taylor 2019).[1] And there is a corollary to this corollary. If the head of maths has done what happens in many schools by putting her 'best' teacher in charge of set 1, then she should at least be aware of Wiliam's (2018: 52) recent finding that she will need eleven years' worth of evidence on her colleague in order to produce a statistically robust measure that this teacher is indeed the most effective. Is it really fair that the best teachers, or what are widely perceived to be the best teachers, commonly end up with the most able pupils (Boaler et al. 2000: 22)?

If we are serious about tackling the excellence or advantage gap we should not wait a generation for definitive research findings, but should take a leap of faith and follow Mary Myatt's persuasive suggestion that, in practice, setting means pupil ability too often bears a closer relationship to their postcode than their prior attainment. As she puts it, 'We do not truly know what anyone is capable of until they are given interesting and difficult things to do' (Myatt 2017).

---

1 See also https://www.mixedattainmentmaths.com/mixed-attainment-schools.html for a list of schools following mixed attainment maths teaching.

So, teachers make a difference and schools make a difference. My own confirmation bias is greatly comforted by the work of Sarah-Jayne Blakemore's team in finding that non-verbal reasoning is not a fixed ability. Applying this to the hypothetical example on page 39, if Yolanda engages in the deliberate, purposeful practice of non-verbal reasoning skills for ten minutes a day for a month as part of her toolkit of strategies to compensate for Asif's heritable processing advantages, those skills will improve. As Blakemore says:

> The funny thing is that everyone I work with in my field would say, 'Of course it's not [the idea that non-verbal reasoning is a fixed ability]. Nothing is fixed. The brain is plastic. You can always train.' But it comes as a surprise to people who, say, set grammar school entrance exams. (see Amass 2017)

As an aside, a plastic, malleable intelligence may make it better for Yolanda to wait until late adolescence (16–18) to learn and improve her higher level cognitive skills in context, rather than trying to do it all in early and mid-adolescence. This, in turn, adds logical weight to arguments for a French- or German-style baccalaureate examination at 18 rather than national testing at 16.

Some questions to consider

Names and labels

- Are you happy with how you label and describe high-attaining students in your school or college?

- Are the terms you use understood by your whole school community, including parents?

- What do these labels say about aspiration to excellence for all pupils?

Is it working?

- How do you know if your high-attainer programme is working?

- Does your high-attainer programme actually help to close any attainment or excellence gap in your school or college?

- Can pupils move in and out of your high-attainer programme – and do they?

- Does your G&T coordinator get into lessons regularly?

Curriculum challenges

- Does your curriculum foster domain-specific skills or generic skills?

- Do your departmental colleagues understand how to help create changes in long-term memory in your subject that help to make students more intelligent?

- Does your attainment grouping policy conform to evidence-based best practice?

Summary

Obsessing about names and labels for students (and for teacher leads) is to put the stagecoach before the horses. What matters more are the approaches we adopt and the values we foster in our daily interaction with all students. Calling a high-attaining Year 7 child gifted is diminished if neither she, her parents nor her teachers fully understand the opportunities and expectations the term carries with it. However we choose to select and identify our high-attaining children, we need to think carefully about our justifications for our choice of terminology. What will be the implications for all concerned?

Ability and attainment are different and we should be careful not to confuse them. Rather than thinking about the lucky break which enables a student with a genetic head start to find playing the piano easy, for example, we might look at high-attainer provision in a more democratic and evidence-based fashion – that is, if we consider intelligence to be receptive to stimulating classroom environments and capable of contributing to high attainment for many more students than is currently the case. Attainment grouping in schools and colleges needs to be reviewed and perhaps reformed: it often happens for the wrong reasons, it caps potential and it traps students and teachers in a modest cycle of expectations and outcomes.

Expert learners are made, not born. Research evidence in this area is contested, but it may be a fair summary to say that while some aspects of intelligence are largely fixed, potential is not, and schools can help to improve intelligence using the wonderfully versatile and malleable ability of the human brain to store and retrieve unlimited amounts of knowledge from long-term memory. Children's genetic code may tell us what is but not what might be.

Chapter 2

The Ideal Lesson

Adults Teach, Students Learn, Students Lead

All I am saying in this book can be summed up in two words – Trust Children. Nothing could be more simple – or more difficult.

John Holt, How Children Learn (1967)

Key themes

- Asking your students to consider in detail what their ideal lesson would look like will help you and them to undertake a remarkable learning journey of more creative and stimulating lessons.

- Although many of these ideas may seem challenging, and will literally take you outside your classrooms in some cases, there is research evidence to underpin them.

- Really listening to your students talking about ideal learning environments creates a dynamic conversation of adults modelling, students learning and students modelling.

What happens when you ask your students to design the ideal lesson? I tried this recently at my school in an off-timetable session held to get our Scholars from Years 8, 9 and 10 really thinking about their learning. The activity was led by Russell Earnshaw, England Under-18s rugby coach, teacher and educator. The students put themselves into groups and came up with a long list of ideas, including a diagram of an ideal learning area. I'd like to spend some time considering their thoughts as professional learners, since that is what they are. The implications of some of their ideas are far-reaching. What would your students come up with during a similar exercise?

I'm sure that you will concur that this is an intriguing thought experiment. After all, if we want to put our institutionalised thinking into a broader context, as we all have to from time to time, a valid way to do so is to ask an outside expert to come in and offer some fresh insight and experience to challenge our assumptions. It is remarkably easy to lose sight of just how closed our in-house experience can be: we do it that way because ... we just seem to do it that way, give or take the odd renaming of a process or role, or the introduction of a new piece of expensively licensed software. Likewise, many schools and colleges have school councils or similar bodies, use student voice a good deal in offering feedback to the SLT about what really happens in lessons and with homework, and use students as part of interview panels for staff appointments. My school recently appointed a new head teacher, and a student panel was integral to the interview process.

And yet. Confirmation bias and habits of mind may cause us to shrink away from accepting and implementing either outside advice or internal student review. We nod approvingly and then go back to where we were. It's a natural human response individually and collectively, but rather than condemning it we might do better if we recognised it as a starting point. If you and your institution are happy with the status quo, and you have evidence to demonstrate that your high-attaining students really do make as much progress as you or any reasonable outsider could expect, then it is hardly for this particular outsider to interfere. But this is not the case in many schools. Research into the national and many local contexts of provision for more able students paints a grey picture, and in some instances a black one.

Listening learners

As I set out in the Introduction, we can start our learning journey to supporting high-attaining pupils with Ofsted's *The Most Able Students* reports (2013, 2015), which we can then connect to what our own students have to say. What follows is a rough modelling of that process. This approach has the merit of testing evidence against our own experience, and vice versa. I trust that the outcome will be uplifting and forward-looking if you undertake this in your school.

Both Ofsted reports offer recommendations for improvement and common characteristics of schools that do well by their most able students. The 2013 report offers ten such characteristics and this chapter will touch on five of them, linking them to what my students told me:

1. Leadership that is determined to improve standards for all students.

2. High expectations among the most able students, their families and teachers.

3. A flexible curriculum allowing stretch and challenge.

4. Groupings that allow stretch from Key Stage 3.

5. Expert teaching, supported by effective formative assessment and purposeful homework, to stimulate students' enjoyment of a subject.

In this chapter, I will argue that our high-attaining students can help to take us on a new and refreshing learning journey through our schools. By this I mean a physical journey out of our classrooms and into other school spaces. This is the most straightforward part. But it also encompasses a journey through the curriculum because the implications of this approach cross traditional subject divides in attitude and approach. This pilgrimage also traverses the year groups in schools because these ideas are relevant to every age group: they develop and flourish with practice and experience, and the behaviours they produce become lifelong through practice and consolidation.

Having an innovative, skills-based curriculum in Year 7 to aid a meaningful, not-standing-still transition from primary to secondary school is a fine start, but what happens thereafter? This learning journey needs to continue through to Year 11 or Year 13, not stop in July of Year 7 or September of Year 9. It is the most important journey our children will ever take, since it will last their lifetimes. This pilgrimage will cause us a few missed heartbeats and will take us literally out of our comfortable spaces, but like many such difficult journeys it will surely be worth it if we are to turn our learners into remarkable young men and women.

Intriguingly, there is plenty of research evidence to underpin the ideas that students express about their ideal lesson. The celebrated educator John Holt wrote:

> When we better understand the ways, conditions, and spirit in which children do their best learning, and are able to make school into a place where they can use and improve the style of thinking and learning natural to them, we may be able to prevent much of [this failure]. (Holt 1967: viii)

Heaven forfend lest this should sound like a hippy dream, a throwback to the 1960s and ideas of self-regulating communes of students scorning exams for discovery learning and self-realisation. If we trust our students sufficiently and listen to them, as opposed to just hearing them, we will find that many of their ideas are rooted in practicality and are sufficiently hard-edged to equip them for the rigours of twenty-first century GCSEs and all the exam pressures our modern education system has in store.

A body of challenging official reports and research evidence is telling us that what we've tried hasn't worked as well as we would have liked. We can't continue with same old, same old. Perhaps this sorry picture can encourage us to do something similar to what I'm aiming to do in this chapter:

- To get your high-attaining students off timetable for a morning or afternoon, working with a different teacher or someone with an alternative approach and asking some big questions.

- To listen really carefully to students' ideas about what makes successful learning (or whatever questions you put to them).

- To test those ideas against your own specific context and against your knowledge of the research evidence and the national picture of more able provision.

The beauty of this approach is that your conclusions will be irrefutably appropriate to your own school or context. This is not the nightmare CPD of a self-publicising blogger being bussed into your school hall and telling you how to do behaviour management. There's no one at the front of the hall espousing the latest commercially sponsored voo-doo about Brain Gym or learning styles. We've all sat there and it's criminal. Your approach will necessarily be anecdotal and unscientific, and I'm not going to pretend for a second that what follows deserves to be called 'educational research', but it has the great merit of being entirely right for you. It will produce ideas and possible directions of travel on the ideal lesson and curriculum for your school, here and now. It is based on the freely given and heartfelt thoughts of true experts and professional learners – the children you teach. It can be appraised carefully, discussed, challenged and tested against the bigger picture of what other comparable schools are doing and what the national picture of provision (or its absence) suggests. It will give you a good basis on which to come up with credible strategies to improve curriculum design, the school timetable or whatever else your findings suggest.

The ideal lesson

Here is what my students wrote about what they want from their ideal lesson:

Learning positives: hands-on, no lecturing, choose classes, be with people you like, moving around, interactive, comfy chairs, music in the background, food, lessons in different places, no seating plans, optional homework, engaging teacher has a big interest in the subject, classroom discipline, able to explain things, debating, engaging, Kahoot!, freedom, respect

Learning negatives: no tests, just teaches based on exams, too many sheets, no blazers if not wanted, no judgement, no homework

Here is Russell Earnshaw's own summary of our session that morning:

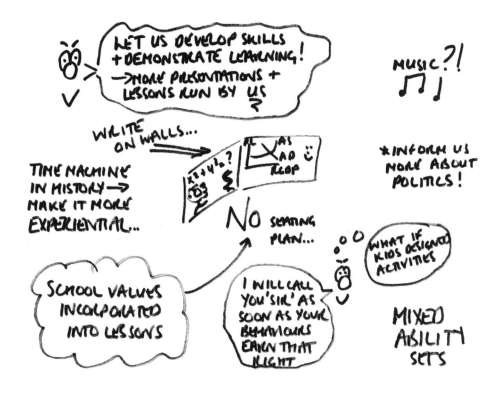

I have taken the thoughts of my Year 8–10 students, along with Russell Earnshaw's contributions, and organised them under four rough headings: environment for learning, thinking in lessons, modelling in lessons and sharing remarkable work.

1. Environment for learning

Comfy chairs, music in the background, food, lessons in different places, no seating plans, choose classes, be with people you like, moving around, classroom discipline

My first thought was to dismiss these points as impractical and idealistic. Give a group of young people a chance to design an ideal space, and snacks, slouching and sounds won't be too far from the top of many lists. Then I thought again and reconsidered my lack of respect for young people who typically spend eight hours each day literally immobile. At the start of this academic year, my own school issued a guideline about pupils remaining seated throughout a lesson.

'Ready to Learn', the current behaviour management approach in my son's school and one which is increasingly popular nationwide, typically requires that students are ready to learn; if not, their name is written on the board. A second warning in the same lesson for being off task or, for example, talking over another student or the teacher will result in time spent in an isolation room. I will talk more about behaviour management in Chapter 5; the point I'm making here is to question whether allowing greater flexibility in learning spaces will necessarily result in behavioural issues.

We glue our children to chairs in rooms with poor acoustics, in adult-controlled spaces of remarkable uniformity, and we ask them to be amazingly creative under these conditions. We demand that they produce (to quote what is needed for success at A level history, to take only one example very familiar to me) 'unexpected judgements' about complex situations in the past. Perhaps our thinking about learning spaces needs to be a lot more imaginative if we are looking, quite rightly, for such remarkable outcomes.

Snacking is an interesting idea. Hold back that flood of protests, stem that tsunami of objections, because I know them all. I merely put my head above the water to observe that it was only very recently that some schools were falling over themselves to buy in crates of bananas and boxes of healthy snack bars, not to mention gallons of bottled water, because they thought that it might produce 'marginal gains' in exam performance. So, schools can allow munching and slurping at designated times? What my students seem to be saying, perhaps stretching their point a little too far, is that if Mrs Smith wants to allow her Year 10s to bring in biscuits on a Friday or if Mr McKenzie enjoys sharing cake with his Year 13 A level set at the end of term, then more good is done to the professional relationship between those teachers and their students than harm. A learning environment which contributes to respectful professional relationships in the classroom is a matter of judgement between each school, each class and each group of students. One Ready to Learn size does not fit all. Can we be more creative here? Yes. But I'm with you on chewing gum. It's just a no, because I say so.

Music? The same thinking applies. There are many teachers who love to play or allow all kinds of music in their lessons as background, stimulus or for a plethora of different reasons and purposes. Russel Tarr's super-creative website (www.classtools.net) has fun music for lesson countdowns. The BBC Horrible Histories 'English Kings and Queens' song lists every monarch, and so can Year 7 pupils if they hear the song and learn it by heart. How do we respond when a class asks to have some tunes on in the background? I think there are bigger things to worry about, just as long as this isn't done on the justification that it will make learning easier for 'auditory learners'. Evidence to support the existence of VAK learning styles can be filed alongside that for unicorns.

The need for a department to match its own learning environments more astutely with the learning needs of its students will always drive these decisions. These can profitably come from the bottom up – namely the needs of students and classroom practitioners. This is infinitely preferable to alternative drivers such as a commercial incentive, a common practice imposed by an academy chain, an ambitious SLT member eager to show evidence of an 'outcome' or by any of the myriad pressures bearing down on schools. Context is all. A few schools have axed or pared down their school libraries and replaced them with e-learning. That was their decision, but it is not ours: at Bristol Grammar School we prefer books, journals, newspapers and desks. Other schools have adopted flexible learning spaces with hot desks, magazines and comfortable seating. Excellent: they are thinking about what suits all their learners.

Returning to my students' ideal lesson, I'm sure that none of them would agree that just by introducing more comfortable seating or allowing snacking during lessons that motivation and learning would dramatically improve. This nails the issue precisely with one-size-fits-all changes to our learning environments introduced with heart and hunch ruling head. By themselves they are tokenistic and random.

If we want to help the young people in front of us to demonstrate their remarkabilities more of the time, or even all of the time, what their comments suggest to me when taken together is an approach to their learning environment that is joined up and coherent. It's not the bean bags, the music or the coffee that they are really asking for, but a carefully considered and thoughtful way of constructing a sequence of lessons. 'Be with people we like' is a way of acknowledging that we often learn better when we are with our friends. Don't we sit with our friends on teaching development days? 'Groupings that allowed the students to be stretched from the very start of secondary school' is one of Ofsted's (2013: 8) common characteristics of schools that meet the needs of their more able students, and here it is in practice. 'Moving around' seems to be a plea for more flexible use of the spaces we have, however inadequate they may be.

Listening to learners on learning

Not convinced? To take two stereotypical ends of the spectrum, perhaps your practice (or that of your department) is to have students in rows in your classrooms, with you as the main focus for most of the time. Alternatively, perhaps your view is very much that desks in clusters work best for your pupils, so they can readily work with each other but still see the board, and you, as needed. To repeat myself, it is not for me or anyone else to tell you how to organise your classroom. There is no right answer from any so-called expert to trump your knowledge of your students in your classes. So, whether you sit at one end of this imaginary continuum or the other, or like most of us if you are somewhere in the middle, it doesn't mean that the point my students are suggesting to me is invalid. What they seem to be pushing for is a common-sense middle ground. If I could presumptuously put words into their mouths, they might be saying:

'Miss, can we mix it up more, more of the time?'

'Sir, I get why we have to be like this in classes a lot, but always?'

'Could we have our lesson or part of it in X? It will really help because ...'

To ignore students' views is to deny their own metacognitive appeals. There is an assumption that in many cases students don't really see the pattern of their own learning: the bigger picture is invisible or hard to discern because of the necessary fragmentation of knowledge acquisition into chunks called lessons. This may indeed be the case, but it is not a given. It remains an assumption, open to challenge according to the particular context and circumstances of a class. In addition, what might be the case at one stage of a student's learning journey may well differ later on under the influence of the very modelling and purposeful practice routines discussed elsewhere in this book. 'Metacognition' may still appear as a topic on teacher training courses, but the term will ossify unless schools demystify it and make it mean something in their own contexts. It could profitably form the basis of a year-long coaching focus for several clusters of teachers who then take time to implement and improve it in departments before modelling the practice more widely, not least to students. A small-scale pilot scheme shared with, and owned by, students and teachers, rather than imposed on them from on high, will be another step on the journey from able to remarkable.

Students will take responsibility for their learning if we trust them, just as John Holt urged all those years ago. If they suggest a more imaginative and flexible use of our learning spaces – this classroom or gym, that hall or art block – it is not necessarily a diversionary tactic, if we handle their requests professionally. By this, I mean matching an appropriate learning environment to the content and activities of a sequence of lessons as we plan them. The 'where' needs consideration alongside the 'why' and the 'how'. It may seem idealistic and naive to enlist student support in planning a sequence of lessons, but this is what listening to learners on learning means at the chalkface. It is this premise that underpins the idea of co-construction (discussed in Chapter 7). The fact that this is a process of shared professional responsibility, with an emphatic emphasis on the 'co', stops this becoming a wildly impractical exercise in wishful thinking.

Some questions to consider

- What comments do your pupils make about using your school or college's learning spaces more creatively?

- What comments do your pupils make about how to match your classroom/seating plan to a particular sequence of lessons?

- What does your department think about how well suited your learning spaces are for particular sequences of lessons or specific topics?

2. Thinking in lessons

Hands-on, no lecturing, optional homework, engaging teacher has a big interest in the subject, able to explain things, time machine in history – can we make it more experimental?

It would be foolish to try to summarise or comment on all these ideas, since each one is a compressed, tweet-like summary of some big thinking, but several themes strike me about what my students have to say. The first is that for these high-attaining students learning is about behaviours, not processes. Having active, engaged and engaging lessons across the curriculum is seen as paramount, to the extent that these qualities were consistently among the most commonly chosen attributes of an ideal lesson. The behaviours have to be learned by the students, having been modelled first by teachers: *adults teach, students learn, students lead*. Clearly there had been some modelling in some lessons at some points in the past for these thoughts to pop up on the day, but more was desired and required. These behaviours have to be learned or relearned by teachers who, for whatever reason, are not willing or able to offer these practices sufficiently often.

The second is a sense of learning as part of a group – it's much more fun to play Kahoot! in a class or team than on your own; likewise, 'hands-on' learning has an implied sense of taking place in a community of peers. This again challenges the idea of the role of an elite, more able group within a class or school. In my experience, students are often less concerned with nominal roles and labels and more concerned with what really matters in the here and now. This might mean not whether Emma is on the gifted and talented programme but whether she helps those around her, contributes positively to the lesson and is generally onside. 'Hands-on' means more work for students in a lesson, not less, so this becomes part of the learning contract that accompanies the transition from able to remarkable.

Lastly, I take from these comments an interest in learning itself and how it happens. Metacognition is always there just below the surface. Whether we agree or disagree with the list of positives outlined here – or those your own classes might produce if you were to run a similar exercise – it strikes me that our students are just as able as us to organise and lead the equivalent of a TeachMeet, teaching and learning conference or twilight INSET session, and would show just as much interest in what constitutes good and effective learning as many of our teaching colleagues. Students want our lessons – *their* lessons – to work.

Research evidence: low-stakes quizzing

Back to the context of your subject and lessons tomorrow. I'm starting from the assumption that children like to know things and like to get things right. They like knowing 'stuff'. If they know stuff then they start to know what they can do with it, particularly more creative things. But we tend to jump past the simple 'knowing' and fly straight to what is often (wrongly) perceived as the apex of Bloom's taxonomy (i.e. analysing, evaluating and creating) before we've built the foundations of knowledge. There is nothing wrong with the ambition – after all, it's a kind of teach to the top – but it is to put the pudding before the starter. If your students, like mine, want their lessons to be more 'hands-on' (as they told Russell and me) and to absorb some of their teacher's big interest in their subject (which is what we all profess to want, too), then we have to strengthen their chances of knowing what they need to know.

Cognitive science research suggests that we might all benefit from putting more emphasis, more often, on how to help our students move information from their working memory into long-term memory, from where it can be retrieved. As Barak Rosenshine (2012: 39) puts it in a seminal article:

> Research has found that even at the secondary level, classes that had weekly quizzes scored better on final exams than did classes with only one or two quizzes during the term. These reviews and tests provided the additional practice students needed to become skilled, successful performers who could apply their knowledge and skills in new areas.

The idea is that until they really know the sequence of events in *Macbeth*, they are ill-equipped to comment on changes in the role and attitude of particular characters, such as Banquo or Lady Macbeth. Learning quotations from the three witches is of limited value if the changing context for their evolving prophecies is not grasped. Rosenshine's principles have been adapted by Tom Sherrington (2019) in a short primer which marries research into learning with straightforward methods to use in the classroom.

I've been using low-stakes quizzing with my GCSE history classes for several years. It's very simple. I see each class twice a week for an hour. In one of those lessons I will drop in a 'pop quiz': ten questions, one-word answers. One question will be on music, typically from the 1960s to 1990s because I'm a bit old school – name any album by Pink Floyd, name one Beach Boys song … They get a mark, and if they or their parents have the good taste to explore some of my random but immaculate likes, then so much the better; if not, there is no disadvantage. It's idiosyncratic, but it's my space and builds my relationship with my students. If they gain some cultural capital along the way, that's a bonus. The other nine questions are more focused and serious, of course, and will test their recall of major events, dates and personalities of the Cold War or whatever recent topic we have been studying.

The twist is that some of the questions are repeated across pop quizzes, often several times, and only a few are new. I'm trying to give them repeated chances to absorb and internalise key moments, to give them building blocks on which their selection, deployment and analysis of key events can be built. They will be unable to explain to an examiner the effects of one key Cold War development between 1947 and 1949 if they don't know their Berlin Blockade (1948–1949) from their Berlin Wall (begun in 1961). Establishing timelines and sequences of events is simply too vital to wait for an end-of-unit test or summative past paper question. I want to use testing formatively. To that end, I don't take in marks: the questions are peer marked and lavish praise is offered, especially for students whose scores have improved (according to my memory). Pop quizzes are simply dressed-up retrieval practice.

I'm not so naive that I don't think the students won't recognise a test when it comes their way, but I do hope they recognise that this is testing for learning, not for ranking and measuring. They like to know things, and I'm helping them by using research into how the memory can help or hinder revision and learning.

Still not convinced? Daniel Willingham makes this an important element of his book *Why Don't Students Like School?* He uses the metaphor of the memory system almost self-consciously 'laying bets'. If you think about something carefully, you will probably have to think about it again, so it should be stored. He has coined a phrase which has itself become memorable: 'memory is the residue of thought' (2009: 210). Willingham argues that 'Learning is influenced by many factors, but one factor trumps the others: students remember what they think about' (2009: 79).

Willingham's research tells us that cognitive skills require background knowledge. Even when we think we are looking at skills in languages, or playing chess, or cooking, or science, or sport, we are often looking instead at an ability to access background knowledge stored in long-term memory. This allows the space in working memory to be kept free to combine information from the long-term memory with the problem in front of us.

Considering how and why we test as we do are questions which have intrigued Daisy Christodoulou, and I believe her influential work can be linked to what my students are asking for in their ideal lesson. As I interpret what my pupils are saying, they have no objection to learning per se; it is the routine chalk-and-talk, lecturing and note-taking which they feel they are receiving, rather than helping to generate or influence, which they are questioning. Christodoulou (2017) also references the 'knowing–doing gap': pupils often know what they should do (e.g. start a sentence with a capital letter) but don't always do it. A deliberate practice model of working on this particular sub-skill in different, focused but interesting ways is more likely to improve outcomes than, for example, writing a creative essay paragraph where working memory becomes so overloaded from juggling various skills that capital letters again fly out of the window.

Willingham concurs. If we attach meaning to learning, we think about it and it sticks. If Year 10 can see that a Quizlet session is helping them to store and retrieve core knowledge, they will enjoy the process more. I don't want to impose a high marks, interpretative question which I can pretty much predict that some students will struggle with until I am happy that the whole class – via low-stakes quizzing, flashcard creation and other methods – have the building blocks to flourish. As for the time machine, which Russell Earnshaw tells me some students want in history lessons, I haven't yet cracked that one. But maybe my pupils could ask their physics teacher and report back.

Finally, the idea of 'no judgement' is intriguing. What did this student mean – teacher assessment or peer assessment? No positive feedback or dedicated improvement and reflection time (DIRT) or no judgement of any kind? Assessment certainly seems to be a barrier to risk-taking learning and creativity. I can't offer my students 'no judgement' and I don't know an education system which could, but the implicit message of choosing appropriate means of assessing work (Why not oral? Why not peer?) more often might help to restore some creativity in the classroom, which is one of my aims. Regarding homework or home learning, it is perhaps unsurprising that learners ask themselves whether everything we set is necessary or useful. They would hardly be questioning the purpose of homework if they thought it worked. Teaching to the test is no one's idea of creativity, however much we think it necessary, and high-attaining students can spot it at 600 paces.

Some questions to consider

- What comments do your students make about engaging, engaged lessons and how these might happen more frequently?

- What comments do your students make about learning and how they think it happens in lessons?

- What does your department do to help students take a lead in thinking about retrieval practice and revision?

3. Modelling in lessons

Kids design activities, let us develop skills and demonstrate learning, Trump? Brexit? inform us more about politics, I'm a C-class linguist, mixed-ability sets, more self-study, prepare for university life, more applicable content/CVs, able to explain things

It is sometimes said that the essence of good teaching is modelling. We explain, they do. Fair enough, but they can explain too – to each other, to the whole class and to us. This is what I'm referring to throughout this book as becoming an expert learner. This doesn't necessarily mean the most successful pupil with the best marks in tests and exams. It is more a question of displaying appropriate attitudes of support and empathy, for example, as well as practical techniques which will help with collaborative learning. Modelling to the top carries all learners with it because 'the top' equates to that alchemical combination of our top and the class' top. This peak is one of a range of mountains, not an isolated summit – even Everest is part of a chain of Himalayan peaks. Some in the class haven't got there, yet. But many have the ability to at least get to base camp. How will they find the path unless we show them? Perhaps by showing each other, since they are rather good at it.

Mixed-ability, singular success

What emerged quite strongly from Russell Earnshaw's ideal lesson snapshot was a preference for mixed-ability teaching. Critics may say that this is a classic example of confirmation bias: we were unconsciously looking for this conclusion, and therefore it emerged in my own notes and in Russell's diagram (on page 51). They may have a point. His approach to rugby coaching is to break down roles and to challenge orthodox coaching and thinking: it's not forwards and backs but low numbers and high numbers; it's not fixed routines and predetermined outcomes but rapid transitions, flexibility, versatility and decision making at speed and under pressure. Which sounds to me like exams, if not more so. At least when Anna and Tom are illustrating the functions of a kidney during their biology GCSE exam they don't have a crowd of people literally shouting at them about what to do and then instantly assessing how well, or how poorly, they just did it.

I'm making a laboured point here about the similarities of pressure situations on the sports field and in the exam room, but it's a point which stands up to some scrutiny. If we treat

Maya like a 'C class linguist' (whatever that means) the point is that we are capping her ability, restricting her progress and demotivating her. Setting and streaming doesn't have to be like that, of course; it can be operated flexibly and humanely.

What does strike me in terms of educating high-attaining students, however, is that the kind of class-centred, participative learning I've been outlining in this chapter is more likely to produce more students delivering more progress across a sequence of lessons (or a term or a year) than any other method or combination of methods I know. Ofsted's report on *The Most Able Students* states:

> In many cases, particularly in foundation subjects, students in Key Stages 4 and 5 were successfully taught in mixed ability classes by necessity because there were too few students to make sets viable. The fact that these classes were delivering mixed ability classes successfully suggests that the organisation of classes by ability is not the only factor affecting the quality of teaching. (Ofsted 2015: 11)

This finding is just one piece of evidence, and it is drawn from only forty secondary and ten primary schools, but it adds to the argument discussed in Chapter 1 that mixed-ability classes are as capable of producing high-attaining pupils as any other curricular arrangement, although perhaps we should be calling them mixed-*attainment* classes?

Play your CARDS right

The equivalent of setting or streaming in rugby coaching and many other sports is to divide players into first and second (or A and B) teams. Russell Earnshaw will have none of this: he deliberately mixes up players. His core belief is that a prop forward limited to the second team will always play like a B team prop forward. He wants a prop forward to run like an A team winger and kick like an A team back. Who knows whether this is possible without the chance to train and practise with the expert modellers of the first team? Russell and his team of England coaches use the acronym CARDS with their players: *creativity*, *awareness*, *resilience*, *decision making* and *self-organisation*. This approach is under evaluation from Edward Hall (forthcoming) at the University of Northumbria.

This is not a self-indulgent experiment or academic exercise. What is at stake for some players is nothing less than success or failure in the professional game. There are serious implications for England's senior rugby team, which is often accused of relying too much on brawn, not brain. Not all coaches go along with the CARDS approach in hockey and rugby where Russell uses it, arguing that it may suit some players and situations more than others. But that is how it is in our schools every day, where, just as on the coaching field, some students can and do make astounding transformations.

Their learning journeys take them to some astonishing places. Alongside the hard evidence of GCSE outcomes, I see students on a daily basis who have impressed me by doing what I never thought possible or advisable. Somewhere along the line, some modelling has taken place of behaviour, revision techniques, classroom participation methods and learning which have helped to produce very positive outcomes for that student. Promised land? Perhaps, but at least let's all die in the attempt to get our students to the promised land, rather than denying them the journey for the sake of some bad moments, subjective impressions or overly prescriptive and premature B team labelling.

Research evidence: Allison and Tharby on modelling

The diagram on page 62 is admirably self-referential: it explains and models explanation and modelling. It simplifies the complex but throws in the rich promise of questioning, feedback and challenge for good measure. Shaun Allison and Andy Tharby's justly popular Making Every Lesson Count series has the great virtue of outlining and developing what we all do, or could be doing, on a daily basis without reducing the mystery and complexities of learning and teaching to catchphrases or simple solutions.

In the context of the ideal lesson, modelling is the spine holding all the other parts of the skeleton together. Moving from good to excellent, and developing techniques of gallery critique and DIRT, is modelling in action, with keys to success including the creation of a peer culture of positive praise but also honesty and repetition. Too often, we try techniques because we have read about them in the *TES*, a tweet or blog and then, for 101 good reasons, we don't return to them, even the quite successful ones. Modelling and deliberate practice go absolutely hand in hand. If we want more students to become high attainers, to develop more of their range of abilities and become remarkable, then practice is the duller reverse of the shiny obverse of success. A coin needs both a head and a tail. Just for good measure, the coin can have a milled edge bearing a Latin inscription about thinking hard about thinking. That should do it.

Modelling can apply to attitudes as well as values. It isn't just methods of classroom management which need our attention. As professional lesson observers, students will have opinions about different seating plans for different activities and about alternative ways to test and retrieve information and ideas. Our pedagogy is in essence a shared responsibility. Pupils accept our explanations and modelling, so perhaps we could be more flexible in accepting theirs?

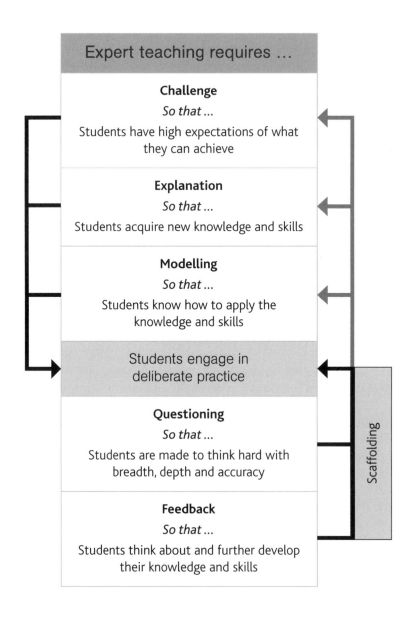

Source: Allison and Tharby (2015): 7.

Still not convinced? There are some good examples out there of colleagues who freely offer the support and example of their own take on direct instruction. John Tomsett, head of Huntington School in York, has blogged about live modelling and getting out of his own comfort zone in order to show his students exactly what they need to do, quite literally, from the moment they set eyes on an exam paper: John has live modelled to the whole of Year 13 an answer to a thirteen-mark A level general studies question (2017). What are the thought processes we want them to acquire and practise, rather than in some way expecting them, mysteriously, to just know? *Adults teach, students learn, students lead.*

Repeat, relax, learn. My suggestion here is that lessons become laboratories for thought experiments. White lab coats may not be needed but this is the practical part of the session after the theoretical introduction. After all, one quality of a successful scientific experiment is replicability: you can do it again with the same materials and the same result will occur. Reflecting on the thinking processes needed under exam conditions is too little and much too late to trust to a revision session the night before – or, as some schools increasingly seem to offer, a briefing session minutes before the exam itself. By this time habits need to be ingrained and routine, like a set play in soccer or mirror-signal-manoeuvre when driving. And this is to take only one example (and a slightly extreme one at that) of modelling in practice. Thought experiments should be happening all the way through the year, the course and the unit of study. A willingness to demonstrate to all students these explicit thinking processes will show them how expert minds unpick a rubric, a question and ultimately an entire exam paper for success. *Adults model, students learn, students model.* As Tomsett (2017) observes, 'We need to model explicitly the mental processes involved in learning which we, as teachers, can often take for granted.'

Finally, in offering their thoughts on an ideal lesson, some students mentioned politics (discussed more in Chapter 5) but also CVs, relevant topics and preparation for university life. My students are clearly aware of the need, as I mentioned earlier in this chapter, to put our mission statement and core values to the toughest test available – not external visitation but the daily routine of classroom practice. Ofsted (2013, 2015) has been critical in the reports mentioned in my Introduction of some schools' limited aspirations in terms of university application and life after school, so this is not to be taken for granted.

Do we do what it says on the tin? Does corridor life mirror the website? My argument in this chapter has been that there is no structural or intrinsic reason why it should not. If we listen to our students, and that means really listen, we will be on the right track. What we will be listening to will be a checklist of the qualities needed to make a flourishing career at university and beyond more likely. They will be qualities which turn 'independent learning' (whatever that means) into a critical, enquiring frame of mind where students take responsibility for, and ownership of, their learning because they have ownership of their thinking. I can't see the students who come from classes, schools and colleges following similar ideas to the ones I've set out in this chapter sitting passively in seminars and lectures. I don't see them abandoning habits and practices which they have seen being modelled, and have themselves modelled and practised, for a couch potato approach to learning. I believe that the habits of successful students will be with them for life – open to change, modification and overthrow as appropriate.

Working with an outside expert, in my case Russell Earnshaw, was revelatory to me both in terms of challenging my scepticism about student voice and his attitude to the young people he works with at a very high level. If he fails to command instant respect through his attitudes and actions, they will simply refuse to do the crazy, challenging things he wants them to do. This is not a unique quality. Many schools and colleges already have on their staff a colleague who can elicit similarly fruitful responses from their learners and bring out equally reflective and interesting ideas at no financial cost. Asking this colleague to give up their time to bring a fresh perspective to a year group or subject will create a debt of obligation, but many institutions have smart ways to compensate in the form of duty swaps or free time. It is time very well spent. If we want to build remarkable young people, then starting from the inside by drawing on the insight and credibility of a 'critical friend' and working outwards from there seems to be a good way of going about it.

Some questions to consider

- What opportunities does my department offer to pupils to model explanations to each other and to their classes?

- What examples can we share of modelling attitudes and values with classes, not just explanations and procedures?

- Are we offering opportunities to make thinking processes in our subject explicit and habitual?

4. Sharing remarkable work

More presentations and activities run by us, writing on the walls/windows, school values incorporated into lessons, I will call you Sir as soon as your behaviours earn that right

'Presentations and activities run by us': I take this to mean rather more than a student simply standing at the front and sharing their PowerPoint on volcanoes in Hawaii. Rather, what is being requested here is something closer to Tom Sherrington's idea of co-construction (see Chapter 7), where students take responsibility for delivering and assessing a series of lessons. This is a step change from what is commonly attempted by way of student participation. It's an immersive exercise and, having tried it, it can be transformative. But like everything else in this book, it is a hexagon in the patchwork quilt we are trying to build rather than a stand-alone solution to a problem. When students ask to be more involved in the set-up and running of their lessons, it is hard for us as the adults in the room to let go, and it is unlikely to be achieved without a lot of careful forethought and preparation. This is one of the many ironies of student-led lessons: teacher workload does not go down. It shouldn't rise either, but the idea that a teacher can sit at the front checking their email while the kids get on with it is not a route to successful flipped learning.

But that doesn't mean finding a myriad of excuses for it not to happen. If we are serious about helping our high-attaining students to thrive, and crucially about supporting more potentially high-attaining students to join them, then we need fresh thinking, not same old, same old. That's why I like 'writing on the windows'. Leaving aside the practicality and slight nuttiness of the idea, what it stands for is revolution, not tweak, and sometimes that is no bad thing. The learning revolution I've tapped into here with my unsystematic, random and non-evidence-based borehole is one driven from below, so in my mind that gives it all the more credibility. Writing on the windows and walls has a touch of *sous les pavés, la plage!* ('under the paving stones, the beach!') about it – a spirit of radical change.

This idea can extend forward to 'school values incorporated into lessons'. Your SLT will argue that this already happens. They will be able to take me on a tour of your school or college and point to posters in pretty much every corridor and classroom which enshrine what you stand for. Allow me to predict some of them: resilience, grit, determination, effort, energy, hard work, courage, politeness, fairness, tolerance, love, hope, respect, community. You may even have some Wordles and perhaps a quotation or two from Einstein and Churchill, each of whom seems to have spent what little free time they had producing social media sound bites. I'm not criticising these displays as such, still less the values themselves – heaven knows, we need them all and more. Rather, the gentle question I'm raising, having listened to my own students, is whether what happens in daily lessons reflects, contributes to and reinforces those values or not. My students are aware of a disconnect between what is professed in my school and what actually happens, at least sometimes. If that's not the case in your context, that's great. But it can happen, even in situations where the values derive from the students themselves and appear on a wall display.

An interesting implication is that the approach high-attaining students adopt in the classroom will in itself contribute to and influence school values. Rather than being stand-alone words emblazoned across a prospectus, school values are there in the classroom. If you want to know what they are, arrange a visit or taster day and see them in action, sit down and join in, talk to the people putting them into effect and changing them every day

– students and inspiring classroom teachers. These values have their origins in small steps and incremental change, not top-down imposition.

Still not convinced? If you take my advice and replicate the approach outlined in this chapter and drill down into your students' ideas about the values they see being demonstrated in their daily lesson lives, you will find some ways forward to the benefit of every student. My own exercise reminded me of a session I attended several years ago at a wonderful event called Teaching and Learning Takeover (TLT) Southampton. I go to this every year and never fail to be inspired. On this occasion, a session was led by the admirable Vic Goddard, head at Passmores Academy in Harlow. Vic spelt out in no uncertain terms his commitment to every student in his school and his determination not to let any of them fail, whatever that might mean. Some of these students come from families and circumstances which are very difficult. Vic's core guiding principle is 'unconditional positive regard' – simply that. He asserts that all adult relations with children begin from this premise. Why should they deserve less? Of course, they will test that regard to the limit and beyond, but the principle holds firm. Vic's mantra isn't up on my classroom walls but it is deeply embedded in my consciousness. I manage to live up to it most days – but when I don't, even the knowledge that it is there, somewhere, does me good.

What should be displayed on our walls, if not boring posters about the feudal system (which didn't exist, by the way) or vacuous promptings about effort? Students' work should: showing the process, not just the outcome. Writing in unconventional spaces (e.g. the windows and walls – using special pens) is an interesting idea. If we are serious about taking pride in the thinking which goes on in our lessons, why are we so quick to rub it off the board or remove any traces of it before the next class of students comes in? There are all kinds of contextual limitations to what is possible and desirable here, but perhaps students are articulating that we should not lose sight of what matters (i.e. the ideas and outcomes captured in a lesson) simply through over-tidiness and zealous cleaning. Rachel Jones has an imaginative chapter in *Teacher Geek* (2015) called 'It's Your Learning Environment: Make It Mean Something'. She shows us how to relinquish the space and to use everything from the floor to the windows so that pupils buy into what you are collectively trying to achieve.

Research evidence: gallery critique

The solution to sharing remarkable work in the classroom is cheap, simple and uplifting – and we may already be doing it. In *An Ethic of Excellence* (2003), Ron Berger argues for the importance of gallery critique. This means setting out work on desks and putting it on walls for all to see and comment on. The students offer feedback on what they are seeing with a view to improving both the task itself and future outcomes. Berger makes clear that this idea flourishes in a context of mutual trust and respect in the classroom, which chimes well with the 'no judgement' idea discussed on page 58. However, there has to be judgement but for the right reason – to produce an improvement to the design, paragraph or exercise. Berger's advice is to ensure that peer feedback is kind, helpful and specific. With those qualities uppermost in their minds, the students can be encouraged to offer feedback that is diverse, supportive and constructive – and, what's more, it can actually improve outcomes for all learners, regardless of prior attainment. Never settle for less than excellent. Train your students to become expert learners by helping them to become expert critics, in the broadest and most inclusive sense.

If this still seems too idealistic, gallery critique has been put to the test by both David Didau (2013b) and Andy Tharby (2014a) with positive results. Both note the caveats and cautions needed to make the idea work, but that should come as no surprise: as always, the context of your lessons and your students overrides everything else. For me, gallery critique is evidence to support what my students want from their ideal lessons, which includes more ownership of what they do and more control of the physical space around them. Displaying examples of work on the wall is hardly a new idea, but gallery critique strips away the mystery of how to improve. It uncovers the naked reality of what good work on this task actually looks like. It wasn't excellent just because Anna did it and she is starting to do really well in English, and nor is it excellent just because Asif is a poetry analysis genius.

It isn't on the wall simply because it is excellent and a parent might come in. The work has gone from OK to good to excellent because the intestines of the task have been exposed and the inner workings of Anna and Asif's minds have been shown to be perfectly normal and capable of being understood and matched in a series of logical stages by every student in the class. Gallery critique is just one of a number of methods which are tried, tested and inspirational. If we allow our students more ownership of DIRT, so they can immediately show each other how to get better, we all do well. Our professional skills and judgement sit alongside, and not on top of, this process. We can give up more of the classroom to the students and take public pride in their improvements, not just their attainment. Now that would be truly remarkable.

Some questions to consider

- Who would your students identify as the colleague most likely to bring out their honest feelings about learning environments and ideal lessons?

- What comments do your students make about their actual and ideal classroom spaces: walls, windows, posters?

- What does your department think about gallery critique and similar methods to allow more student control of DIRT?

Summary

High-attaining students (which is to say all our students, potentially) are made, not born. Several generations ago, John Holt asserted that only a few children in school ever become good at learning and that most become humiliated, frightened and discouraged:

> When we better understand the ways, conditions and spirit in which children do their best learning, and are able to make school into a place where they can use and improve the style of thinking and learning natural to them, we may be able to prevent much of this failure. (Holt 1967: viii)

Holt overstates his case but the point has merit. Not least, pupils tell us, explicitly or by strong implication, that they want to learn. It becomes clear from listening to them, really listening, really really listening, that they care enormously about constructing their ideal lessons and would dearly love more of their lessons to approach what they would like and need.

Of course, we need to filter our students' comments about what they would like in a perfect world through our own adult, professional lenses, and make the customary compromises and allowances. But, dare one say it, they are the learners in the room and experience a more intensive daily diet of instruction and learning than we do. We dismiss or ignore their comments at our peril; we cannot then claim to be responsive to pupil needs. Your context will be different to mine, and our students will look and sound different, but I'm willing to bet that more unites them as learners than divides them.

Part 2:

The Expert Learner

Chapter 3

Purposeful Practice

One benefit that a young student – or anyone, really – gets from developing mental representations is the freedom to begin exploring that skill on his or her own. They no longer need a teacher to lead them down every path; they can head down some paths on their own.

Anders Ericsson and Robert Pool, *Peak: How All of Us Can Achieve Extraordinary Things* (2016)

Key themes

- Teaching to the top means teaching, coaching or mentoring, not merely allowing high-attaining students to get on with it while you teach to the middle. Modelling success is crucial.

- The top is the highest level to which you and your students can aspire. You know them better than anyone and you are uniquely placed to show them what expert performance and achievement looks like.

- If students wish to improve then they need to develop purposeful practice skills in the classroom and at home which will keep them in their struggle zone. They need to know what success looks like and to have a mental model of how to acquire and recall the knowledge and skills they will need.

- Every pupil wins by this approach because no one is excluded by notions that they have no natural ability in a whole range of subjects or no talent in a set of others. Success is available to all – including, crucially, learners disadvantaged by social and economic circumstances and at the wrong end of the excellence gap.

The top

I want to start at the top, since this is a book about provision to help children achieve to the best of their abilities. Where are my students starting from? How do I want them to get there? How will I know when they arrive? Assuming I want them to get to the top, what do I mean — is it the top level this class can attain or the highest level available in this school? Is the top the highest level of a specification or is it university level? Am I limited by my own ability and knowledge in getting them there?

The top is the highest level to which you and the pupils before you can aspire to achieve. Barak Rosenshine's celebrated article 'Principles of Instruction' (2012) describes the instructional support that teachers provide in the form of scaffolds — temporary supports that can gradually be withdrawn. This 'cognitive apprenticeship' is, in my view, too often applied to lower and middle ability contexts and too seldom to the benefit of high-attaining pupils. Rosenshine (2012: 18) summarises the research supporting this idea:

> In some studies, students were provided with expert models with which they could compare their work. For example, when students were taught to generate questions, they could compare their questions with those generated by the teacher. Similarly, when learning to write summaries, students could compare their summaries on a passage with those generated by an expert.

The top should certainly not be defined by an exam board or a departmental scheme of work. There is no limit to the top to which you and your students can aim. It may help to see the top as a collection of Lakeland or Himalayan peaks rather than as a single high or famous mountain. Like Scottish Munros (peaks above 3,000 feet), it may take a lifetime to bag them all, but that is what school days should be a preparation for. Perhaps in our collective angst to provide the best classroom experience possible, at times we forget that everything we do in schools is preparatory to a lifetime of learning.

In some ways, it is easier to say what the top is not: to reiterate, it is not defined by an exam board. A BTEC Level 2 Distinction and an A* at A level are superb achievements, of course, but they do not necessarily encapsulate all, or even the best, that our most able students can achieve. They are benchmarks, waymarks, signposts of success along the journey, but no more than pilgrim halts: convenient, necessary, but not in themselves destinations. This journey lasts for life. Have you ever had the experience of teaching a student or a class which has outgrown the confines of a specification or, indeed, the school itself? Year 11 or Year 13 students can mark time when they could instead be coaching others in their year group (or below) to climb the peaks with them.

Wise curriculum planning points them towards the next summit – accessible but just out of reach at the moment. What do pupils need to do to get there and can they plan their own learning journeys (akin to participants on the Duke of Edinburgh's Award scheme reading a landscape for safe yet challenging paths)? There is evidence on a national scale that, in terms of pupil well-being and pupil learning, we don't manage the primary–secondary transition well. Levels of attainment are commonly held back or even reversed. Some of our Year 7 pupils would benefit from greater teacher knowledge and expectations of what their new charges can and could achieve. The brilliant work done in many primary schools becomes summative and not formative. If Key Stage 3 teachers were transplanted into feeder primaries for a day or two they would return to base with a much better idea of how to share knowledge appropriate to high attainment for a Year 7 group.

The top is similarly not defined by a head teacher, board of governors or Ofsted. Naturally, teachers and professional bodies have practical experience of what tends to be roughly appropriate or typical for the different age ranges and abilities of children in our care, but at times we get it wrong. I'd say the same about myself as a parent. 'What tends to work' is often about as good as it gets. Leading universities offer good leads about high-attainer aspiration, even if they fall short of excellence in other respects (as I argue in Chapter 10). Some Oxbridge colleges and Russell Group universities welcome students from as young as Year 8 and 9 for experience days in order to dispel myths and raise expectations. Putting to one side the marketing motivations behind such schemes, they are at least trying to address some of the social mobility and aspirational issues raised by the Sutton Trust over recent years (Montacute and Cullinane 2018), while themselves admitting that they need to work a lot harder. Perhaps we could all be doing more to acknowledge that our own political judgements and fears about supporting an 'elite' should not get in the way of challenging our students to think big. There are many obstacles to disadvantaged high-attaining students getting into Russell Group universities, Oxbridge or Imperial College London, but our negative attitudes and preconceptions should not be one of them.

Nor is the top capped by personal knowledge and ability. I have regularly taught children who are cleverer than me and know more. To be honest, this doesn't often happen; after a lifetime of learning and teaching I can normally tip the scales in my favour in terms of subject depth and overview. What distinguishes these students is that they can do more with what they know, and much more quickly. They see problems differently and more perceptively. They make links and see threads where I am at best partially sighted. Very rarely has one of these students made me feel embarrassed or humiliated, and even more rarely was this deliberate. Their top is beyond my own, so there is a gentle, unspoken agreement that I point them in the right direction to continue their journey beyond school and its boundaries. What they need, and are grateful for, is my experience of how a specification and examination works in practice, its quirks and its pitfalls. High-attaining students are as vulnerable as any others to the academically untenable but still common inconsistencies and failings of particular exam boards, subjects and papers. They also need a relationship which helps to build their academic and personal self-esteem and well-being.

Our high-attaining students may share characteristics such as:

- Questioning the validity of the questions we are asking them.

- Offering a new dimension to a problem.

- Sharing factual knowledge of which we were unaware.

- Making a connection within a subject or across disciplines.

- Taking a project or extended project qualification in a whole new direction.

- Writing a well-argued and well-supported essay demonstrating complex thinking and unexpected judgements under timed conditions.

These students are a huge and underused resource. We can benefit from their goodwill and perception in setting the bar as high as possible. They too can be pathfinders and way-markers working alongside us. They are potentially expert learners. High-attaining students want to succeed, of course, but they are usually willing to have others succeed with them. Winners like to be part of a winning team.

Anna is ready for her natural sciences course at Cambridge in the spring of Year 13, and has been reading a first year undergraduate text in order to enrich her application. This can't replace, as she is the first to admit, the careful support of my biology colleagues in preparing her for the time and specific question pressures of a public exam. They are not merely teaching to the test. Anna has been shown the many directions of travel beyond it and has decided her route, but at this point in her learning journey the peak of this particular academic mountain is one she needs to 'bag'.

But is even this the best to which Anna should aspire? Matthew Arnold wrote a famous series of essays collected as a book in 1869 entitled *Culture and Anarchy*. He argued that we should aspire to know 'the best that has been thought and said in the world' (2006 [1869]: 5). I have deliberately removed Arnold's idea from its specific context here: I certainly don't see, as Arnold does, the virtues of an elite class pouring sweetness and light onto a raw and blind populace for their greater good. Rather, I'm extracting his idea that we should all be introduced to, and experience, the best music, art, design, literature, mathematical thinking and so on. Does this have any relevance for our bid to turn more able students into remarkable young men and women? I think it does.

Martin Robinson agrees. *Trivium 21c* tracks a very personal quest for a good education for his daughter, a quest that will enable her to accrue wisdom and lead a good life. His approach is an updating of the classical trivium – mastery of the three ancient arts of grammar, dialectic and logic for today's world:

> Autodidacticism, the art of teaching yourself, is something we all need to be able to achieve. I do not expect my daughter to leave school knowing everything there is to know, but I would like her to acquire the habit of learning on her own, of having knowledge, processes and criteria by which to judge what she is yet to learn. The trivium is a *way* of learning rather than just the *what* of learning.' (Robinson 2013: 50–51; original emphases)

Martin's courageous, idiosyncratic and uplifting reimagining of the benefits of an older model of education for the twenty-first century has been influential on my own learning journey.

Certainly in humanities subjects, there are countless ways in which essays in religious studies, English or history can achieve full marks because there is an element of subjective interpretation attached to descriptors such as 'analysis' or the extent to which an idea has been developed. Yet as teachers in the humanities, I believe we are reluctant to award 25/25, even if Tom hits one of these golden pathways and matches the mark scheme criteria. Perhaps we fear devaluing the currency in some way or demotivating our highest attaining students who, having reached the top once, might thereafter reduce their reading and efforts. Were we to acknowledge their ability more generously, we could benchmark a summit performance and yet still indicate the next pathway, with more reading at undergraduate level or the acknowledgement of an approach used in another discipline, perhaps anthropology, psychology or geography. We can hardly accuse exam boards of meanness and an inability to recognise outstanding achievement in source analysis or essay writing if we constantly practise an ungenerosity of reward in spirit and practice ourselves.

Putting this alongside what has been said above, the top is a fusion of your achievements and aspirations and those of your students. Increasingly, schools are not able to match public exam classes to teachers with a university training in that subject. This is difficult all round, not least for the chemistry teacher encountering A level biology, for example, for the first time since their own sixth-form studies. It would be easy and understandable for that colleague to aim for the safe middle ground of the ability range of the set in the hope that the good biologists will somehow look after themselves. Having the courage to pool student energy and expertise with that of the teacher in an open and collaborative fashion may instead open up a range of 'tops' hitherto obscured or denied. This approach may also inspire others to raise their sights and endure the ups and downs of the collective class rollercoaster. The teacher may also at times be hanging on for dear life.

Scaffolding for a top-level essay to enable full marks is just as important, and just as necessary, as support for a borderline grade 3/4 GCSE candidate looking to secure a pass to enable access to a college course. The framework may be different: it might be the recommendation of a particular chapter of a book or highlighting on a mind map a particular feature relevant to the planning of this particular question. It might be oral prompting and urging of a motivational rather than a technical kind. It might be close annotation of an exemplar paragraph written by you earlier in the lesson or by another student in a previous year.

If we don't provide this support, are we in danger of leaving it to instinct, natural ability or the luck of the draw on a particular examination day to determine a high-attaining student's chances of gaining, quite literally, the top grade in the mark scheme? If so, we need to be open and honest about this because of the implications such an approach carries, implicitly or explicitly.

Is teaching to the top elitist and unjustifiable? That is a discussion to be had in your school or department. Can Tom safely be set aside in religious studies, in the nicest possible way, because he has so much innate ability to think critically and deploy apposite examples from the texts he has studied that you can safely divert your care and attention to other students in the class? After all, for every Tom there is a Rosa or a Rajveer in the next tier of attainment who also deserve a crack at the top grade and who, unbeknown to them and us, may have a chance of getting it if we stretch them.

Has your college or academy taken the decision, consciously or unconsciously, to provide all the necessary ropes, ladders and equipment for the middle-attaining students and/or the low attainers, but to leave the high-attaining free climbers with the equivalent of a map, a compass and some prayers? Again, context is all, and it is not for me to judge or condemn. But it is for me to argue that supporting all to the summit in a collaborative fashion will increase the chances of every student achieving to the highest of their ability and potential, however far that takes them. The extra effort spent on Tom could mean that the mental models of success he develops, models and explains to others could make all the difference to how far up the slopes the whole set reaches.

The top is infinity plus one. It is not criterion referenced.

Anders Ericsson and peak performance

How should teaching to the top happen? There are no easy answers here and there remains a gulf between the research laboratory and the classroom.

Let's run a little thought experiment here: a research paper is published with relevance to learning and teaching – let's say it's tagged as 'gifted and talented education'. Its findings are distributed via an online journal behind a paywall and also via Twitter and other social media. Bloggers, re-bloggers and commentators add their takes on the findings. The circle is closed as the paper's authors comment on how their findings have been interpreted.

Brave teacher Ramona, who is attacking this particular Castle Clever looking for the latest nugget of learning and teaching truth, has to negotiate the ditches and palisades of misinterpretation and misapplication. It's 8pm and she has just put her daughter to bed as she naively opens Twitter and clicks on a link. 'Interesting,' she thinks, 'this could really help with Year 10 planning.' She storms the concentric walls of misinformation and refuses to be led along the paths of misdirection. Trebuchets and mangonels land heavy blows as fair and necessary criticism of the original paper now lie in wait, but Ramona dodges the shock-waves undaunted. Was that my daughter asking for a drink? Finally, the innermost defences of Keep Clever await. She approaches the grail. A technique! An approach! From nowhere appears a final and most unexpected hazard – shrieking denial and the screaming of foul play. It's the report authors themselves: 'We never intended this! We're just some postgrads who asked some of our college mates in Kansas to fill in a questionnaire. Now we're being invited to international education seminars!'

As our disappointed colleague multitasks with beaker of water for her daughter and a deep wine glass for herself, she spots a thread featuring fellow pilgrim Theo, who she met at a BrewEd event. He has been wise enough to avoid the lures of Castle Clever in favour of bigger and more strategic targets. As she gets to know Theo's Twitter-verse, he introduces Ramona to teachers, academics and writers worth following, and she starts to understand their ways – some of them very strange indeed. They too are not immune to misdirecting themselves and each other, and sometimes they drink long and hard at the Inn of Waffle and the Tavern of Self-Regard, but by and large they are a collegial and supportive bunch. They are the Knights of the Education Round Table, and their filtering of the relevant from the faddish and their assessments of the necessary rather than the desirable are pivotal on our journeys. Their names are scattered throughout this book and it owes much to them.

However, I would advocate complete faith in no individual guru or grail-hunter. Many have much to contribute, and some a lot more than others, but the lab is not the classroom – and producing school-based research evidence of statistical validity and reliability is hard.

Even Harrison Ford would draw breath. Yet, outstanding teachers and school leaders won't just give up and leave it all to university departments. Big strides have been made on this particular journey in recent years since the foundation of the extraordinary researchEd (https://researched.org.uk), led by Tom Bennett, which is committed to the idea of championing evidence-based interventions in schools. On a parallel strand, research networks of schools have been set up to increase the evidence base for research, to share what works and to offer ideas. The Research Schools Network (http://researchschool.org.uk), based in York, is pioneering evidence-based practice as a collaboration between the EEF and the Institute for Effective Education. It is at the gritty interface between academic and scientific research, on the one hand, and hard-pressed and increasingly underfunded schools, on the other, that some of the most cost-effective and worthwhile strategies are being investigated and applied. Teachers like Ramona and Theo looking to model good learning and teaching by improving their own professional practice could do a lot worse than to keep up to date with this body of work.

There is always the hazard that teachers jump from one set of half-understood ideas to another, leaving them confused and none the wiser. I say 'jump' but perhaps 'pushed' would be nearer the mark. The world of more able education is frighteningly vulnerable to the latest fashion, fad, Twitter storm or bestseller on mindsets, motivation or metacognition. We don't have time to do more than sip from the fire hose, still less reflect, discuss and choose what might be most appropriate for our classes in our college in our contexts.

At the risk of falling into the same trap, I doubt very much that Anders Ericsson's work over thirty years on expertise and peak performance can be dismissed as lightweight or transient. If we apply one common-sense test, namely what we think the picture of high-attainer provision might look like in 2050 or 3000, it seems very likely that Ericsson's research on successful learning will still be seen as relevant and appropriate.

What does Ericsson mean by the top? The top means Nobel Laureate physicist Paul Dirac. It means Picasso. It means American swimmer Natalie Coughlin (who won twelve Olympic medals). It means competitors who play Scrabble or Go to an extraordinary level. It includes violinists in the Berlin Philharmonic and chess grandmasters. Summarising Ericsson and Pool's (2016) ideas here will not do them full justice, but I hope that I can distil from their essence some points which are relevant to our students' learning journeys to the top.

Expertise not genius

We may loosely term Marie Curie or Tiger Woods a genius, and there is no harm in that. But it is a dangerous term if we imply that the abilities of a Dorothy Hodgkin or a Mozart are beyond us and people like us. It may seem that we are in the presence of superior mortals when we watch our favourite band or entertainer or read the latest novel by a Nobel Laureate in literature, but if we use the less glamorous term of expert instead, it may help us to realise that these remarkable human beings are mere flesh and blood trained to an exceptional level. When researchers such as Ericsson search for genius, they find deliberate, purposeful practice. Not simply deliberate practice, as we shall see, but always a lot of it. There is no gene for genius, and the recent unlocking of the human genome has not produced a DNA blueprint for perfection. Picasso was, first and foremost, an expert draughtsman.

Expertise not innate talent

Nor is expert performance about innate ability. Darwin was not innately talented as a scientist. Sir Isaac Newton did not possess mathematical processing power so great that contemporary rivals such as Hooke and Leibniz shook their heads in disbelief and gave up their own brilliant work. Mozart was not a prodigy beyond explanation, a child performer writing symphonies before our children sit their SATs. When we strip away the myths and accruals of history and popular culture we find extraordinary individuals, but they were and are often working in exceptional contexts (not the full answer but part of it) in cooperation with, or in competition with, other like-minded people, often guided at some points by a mentor or teacher and working very hard in a focused zone of struggle.

Newton was an exceptional thinker about the principles of mathematics. If he were just a genius capable of seeing solutions and answers to problems which baffled his contemporaries, why did he spend a large (and I mean a seriously large) amount of his professional time in the pursuit of alchemy? Yes, Sir Isaac Newton, of gravity and banknote fame, sought for years to turn base metal into gold. We overlook this. Turned on its head, what this tells us may be more interesting. Such was his capacity for thought experiments and the pursuit of *scientia* (or wisdom) that Newton was unwilling to close off avenues of enquiry. This may make him less of a genius, if that is a label people wish to stick to, but in my mind it makes him more of an expert learner.

Expertise not 10,000 hours of practice

Ericsson's work has inadvertently given rise to another myth: that putting in 10,000 hours of practice will allow almost anyone to become an expert. The idea came from Ericsson's work on violinists, and was taken up by Malcolm Gladwell in his popular work *Outliers* (2009) to be the approximate amount of time that Bill Gates put into computer programming or The Beatles put into their Hamburg shows in order to become experts. As Ericsson ruefully points out, there is nothing special about 10,000 hours, a number both under- and overshot by many expert performers. More damagingly, the misuse of his research implies that any kind of practice will do because it is the quantity of it that matters. It won't and it isn't. This serves as a salutary reminder that dangers lurk in popular misrepresentations of neuroscience and educational psychology. For every bona fide researcher and expert there are many interpreters and popularisers who, consciously or otherwise, fail to explain some complex ideas in context and with subtlety. Simple catchphrases sell books and ideas, but the casualty is truth.

Mental representations of success

The research is understandably more provisional when it comes to mental representations of success. After all, how can we reconstruct what was in Picasso's mind as he worked on *Les Demoiselles d'Avignon*? But we should die in the trying and make advances where we can. Taxi drivers learning their trade on the notoriously difficult streets of London have had their brain activity studied extensively by Katherine Woollett and Eleanor Maguire (2011). They found remarkable physical changes in the rear hippocampus of licensed cab drivers. Success in acquiring 'the Knowledge', and applying it daily to problem-solve journeys, produced the equivalent of extra neural muscle. Presumably, the mental representation of success here was the successful completion of the journey in the shortest possible time.

Similarly, Ericsson's work with Bill Chase on memory experts who learn to recite sequences of numbers unprompted suggests that no amount of trying hard and resilience will suffice by themselves (Ericsson and Pool 2016: chs. 1 and 2). These expert learners seem to create mental patterns and frameworks in order to process and retain information – systems which allow them to retrieve that information with seemingly little effort. Ericsson identifies mental representations of success in a particular field as a key attribute of peak performance; therefore, 'The main purpose of deliberate practice is to develop effective mental representations' (Ericsson and Pool 2016: 75).

Deliberate practice by itself isn't enough – and this is a vital message for schools. However, it is one of the biggest elements missing from conventional accounts of how we can raise pupil performance – because without deliberate practice the model doesn't work.

Deliberate practice

Research indicates that what helps to elevate very good performance to the level of excellent performance is deliberate practice. It's about the quality of particular training, repetition and practice, not simply the number of hours. No teacher consciously sets a class mindlessly repetitive work but this may be how a pupil perceives it. This is common sense in some ways. 'Learn your perfect tense French verbs for a test' is a type of purposeful practice, assuming that students such as Maya and Tom are keen to improve in French. However, a focus on verbs taking *être* is deliberate practice because this is tough grammar that, once learned, opens up accurate and complex sentence structure using past tenses. But I would suggest that even this isn't enough for an improved outcome in the classroom. The craft of the classroom teacher is to build in that little element of motivation which will help the class to see what success with those verb endings looks and feels like. It is this combination of deliberate practice, motivation and a picture of successful progress which makes the approach irresistible.

Identifying an area of weakness and breaking it down into smaller chunks of analysis and repetition is something that Ericsson found was common to expert musicians. This makes the mindless mindful. Simply practising scales or playing a whole piece repeatedly is no substitute for butting up against the difficulties of the transitions between bar 12 and bar 24, where particular repetitions (or retrieving from memory a similar transition) will stand more chance of being effective. A good teacher or coach will help to make practice purposeful (extrinsic motivation), but it needs to be accompanied by an intrinsic motivation and a self-generated model of success. Ericsson and Pool (2016) advocate the three Fs: *focus*, *feedback* and *fix it*. As obvious as it sounds, by identifying what causes a process to break down and then designing a practice technique to work on this specifically is a method proven to work.

Motivation

Of all the features found in the work of Ericsson and others, it is motivation which is most familiar to teachers in schools. After all, it is our daily task to encourage pupils to complete the work we give them, and to do it well. How can insights from expert performers in tennis, chess or music help to improve students' motivation? Above all, we should help them to understand that these men and women do not have a decisive genetic advantage in their mental make-up labelled 'extra willpower'. Rather, they have consciously developed the motivation to keep practising and not to stop, perhaps from a combination of intrinsic and extrinsic stimuli from family coaches and teammates and a peer support system that can be called on flexibly as different circumstances dictate. For example, guidance from a teacher or coach may help a learner to recognise the distinctive differences between various roadblocks to progress: is this a 'plateau' moment where consolidation and repetition will suffice to move the learner on or a 'new technique' moment where a fresh approach may be needed from a different source?

Piano teachers secure repeat visitations from once-reluctant teenage charges by weaving the stories of how great songs are written into the necessary diet of scales and theory. There are no better stories than those associated with The Beatles. Very occasionally, Paul McCartney would wake from a dream with a song fully formed in his head, most famously 'Yesterday' – the most covered song of all time. Such was McCartney's disbelief that the song didn't already exist that he played it repeatedly to people using nonsense lyrics until he accepted his own authorship and was ready to record (Miles 1998: 201–209). Hardly an example of deliberate practice, you might think, until you remember the years of hard graft in clubs in Hamburg and Liverpool.

Another justly celebrated song, 'Strawberry Fields Forever', was entirely different: its creation was an epic struggle of doubt and confusion for John Lennon. He can't seem to get what he's hearing in his head onto tape. There are huge differences (and 55 hours of studio time) between the acoustic guitar demo version and the final song featuring cellos, Mellotron and Indian zither (MacDonald 1994: 188–194). Finally, what finer example of collaboration could there be than 'Hey Jude'? So embarrassed was McCartney by the line, 'the movement you need is on your shoulder', that he offered to cut it on playback to Lennon, only to be told in no uncertain terms that it was the best line in the song. Lennon later told McCartney that it was the best song his partner ever wrote (MacDonald 1994: 264–266).

It's difficult to conduct a thought experiment in which your favourite songs don't exist or only exist as demo versions. Musicians, artists and athletes undergo often very difficult journeys requiring the collaboration of like-minded others and the support of a critical friend in order to overcome a plateau moment or similar. Constructing a narrative in the form of a song or an English essay or a piece of creative writing needs different types of motivation and practice: more than just 'effort' or 'grit' and other than just 'try harder'.

Footballers such as David Beckham are regularly mocked because of a seeming lack of intelligence or fluency in front of the TV cameras, which conveniently ignores the hours of deliberate practice of free kicks and corners which they put in after regular training sessions were over which helped to make them successful. This is a different kind of intelligence: an expert footballer is created through expert learning, which is just as deliberate and self-aware as any classroom motivation. Expert players don't simply practise generic kicking or passing, but look at particular techniques and strategies for different situations, 'chunking' practice at regular times and rhythms until a particular strike of the ball has become second nature – at which point their talent seems so natural that they are mistaken for an effortless genius.

Pulling this together: creativity in the classroom

So far, you might be forgiven for thinking that the school or classroom that I'm outlining here would have more of the qualities of an industrial workshop or gym than somewhere you would like to work. Practise, test, find inner motivation, don't trust to inspiration or talent – it all sounds mechanical and reductive. In fact, the opposite is true. The takeaway message here is that successful outcomes are available to all learners. Ironically, we can acquire the good habits modelled by elite and exceptional performers that are appropriate to every learning environment.

Some research findings are provisional and will need careful application to any specific college or school context, but we are now in a better position to understand what will democratise our schools by demystifying what might make some students better learners than others. An expert learner has developed a mental model of success by means of a programme of deliberate practice for which he or she has found, within themselves or with the help of peers and teachers, motivation and commitment. The reverse of the grey industrial 'factory of learning' applies: as teachers understand learners and learners understand themselves, the lights come on – but not the light bulb over Einstein's head or the reflection of a gold medal on an Olympic winner's chest. It is the stage lights of creativity illuminating the whole school.

Helping high-attaining students to improve will take more than a few slogans. You may well be a growth mindset school but what does that actually look like on the ground, and how might it be different from a neighbouring school of similar size and intake? 'Teaching to the top' and 'purposeful practice' will likewise be no more than empty refrains unless they can be translated into daily school routine. The good news is that this has already been happening in schools and colleges, so there is no need to start from a clean whiteboard. There are dozens of authors and bloggers who have championed practices based on the rapidly developing fields of neuroscience and educational psychology in the past twenty or so years, and thousands of teachers have absorbed their work, challenged it, refined it and made it relevant to their particular contexts. Applying some of this research to high-attaining students will have a wholly beneficial effect on all learners.

Our pupils are novice chess players rather than grandmasters. They are learner drivers not London cabbies possessed of 'the Knowledge'. At regular points on their learning journeys they need to develop, with our help, the means to chunk information into meaningful shapes in their long-term memories. The very process of developing and creating this framework will itself help the rapid retrieval of this knowledge. We are looking at this the wrong way around if we believe that only memory experts and chess champions can see strings of figures or a sequence of possible moves on a board. It is a potential that every student in our care possesses – one which we all have but so often choose not to use.

To reiterate, we can all create – to a high level – the mental patterns and frameworks in which to store chunks of knowledge. It is avowedly not an elitist or special intelligence, otherwise none of us would be able to speak, drive a car or do a crossword. All our students can do it, regardless of their ability and prior levels of attainment. My argument is that some of them – more than we think – can use and improve their existing skills in chunking and retrieval more efficiently and more often. When added to the right motivation and encouragement, and lots of deliberate practice, the improvements can help more students to become more expert and to become higher attainers. Existing high attainers can become experts. 'People do not stop learning and improving because they have reached some innate limits on their performance; they stop learning and improving because, for whatever reasons, they stopped practising – or never started' (Ericsson and Pool 2016: 225).

At my school, we have an annual 'Pi Day' where students may, if they wish, recite pi to as many decimal places as they can in an assembly, checked by a maths teacher. I've seen a student recite pi to 200 places and the school record is currently 708. Since this friendly competition has been running for several years now, more students (and staff) are taking part (it's up to about fifty now), and a few of them have pushed up their individual scores as they have practised and improved their memory recall methods. Struggling, planning, chunking: it's all painfully exposed. Listening to some students it's clear that they are recalling strings in an almost musical fashion, with a rhythm to the number sequences they recite. Other methods are not so readily apparent. I think that each student must also have previewed what it would be like to stand in front of 150 people and call out the numbers. I salute their skill and bravery. It is fascinating to see these skills develop and interesting to speculate how much further some of these students could go.

Another way to consider the process of chunking is to look at recent research on metacognition. The EEF's report on *Metacognition and Self-Regulated Learning* offers insight and practical guidance about what this might mean in practice. One of the key findings is that teachers need to model explicitly and share metacognitive strategies so that students can monitor and evaluate their own learning. A worked example takes us through a student's thought process as they attempt a self-portrait in an art class (Education Endowment Foundation 2018b: 12–13):

- Planning: what materials do I need in order to succeed here? What have I learned from my past experience of doing this or a similar task?

- Monitoring: How can I improve this? What techniques would make this a better portrait?

- Evaluation: Next time, what would I do differently, and why? What other perspectives could I adopt, especially having looked at some other examples?

Some students in our classes may do this instinctively, just as some adults seem to, but many more will benefit from having these stages explicitly demonstrated, modelled and refined. This is why it is so beneficial for the teacher to demonstrate exactly the same process live in the classroom. 'Deeds not words', as the suffragette motto had it. This process is about helping our students to improve in learning about their learning – becoming self-actualised and self-aware learners – without it seeming too heavy or clunky. It is as appropriate for primary school as it is for the sixth form. Indeed, the earlier these skills can be fostered, the better. Didn't Mozart start to demonstrate excellence quite young? *Teachers model, students learn, students model.*

International Baccalaureate Diploma students have to write a 4,000 word extended essay on a subject of their choice. The process requires self-evaluation, which is recorded on a form submitted with their essay and assessed externally. When reading these reports as an examiner, it is clear to me which students (and which supervisors) have engaged whole-heartedly with the research process: changing direction, following a new lead, hitting a dead end, finding enjoyment and fulfilment in the successful completion of what is probably the longest piece of writing they have ever done. It is a pleasure to reward this. Other students have not been shown how to go through these patterns or have ignored them, and it is distressing and disappointing to think what some of them might have achieved 'if only'. The extended essay is itself part of one of the best examples of genuine curricular planning and thinking known to me in the field of education. The International Baccalaureate Diploma is not perfect, but it represents an excellent and considered model of thinking about the depth, breadth and overview it fosters in the worldwide community of students and teachers who undertake it.

Why scaffolding expertise matters for high-attaining students

Expertise can be developed in the classroom by modelling, learning and practice without it seeming like a return to the Victorian classroom. It may be helpful to recap some of the core principles which will help to boost attainment for all students so that as many as possible become expert learners.

Goldilocks shows the way

Learners love to see where they have come from and where they are going. It's fun in January of Year 9 to look again at the maths problems which seemed like hieroglyphics back in September and which can now be manipulated with ease. Back in the autumn the problems lay in the struggle zone because the teacher knew those students better than anyone else: better than the head of department, better than the SLT member dropping in that day, better than the multi-academy trust manager in a shiny suit on a flying visit. The struggle zone is 'ideal porridge for Goldilocks' territory – not too easy. (Although why shouldn't we let students do the really easy stuff once in a while? They love it, just like when we find a simple form of cooking wholly satisfying.) And not too hard. (Although a glimpse of what is too hard now but will be possible, even under timed pressure, come June, is entirely desirable.) In-between, deliberate and purposeful practice in the struggle zone combines elements of both and offers research-backed rewards.

Pitching the lesson at the heart of the struggle zone relies on, for example, checking where pupils' understanding lies by means of hands-down questioning at the start of a lesson or some think-pair-share work to explain a rule to each other. Recap over (and there is absolutely no neat 'time allocation' for this because a 'starter' may need to become the main part of the lesson), the Goldilocks formula kicks in as excellence is showcased via the accurately labelled diagram showing the excretory function of the kidney or the model paragraph analysing Act V of *Macbeth*. How can we teach to the top without the pupils knowing what excellence actually looks like?

But there's more. They also need to see how to get there from where they are now and what the common pitfalls are on this particular learning journey. Planning and chunking methods and outcomes are universal principles applicable to any subject or task in schools.

Plan is a four-letter word

Planning is the best form of preparation and scaffolding. It's a pattern of behaviour which often does not come naturally to young people. Their willingness and capacity to plunge straight into a task or procedure and work it out as they go along is simultaneously refreshing and alarming. 'Plan' is a word students should use more often, and we can help them by building it into a basketball session or a physics lesson. Simultaneously, we can point out the savings in time and mental and physical energy which an effective and agreed plan produces. Planning that presentation increases the opportunities for success in its delivery and assessment. What's the rush? Deep, meaningful consideration of the options before setting out brings the top closer and makes the achievement of excellence accessible to all, not just the quick thinkers. Planning also includes the preparatory stages and build-up to a task, not just its execution.

Chunk it

Deliberate practice often deals in the micro not the macro. My A level history students often miss this point as, with the confidence of youth, they sit down to write their Crusades essay for me in an hour and a half or perhaps two hours of homework. The results may be acceptable but this is nothing to do with deliberate, focused practice. Brilliant history educators like Christine Counsell (2004), Ian Dawson (2015) and Michael Riley (2018) have advocated, for example, breaking down complex questions into smaller, coherent chunks of analysis, with each paragraph following a point-explain-evidence model. Planning a sequence of lessons around an exciting and accessible open enquiry question (e.g. 'How great was Augustus?') has been an area of professional practice at the heart of good history teaching for several generations – not least because it can be broken down into a series of equally interesting and stretching sub-questions (see Riley 2018).

Indeed, the work of the Schools History Project (SHP) during more than forty years of groundbreaking work has led the way in curriculum reform, methodological enquiry and practical strategies to the extent that it has become a model for other subject associations and has an influence across the education world. Scaffolding expertise in SHP fashion does not mean compromising excellence; in fact, the opposite is the case. The inspirational Paula Lobo (2016) has modelled how to use the work of professional historians to help students understand the purpose and use of an essay introduction. Baby steps in constructing mini-explanations and micro-points will encourage intense concentration and clarity of thinking; the fully grown essay will be much more than just the sum of these parts, but without the small pieces the essay will be bare bones.

Inner and outer voices

It is a truism that effective learning needs feedback, and the research discussed above on practice confirms this. Some feedback does more harm than good; some is unhelpfully wrapped up in variations on 'try harder'. Hitting your head against a barrier repeatedly indicates a problem, and it's not with the barrier. Some learners have developed a strong inner voice or have decided to build a powerful model of self-critique which allows them to improve with little external guidance, but the majority of young people still need our support on their individual journeys. Of course, feedback tells improving athletes, performers and students where they've gone wrong and where they've done well. But a particular strand of effective feedback lies in maintaining and improving motivation. Putting in the hours of practice won't be enough by itself to hit the top without the motivation to see and reach the next level. Feedback will be explored more thoroughly in the next chapter.

Teacher, coach, mentor

When reading about deliberate practice, it is still part of my cultural conditioning to think about a tennis player hitting hundreds of serves or a young flautist practising scales repeatedly. It is harder to imagine these methods applying in a classroom, but they can. Doug Lemov's wonderful books in the Teach Like a Champion strand come with DVDs showing techniques that we can all learn and practise to make us more effective teachers. Again, it's often by small steps, and it's always about practice and repetition until something that was worthwhile as a one-off becomes part of our daily toolkit of skills.

Whether your CPD coach is an American high school teacher using finger clicking as non-verbal signalling or a colleague chosen by you to review your recent work on whole-class feedback as part of an enlightened whole-school coaching programme, the principle is the same: show me, model it carefully for me, break it down until I'm totally clear, let me have a go, that's not too bad, now let me have a real go, check in again next week. Repeat. Repeat. Effective learning and teaching to the top is all about teaching, coaching and mentoring. The labels we give to this process don't really matter because it's the care, love and consideration they show that makes the difference.

Ten activities for you to stretch and challenge

Here are ten activities which are regularly set in schools and colleges as extension or 'stretch and challenge' tasks. They are perfectly valid examples which can, as they stand, give rise to excellent outcomes in your classroom. But I want to move my thinking and practice along to enrich these standard strategies with research evidence. These are only suggestions and they can readily be supplemented with many brilliant examples of your own, but they may serve as prompts for reflection (and disagreement) in your department.

1. Extension sheets and questions

Some colleagues believe extension sheets to be the work of the devil. They certainly can be the epitome of the idea that a pupil who completes their maths problems efficiently is rewarded with, yes, more of the same. But they are probably here to stay.

Stretch and challenge this activity

- Daringly, give the sheet to the whole class. How can you be sure that only a few can or want to complete it? Even more daringly, give it out at the start of the lesson so that pupils can be responsible for their own rate of progress through a series of tasks. Maya is unlikely to improve her motivation if she feels excluded from what others are doing.

- Try purposeful practice in just one of the core skills, digging a borehole into the learning underpinning an activity. Depth not breadth.

- Ask them to design a consolidation and practice task for next year's class and get them to gallery critique it using Ron Berger's (2003) 'kind, specific and helpful' principles (i.e. identify strengths as well as shortcomings).

- Connect the learning: can pupils extend an extension sheet by explaining it to a peer/chunking it into units accessible to every pupil/turning it into a quiz, cartoon or diagram/linking it to a website/redesigning it from scratch?

2. Open-ended research task

At worst, the open-ended research task is death by project and an invitation to google randomly. YouTube videos of lava from a Hawaiian volcano consuming cars can be fun, but where is the learning? If you want the class to find out about a famous engineer or architect, expect a PowerPoint of James Dyson's many colourful vacuum cleaners. Digital natives? I'm not convinced that a whole generation deserves the label; some pupils are adept at ICT and others are merely competent.

Stretch and challenge this activity

- Provide a tight, controlled beginning to the task with carefully chosen criteria and modelling so that everyone produces one PowerPoint slide using appropriate terminology of, for instance, volcanic eruptions and a relevant diagram or image, and then use oral feedback from the class to critique kindly for improvement. Only towards the end of the task is it genuinely open ended with student choice of what and how to present, because by then they fully understand that the term of reference is excellence.

- Think about the specific digital research skills you would like pupils to acquire and demonstrate – for example, using Creative Commons licences or crediting sources accurately. Do the pupils see themselves as part of a digital community of enquiry, gathering and then transforming resources for the classroom?

- Upload some extracts from the autobiographies of Zaha Hadid, Jonathan Ive or James Dyson to your virtual learning environment (VLE) and ask the students to create some interview questions for them. Zaha Hadid died in 2016. What do the students think was her outstanding contribution to architecture? Ask them to write an obituary assessing her work.

- Ask the students to review a favourite or famous building from the perspective of an admiring tourist or a critical everyday user of the building. How and why do their perspectives differ?

- Use the brilliant Google Arts & Culture resource – an astonishing collection of tools enabling learners to explore distant buildings, museums and art collections, as well as individual works of art, in great detail. This means going beyond random browsing, especially as pupils could spend hours on this site doing precisely that. Ask them to curate images into their own personal gallery or supplement a geography/religious studies project with extra understanding of the local environment and culture gained from Google Street View tours of the Daigoji Temple in Japan or a petrified forest in Arizona.

3. Picture starter to hook pupils into a lesson

A picture starter can work very well to elicit interest and provoke discussion. It can serve as the basis for useful recap, introduce key content or challenge preconceptions and add a twist to a familiar story or event, among many other uses. However, if used too often or in a token fashion, a picture 'hook' can become something of a millstone around the first part of a lesson.

Stretch and challenge this activity

- Play 'odd one out'. This is one of the best thinking activities and can use pictures or words. You are studying Plains Indians and you offer a word list of relevant terms, inviting the pupils to explain why one word or term does not belong with the others – for example, *fort, reservation, railroad, bravery*. Or how about *buffalo, greed, Sioux, Indian agent*? Classification is an explicit thinking skill made visible. There are no right answers and disagreement is fertile.

- Concept maps: extend this idea using a concept map. Write a key question in the middle of a large sheet of paper (e.g. Why did some women gain the vote in 1918?). Surround it with possible causes and effects. Ask the pupils to forge, and especially to justify, links between the factors.

I owe these ideas to Peter Fisher's excellent *Thinking Through History* (2002), which builds enquiries around photographs, stories and mysteries in a manner guaranteed to provoke pupil thinking and argument.

4. An extra reading list or viewing list (e.g. bibliography or filmography)

Many departments provide paper or electronic lists of fiction or subject-specific extra reading or viewing to enhance and enrich further study, which is excellent. Every science exercise book or folder should contain a list of recommended reading, such as science fiction for students to enjoy at an age-appropriate level. But how do we close the knowing–doing gap by building opportunities into lessons to encourage and monitor such viewing and reading?

Stretch and challenge this activity

- Thread the novels together. Maya is really getting into dystopias. She will not want to read the only one on your list and then feel frustrated by the paucity of the other choices. A genre list of five dystopias from different cultures and periods will give her free choice within the guidelines, thereby improving the chances of sustained reading and exploration.

- Abandon the specification and take a lesson to share your own love of reading and language using extracts from a favourite book or film. Show Maya and Anna what the top looks like in your world.

- Get a local writer to come in and talk about his or her work, perhaps in collaboration with another school. Prime your students shamelessly with questions about writing routines and difficulties to put to them.

- Use Cornell notes (see Chapter 7) to build in self-assessment and regular checks of what students have read and watched.

5. Practice routine at lunchtime or after school

Practising a dance routine or sport enshrines the idea of deliberate, purposeful practice and is a key component of many lunchtime clubs and activities.

Stretch and challenge this activity

- The quality of the routine will reflect the number of hours put into it, but repeating the same sequences in the same way will trigger the law of diminishing returns. It is better to vary the practice, speed up or slow down the pace, chunk the routine or show them a DVD of what excellence looks like.

- Let older students lead the session. What have they learned about motivation – what has worked to get them to practise and improve? How did they get around the barriers they inevitably hit? Ericsson says that finding and sticking to habits really helps because this minimises the reasons to stop. Berlin Philharmonic violinists practise early in the morning when nothing else can get in the way. How do successful older students plan for success (e.g. estimating how long a routine will need to be worked on)?

6. Class debate at the end of a unit

Debates are excellent for allowing free discussion and listening to other perspectives, but too often they degenerate into point-scoring and low quality contradiction. Ironically, what students sometimes think they will enjoy about a debate is the absence of rules and the chance for a free-for-all discussion, whereas what they actually enjoy is a rule- and role-heavy discussion which has been planned by the teacher (or the teacher and the students) as carefully as any other activity – if not more so.

Stretch and challenge this activity

- Ask pupils to come up with their own debating rules. How will they reward listening skills, persuasiveness and modifying or changing views? Offer pupils some texts, facts and knowledge with which to support the debate and ask them to prepare questions for the opposition, so the debate does not degenerate into petty point-scoring. Then swap roles so that each pupil is now arguing against their own prepared position.

- A 'boxing match' debate (or dinner party) with pupils scoring points for the quality of their sparring can work well, with the necessary and obvious safeguards. Pupils love watching verbal 'take downs' on social media, so here is a chance to play one, decode it, assess it and apply it: what makes a knockout 'punch', and why?

- 'Hot-seat' roles. For example, a religious studies lesson on speciesism and animal rights will invoke strong passions, but what is the learning outcome? Putting a succession of pupils into the 'hot seat' as moral philosopher Peter Singer and as a critic is more likely to produce memorable points and ideas. Before you start, give every pupil time to read and interrogate accessible extracts from Singer's *Animal Liberation* (2015 [1975]) plus a critical review of it to prepare for the discussion. The skill of debating is founded on a bedrock of knowledge: statistics, examples, ideas and beliefs. Using knowledge to inform debating positions is crucial: without whole-class knowledge all you have is a shouting match. As the old Monty Python sketch reminds us, there is a whole host of difference between an argument and a contradiction. Yes there *is*!

7. Extra help session dedicated to a past paper

Additional sessions devoted to past papers is a standard expectation for any good department. However, it is only the students who don't need them who turn up to extra sessions, or so teacher wisdom has it. Deliberate practice of past papers is obviously vital to exam success, but how might we help to foster the motivation among more students to attempt another one and how might we move their learning forwards this time?

Stretch and challenge this activity

- 'Start to finish: Sir does the exam!' Model the whole process yourself and turn a past paper into a learning journey. Guide the students through every single stage (albeit speeded up) from the second the paper lands on your desk, through every question and on to the final checks and submission.

- If this really is too important for lunchtime or for many of them to miss – which it is – roll it out across every lesson as part of revision.

- My wife and her department acquire English GCSE papers as soon as they are released and sit down to do them in a classroom under timed conditions. They then know exactly what Maya, Anna, Asif and the others have faced well before results day, and have the basis for some model answers for their own future teaching of that paper.

8. Make a poster for a wall display

The reasoning behind poster-making is sound enough – namely, consolidating the understanding of ideas and condensing this comprehension into an image or text which conveys a message both powerfully and accurately. In practice, posters often represent the lowest common denominator of both thinking and drawing. Posters in history are especially prone to poor execution (which just happens to be a favourite subject for students to draw).

Stretch and challenge this activity

- Model the template of planning, monitoring and evaluating suggested by the EEF (2018b). It really is all about planning and design.

- Impose a strict word limit using examples of successful posters as exemplars. How many words, if any, and why? Must it really be A4 or could it be four times the size? How might the class link this to the geography department's expertise in maps and projections to add another visual perspective? How might we connect the 'triangular trade' to bonded labour in the twenty-first century?

- Gallery critique or 'Austin's Butterfly'[1] type discussions should allow for reflection and improvement in the early stages of drafting and sketching, before committing to any final decisions. Could an art teacher evaluate the end products?

9. Extra vocabulary list – enrichment of topic knowledge

Vocabulary lists are a necessary part of success in modern foreign languages. The more words the students know – and they need to be not just 'test known' but capable of being retrieved from long-term memory – the less pressure there is on active working memory in the pressure of a test or exam. But even high-attaining students can struggle in Year 11 when yet more words are thrown their way.

Stretch and challenge this activity

- Chunking: ask Anna (the student in your class with improving recall skills) to help. She can explain how she creates a pattern or framework to learn new vocabulary or a new tense.

- Show the extra language being used in a real context such as a film or TV clip so that the students see the sheer speed of delivery and how some of the new words are incorporated.

- Low-stakes quizzing: give the students lots of practice by using low-stakes quizzing in every lesson, not just in the traditional end-of-unit test. Use a game or app such as Kahoot! or Quizlet to generate resources and boost motivation.

- There are lists of words in English which every 16- or 18-year-old should know. I give out classic 20cm x 10cm notebooks to A level students and encourage them to write down new words and terms regularly to build their vocabularies.

10. Make some flashcards or a mind map for revision

The current mantra for students to use flashcards or mind maps can be a step in the right direction towards retrieval practice and spaced learning, but it is too often used unthinkingly as a fallback. Similarly, the indiscriminate use of highlighters in notes – or, worse still,

---

1 See https://www.youtube.com/watch?v=hqh1MRWZjms.

textbooks – is often a colourful self-deception. Highlighters belong with chewing gum on the banned list. Revision methods can be a powerful way of understanding what students can and can't do, and why. However, for revision to be a circle (or a loop) there needs to be feedback from other students and/or a test set by the teacher: is the mind map too condensed or wordy? Are the flashcards too random and unfocused? Are they missing key formulae or tenses?

Stretch and challenge this activity

- Flashcards can be powerful aids to knowledge acquisition and retrieval, but just as with every other learning method, their effective use has to be modelled and practised. Why not use them at the start of the unit, model/share/improve them in subsequent lessons, show how they work with mini-quizzes and only then demonstrate improved recall and retrieval in the end-of-unit test?

- Mind maps, flow charts, algorithms and worked examples in maths are also useful acquisition and retrieval aids. Ongoing practice and refinement is more likely to boost retention and recall than one-off attempts which may or may not succeed.

- What does success in this test look like? For Maya it might be accurate labelling of the parts of a kidney. For Tom it could be understanding for the first time how the kidney functions within the excretion system. Are our assessment methods sufficiently nuanced to be able to acknowledge and reward both?

What's in your backpack for this journey?

These ten tasks are deliberately familiar, routine stretch and challenge activities for classes and individuals. I have chosen them to illustrate the point that there is much of value in what already happens in many schools. For teachers such as Ramona, storming Castle Clever to take on and trial a new approach or skill to Year 10, learning is great fun when time and energy allow. But in the meantime, the standard hard-learned and mastered practices work – and can work very well indeed.

Research by Anders Ericsson, the EEF and others simply takes us further on this journey by asking what else we need in our backpacks so that more of our students can become high attainers and existing high attainers can become expert learners. It turns out that we can travel light, more lightly than perhaps we thought when packing. Much of what we need is in our heads already: it is the knowledge that we need to plan, connect, practise and repeat core knowledge and skills. The Swiss Army knife we were tempted by turns out not to have a gadget for genius or a tool for inspiration. That shiny new LED self-winding torch promising to throw light on every area of learning and teaching loses its charge and attraction all too quickly.

Instead, a rather creased and wind-blown paper map allows us that most crucial quality for expert learning – planning. A mundane notebook records the phases of the journey, which has been broken down into sections to prevent it from looking too daunting. This chunking or breaking down of a process makes the journey or task credible and manageable. The bells and whistles on our mobile phone are expendable, but the archived WhatsApp group chat from a previous group who tackled this journey is invaluable. We can now see their reflections on what they would do differently next time. Finally, in the super-lightweight class comes a postcard of the summit of the mountain you are climbing. What will the view look like and how will you describe it? You have, quite literally, a picture of success in your hands.

Some questions to consider

Aiming for excellence

- How could you instantly improve one of the suggested strategies in this chapter?

- In what ways do you provide students with examples of excellence (e.g. questions or summaries)?

- What does 'scaffolding to the top' look like in your subject?

- How do your students perceive excellence in your subject?

- How do you use students as pathfinders to excellence in your subject?

Sharing success

- How does your local research network or similar body help to share ideas and resources in your subject area?

- What do deliberate practice and mental representations of success typically look like in your subject?

- Have you shared examples of tasks where students have followed a plan-monitor-evaluate model within your department?

- What does the 'struggle zone' look like in your subject and related subjects?

Summary

The quotation by Anders Ericsson and Robert Pool at the start of this chapter reminds us of the point of purposeful practice. The aim is for students to strike out on their own and become lifelong, self-aware independent learners. Schools commonly state this as an aim in their mission statements, and doubtless mean it, but are we modelling to them more than one pathway – or any route at all? The top is the highest level to which you and your students can aspire. You know them better than anyone else. You are uniquely placed to show them what expert performance and achievement looks like in your subject and across your curriculum. However, just pointing the way and cheerleading students to try harder and strive for the summit won't do it. Feedback for success needs to be specific. Work on motivation needs to look at maximising reasons to continue and reducing reasons to quit. Habits help; routine repetition rewards. Ericsson's research tells us that working out what expertise and success look like – in other words, having a mental model of success – is the often missed component on this learning journey.

High-attaining students need scaffolding and modelling as much as any other student, and they are superbly placed to become reciprocal sharers and modellers themselves. Expert learners are made, not born. They plan, they estimate, they develop habits and rituals, and they share these with others in their team and classroom. They minimise the risks of failure with extrinsic motivation from the people around them. This conscious, active modelling works, and it is strongly evidence based. Imitation alone won't complete the journey from able to remarkable. That much vaunted and elusive quality called creativity is linked by research evidence to expertise. If we want more creative schools and classrooms, we know how to get there and how to close the knowing–doing gap.

Chapter 4

Feedback

We need to stop looking for the next big thing and instead focus on doing the last thing properly.

Dylan Wiliam, in Greg Ashman, 'An Interview with Dylan Wiliam' (2018)

Key themes

- We should not characterise learners (or indeed ourselves) as simply 'poor at maths' or 'a natural linguist'. Feedback is a valuable form of deliberate, purposeful practice to deploy from our toolkit of good practice. Building it into curriculum design is essential.

- Feedback can be an important part of the process of improvement for high attainers and every other student, alongside praising effort and working to build their motivation to establish effective study rituals and habits.

- Some types of feedback and self-review are more effective than others in helping students to move from being able to remarkable. If this was an easy process to get right, schools would have been doing it successfully for years.

- You can model routines for your learners that will help them to take responsibility for their own self-review, so that it becomes a process they do rather than something that is done to them. In this way, they build their own mental representations of success and share them with their peers. Feedback, done properly, moves learners forward rather than trapping them in the recent past.

There has been a lot of research on feedback in recent years. Indeed, there is probably a larger body of literature on this topic than many others in the field of education. It is impossible to do justice here to the many themes and good practices, so I have selected some strands which tie into the overall direction and purpose of this book. Readers wishing to explore these ideas and others in depth will benefit from reading the works of Dylan Wiliam, John Hattie and others listed in the bibliography. Similarly, we can pay tribute to the creativity and energy of those teachers who are willing to share and discuss what works for them in terms of feedback. We know it's important and we want to get it right. We haven't failed to hear the message.

Like these brave teachers, I've filtered what I've read and heard through my own experience so that what follows has, I hope, a practical bent. Firstly, I outline five reasons why feedback matters for high-attaining students. There are then ten practical strategies for classroom use which encapsulate some of these principles and ideas. If nothing else, they should serve to stimulate discussion in departments about what works in specific contexts – because nothing works for everyone all the time.

I've tried to practise what I preach: an earlier draft of this chapter was nervously submitted to my wife for feedback. Unequivocally, she told me it would be even better if I cut out a lot of the literature review and waffle and focused instead on what works for teachers. Here goes!

Why feedback matters for high-attaining students

Research evidence shows that effective feedback boosts learner progress at all ability levels

It is axiomatic that feedback matters. Influential educator John Hattie argues that the effect size of a feedback strategy that works is among the highest that can be measured. Hattie's critics are less convinced by his statistical methods and their applicability, but for many researchers and classroom practitioners it is clear that feedback makes a difference. The EEF lists feedback among the teaching strategies with the biggest impact: an effectiveness trial in 2018 found that schools which followed an Embedding Formative Assessment programme saw pupils make an additional two months' progress in their Attainment 8 GCSE scores.[1] Rob Coe (2017) and the Centre for Evaluation and Monitoring team regularly cite feedback in their advice to schools and teachers as among the strategies producing the greatest impact at the lowest cost. Dylan Wiliam (2015, 2016) has led the way in arguing that effective feedback, done well, works.

I am doing none of these eminent researchers justice in lumping together decades of writing and thinking about how learners respond to what we tell them or what they tell each other. Extrapolating from what they say, the scale of the impact of effective feedback on

---

1 See https://educationendowmentfoundation.org.uk/projects-and-evaluation/projects/embedding-formative-assessment/.

our students' progress may be much greater than we once thought. We can certainly do it well or badly. Whether we call it marking, testing, peer evaluation, Assessment for Learning or just telling students how they've done, feedback has always been with us and always will be, regardless of educational trends or fads.

My contention is that feedback stands a better chance of working for high-attaining students – and therefore, potentially, for all students – if it is used in conjunction with, and in parallel to, the methods of purposeful, deliberate practice discussed in the previous chapter. Initially, a teacher, coach or mentor will probably need to be involved as an 'outside eye' or 'critical friend' to appraise, prompt, urge and focus. Gradually, however, modelling becomes self-review as learners adopt the metacognitive good habits prompted by the expert feedback of their teacher or coach.

Learning to accept and respond to feedback is what helps to make it effective. Feedback that is tied to deliberate practice is more likely to be specific, targeted and well-received. Put simply, take Anna's essays that you have just reported on at parents' evening. There may have been some natural developmental improvement between Years 11 and 12 which meant that her powers of analysis would have improved anyway, even if you had done little or nothing in class. Equally, some of the improvements in her essays may be connected with brain development, as the prefrontal cortex matures and synaptic pruning takes place. But even more may come from responses to the work undertaken. As you bring Anna's impressed parents into a positive feedback loop, you explain that her class knows how to improve because you've broken down effective paragraph writing in a lesson, you've shared ideas on structure and argument, and you've modelled a paragraph yourself in front of the class in real time (which they liked but also thought could be better, if that's OK, Miss). Now Anna can immediately, there and then, repeat the practice, add effective paragraph writing to her toolkit of self-aware skills and move on. Phew!

As Daniel Willingham (2009: 193) puts it: 'When you think about it, how can you possibly improve unless there is some assessment of how you're doing? Without feedback, you don't know what changes will make you a better cognitive scientist, golfer, or teacher.'

High-attaining students benefit hugely from the 'big questions' which feedback asks (perhaps disproportionately so)

As so often, the best questions are deceptively simple. An aspect of John Hattie's (2012a) work which I particularly like is his willingness to frame research around open-ended, challenging questions:

- **Where am I going?** Hattie suggests that this is the first question which an effective feedback strategy should ask. We have certainly become much better at setting targets and goals for our classes and year groups. They proliferate in student planners, schemes of work, spreadsheets, exercise books and folders. However, much of this feedback is often transactional and performance related. Teachers spend time, often a lot of time, awarding marks and comments to students who duly receive this information. But do they then act, review and reflect? The research suggests not.

- **How am I going there?** The second of Hattie's questions quite rightly looks at the nuts and bolts of peer and self-monitoring. It is perhaps here that the greatest potential for learning can be found. How will your school's (or cluster of schools') feedback processes help Maya or Yolanda to move from starting point A to finishing point B? Or is this more a matter for an individual department? In my school, we issue purple pens and ask students to critique their own work: purple is used for self-correction and redrafting before submission and for comments and reflections afterwards. This is a relatively simple method of initiating a beneficial feedback loop, and it passes the salient test that when PGCE students undertake placements with us they can understand and apply it without stress. Furthermore, purple pens are cheap, which cannot be said for some commercial ICT programs.

- **Where to next?** Sometimes feedback processes start more effectively at the end than the beginning. High-attaining learners may see that they would benefit by reading another novel or two by Stevenson's contemporaries in order to enrich their understanding of characterisation in *Dr Jekyll and Mr Hyde*, but how would they and why would they? Writing a purple pen comment at the end of an essay along the lines of 'Read Conan Doyle for character comparison' is a tick-box exercise if it lacks further planning and follow-up. 'Where to next?' is deceptively straightforward as a destination. It requires careful mapping and planning. This is a paradox of feedback: if we want expert learners to demonstrate spontaneity and brilliance in response to the feedback given to them by peers or ourselves, we have to plan for it and practise the methods most likely to produce it. Autonomy is unlikely to arise autonomously; independent learning needs a lot of scaffolding and supported learning.

Why 'disproportionately so'? My cheeky and unevidenced observation here is that a culture of asking big, challenging, open-ended questions lifts the sights of all learners from the humdrum to the heights, and may especially challenge high-attaining students to see not just a novel but literature, not just a physics problem but a scientific method or approach, not just a religious studies text but an ethical issue for today. The quality of feedback in our classrooms can only benefit from this virtuous circle of asking intelligent questions and thinking about directions of travel to answer them.

High attainers benefit from feedback as much as any other students

Yolanda is a high-flyer in a Year 12 maths class with the potential, the department judges, to sit maths A level in a year and then focus on further maths in Year 13. A double maths qualification which will boost her prospects of applying to a Russell Group university for an engineering degree is not going to happen through ability or hard work alone. Yolanda will benefit from the stimulus and competition of a group of like-minded students such as Asif and, of course, the expertise of a well-qualified maths teacher. This teacher will increase all their chances of securing that double qualification if she can offer Yolanda and her bright peers some mental representations of how to tackle a thorny statistics problem in a particular way, which might have a parallel with a similar process studied previously or be familiar from physics.

Restricting close and detailed feedback strategies to certain sets or classes is understandable. Schools are under immense and unprecedented pressure from Progress 8 and other benchmarks to spend time and share resources with, for example, GCSE grade 3/4 borderline students whose attainment in relation to that cruel line can make or break reputations and careers. It is regrettable that hard choices need to be made. But as a principle, high-attaining students such as Yolanda deserve to be shown habits of self-review on their own terms. They need personal and professional guidance to become aware of, and critical of, their habits of learning. Yolanda can become an expert learner – to the benefit of her class. In doing so, her learning journey may be a rollercoaster, so she will need as much pastoral care as other students.

Feedback faces up to failure – the learning journey will never be smooth, regardless of ability

In Chapter 7, I propose the metaphor of a learning rollercoaster to characterise the thrills, spills, excitement and fear at the heart of student progress. Many teachers find the process of staff review, appraisal, lesson observation and similar processes difficult, and sometimes painful. We build up to it and try to cushion ourselves from its worst blows and buffetings. The process cuts to our professional core. Compare this to how we expect a sensitive, hormone-heavy teenager such as Maya to react, surrounded by potentially critical classmates, when forced to think about why their essay on *Dr Jekyll and Mr Hyde* only earned 8/25. Deep hole, swallow me up.

This is why it is wrong to consider feedback in isolation from the consideration of a whole-school culture. If we are serious about encouraging self-reflection and improvement in our classes, we need to think about how our processes and procedures impact on the well-being of students. As a principle of feedback, this is often overlooked or its power is underestimated. Regardless of the findings of meta-analyses or 'pure' research, some of the most persuasive approaches to feedback are those which locate the process within a compassionate culture of mutual improvement and respect, not competitive, results-driven fear. In a positive environment, some meaning, at last, attaches to the vague platitudes about learning more from failure than success. Such post-hoc rationalisations often ring empty.

I first, unwittingly, came across this notion when desperately struggling in my O level maths class back in the Stone Age, or 1973 as we called it back then. We had moved far from Luton, and I started what we now call Year 11 in a new school. It ran more on fear than love. The maths teacher was strict. I blatantly borrowed a clever boy's book to copy out, literally and totally, the answers. I didn't understand a single line of the maths. I was in for a shock. The boy had left a jokey maths comment for Mr Strict on a previous piece of work. Mr Strict had replied in kind with some maths banter. I was amazed by this, and thought about it a good deal afterwards, which is doubtless why it is easily retrievable from my long-term memory. Dialogic marking has always been with us, and it clearly helped to inspire one very high-attaining student, even if it did nothing for his weak classmate. Would that Mr Strict had melted sufficiently to put an encouraging comment my way.

Feedback must confront failure, whether that is the absolute failure of 8/25 or the high prior attainer's failure of 23/25. In the end it will come down to trust. Students will buy into your urgings and promptings to look at why their explanations of kidney function were below par, if they trust you as a teacher to be sensitive and if they have confidence in themselves to undertake the task. They also need faith in others, if not the whole class then at least their talking partner or their table. Again, these relationships will blossom given the right nurturing. Easier said than done. The benefit will be that peer evaluation and oral evaluation become more possible and more powerful as mutual trust grows, because the sense of teamwork and learning together flourishes and generates its own cycle of rewards and possibilities. *Adults teach, students learn, students lead.*

Self-review becomes a learning habit which high attainers can use to model to others

There is a story told about Marco Polo's famous travels to China. The celebrated Venetian voyager met with some Chinese leaders who asked him what he was looking for. He had travelled thousands of miles and had faced many dangers. He said he was looking for dog-headed people. That's funny, came the response from the Chinese. We've spent years looking for them too.

If it's not dog-headed people, it's those unicorns of the education system – independent learners. They must be out there. Someone must know what they look like, how to catch one, how to harness its powers for the common good. Every school from Barnstaple to Barnsley says it wants to produce them. If we are to produce more self-aware and thinking students armed with a toolkit of lines of enquiry and strategies to test and critically weigh evidence, then the process of reflection and review which we summarise as feedback will play an instrumental role in their creation.

The processes have been modelled to them, and now they can pass them on. Having internalised how to make a measured appraisal of their last piece of work – whether in their heads, to a talking partner or on paper as part of a gallery critique – the deliberate, purposeful practice described in the previous chapter will help to make your students expert self-reviewers. They have been coached to excellence. *Adults model, students learn, students model.*

Ten strategies for effective self-review by high-attaining students

'Anna just seems to get better and better with her essays. Keep going, Anna!'

[I don't have much of a clue about how or why Anna's work is improving. More importantly, nor does she.]

'I must have been through this function ten times with Maya but she's still not getting it.'

[I don't have any idea about how or why Maya is not understanding this chemistry. More importantly, nor does she.]

'I went through the exam paper with the whole class, so they do know how to get grade 9s.'

[It's not my fault if they don't.]

'Is there some extra reading that Tom could do over the summer?'

[Why hasn't this teacher understood how bright my son is?]

Broken feedback loops such as these are familiar to all teachers. It is as if the laces are in the shoes but they are not tied up properly. There is no lack of goodwill or motivation to build improved feedback outcomes, nor do we lack knowledge given the quality and quantity of the research. How do we solve the conundrum and close this particular manifestation of the knowing–doing gap? Here are some strategies to help you do just that.

1. Expert learners

I've been into schools and seen pupils wearing badges saying 'prefect' or 'games captain' but I've never seen one saying 'expert learner'. The closest I can think of are ICT ambassadors, whereby certain schools identify a pupil whom the whole class and teacher can call on because they have great digital and tech skills.

Expert learners are simply an extension of this idea. This is not 'maths genius' Asif basking in his role within set 1 as the highest-attaining student, in a comfortable routine which a grateful teacher is happy to endorse. This is maths expert learner Yolanda, who is able to help the teacher keep an informal running record of where she, Tom and Maya are at, to monitor the class' 'learning temperature', to report back on whether recent work was too easy or too hard and to direct it into the struggle zone. Typically she will be a more able student but not necessarily the highest attainer in every test.

Not all high-attaining students are expert learners, yet. But all expert learners are on a journey to becoming high-attainers. Graham Nuthall (2007) argues from detailed observations that the majority of verbal feedback in class comes from other students, and that most of it is inaccurate. Deploying expert learners may help to redress the balance more favourably. Far-fetched? Hattie (2012b: 131) argues that 'Interventions that aim at fostering correct peer feedback are needed.' Set besides the use of prompts, expert learners may be one such useful intervention or corrective.

Expert learners are not simply unpaid learning assistants, but they could be brought into the learning process much more effectively because of the skills they have learned and practised as learners. They have a facility with purposeful practice and, in particular, self-monitoring from which others can benefit. Expert learners will also have acquired and practised metacognitive strategies. They know about the pitfalls and false promises of learning as well as the peaks and joys of the rollercoaster ride. They can help to keep their own and the learning of others on track. Expert learners can show others the fun of revelling in the DIRT.

2. Revelling in the DIRT

Some of the education books, articles and blogs I most admire are those where everything is not presented as cut and dried, with problems neatly defined and 'answers' elegantly resolved. Learning isn't like that, and learning about learning isn't either. Sometimes something works, and sometimes something which should work doesn't, or vice versa. My own learning journey on feedback and dedicated improvement and reflection time is a case in point.

Schools are using self-reflection in many different ways. As ever, the local context and needs of each school and set of pupils should drive what form the process takes, rather than buying in a one-size-fits-all model. Bottom up not top down. In my department, we typically use self-reflection after a bigger piece of work as a summative exercise to consider what went well and what didn't. But it is also formative in the sense that the comments (in purple pen) should carry forward to the next time some extended writing is undertaken.

Here's how it might work, although I'm sure you will have lots of variations and improvements of your own to suggest. I will remind the class of some of the aims of the exercise – to help them improve in a non-judgemental way, to encourage awareness of their own strengths and weaknesses and to give them a chance to ask questions if they are unsure about why they have been given the mark they have. I will go through the task and the mark scheme and share what worked and what didn't. To save time, I might use a common marking pro forma displayed on a screen, rather than writing similar comments many times in their books. We will remind ourselves (hopefully from previous examples) of the value of writing something positive about the task and how we attempted or completed it. Any self-review should be kind, critical and specific. I will then leave the students to work quietly until one or two of them have modelled some pertinent comments that I can share with the rest of the class to ensure that this difficult process is accessible to every learner.

By the time I have seen all or most of the students on a one-to-one basis, the whole process will have taken most of a one hour lesson. If any time remains, I will use it to signpost what lies ahead in terms of topics and skills – where we've got to, where we're going and why, and how come we're about to look at something as seemingly random and disconnected as seventeenth century witch-hunting, having spent weeks immersed in the political and religious complexities of the Civil War. The same process is carried out in a similar way with both GCSE and sixth-form classes.

The benefits of DIRT are considerable:

- It strongly encourages self-reflection and demands that a class pauses, thinks and adjusts before moving forward.

- It saves time when used alongside a whole-class marking system or a series of marking codes.

- Lengthy written teacher comments which are beautifully composed but scarcely glanced at are replaced by student self-assessment in their own voice.

- Pragmatically, it provides an instant message for a book look, work scrutiny or inspection that these students have been given a chance to take responsibility for their own learning.

- It provides an exemplar in miniature of the metacognitive processes which are part of many schools' professed learning aims.

DIRT is a helpful way of stopping a class in its tracks. Think about your work, right now. Look at where we've been and where we're heading. It's that part of the rollercoaster ride where the class can briefly catch their breath, readjust their grip and steel themselves for what is ahead. It shares the merit of being appropriate for all students because it builds in raising the bar from each student's individual starting point to wherever they can reach and beyond.

For some teachers, DIRT can feel like a waste of that most precious commodity in the school week – time. The pressure to add more content, testing, data collection and pastoral interventions seems relentless, so devoting a large part of a lesson to what may seem like idle musing is never going to appeal. At its worst it can be formulaic and meaningless. Like many other interventions it needs practice, improvement and to fit, and to be seen to fit, into a bigger culture and strategy of collective self-improvement for a group of learners. By itself it may or may not be effective, but when integrated within an approach to feedback which is inclusive, adaptable and meaningful, it moves closer to generating the kind of effect size which John Hattie and the EEF have recorded.

3. Layer up the feedback: task, process and expert layers

High-attaining students can help to improve the quality and quantity of feedback received and acted on by a class of students. This is much more likely to happen if some active modelling and prompting takes place, rather than waiting for it to take place organically (Hattie 2012b).

So, let's layer this up. The bottom layer of prompting is where feedback concentrates on the *task* itself – how well it was done, where it went wrong and whether the success criteria were met. This is where a lot of the classroom feedback that I've seen in lessons and used myself operates: it is classic what went well (WWW)/even better if (EBI). It is all well and good, but it is not sufficient on its own.

Moving upwards, the *process* (or self-review) layer of prompting considers why errors were made and what a pupil's understanding of the concepts and knowledge behind the task might be.

'When bringing this essay together, I got confused about … '

'I never really understood that I needed to do X to achieve Y.'

'I forgot that it worked in class when we did Z and applied it to similar examples.'

The process layer could be carried out collaboratively, since it is likely that there are common weaknesses shared by groups of students.

Finally, and most powerful of all, is the *expert* layer of prompting (sometimes called self-regulation):

'How well did I plan what I needed to do for this task?'

'How well did I monitor it as I was doing it and adjust accordingly?'

'What picture of success do I now have in my head for the next task?'

Task, process and expert layering of feedback using starter sentences or prompt questions is a form of scaffolding to the top from which every student can learn and benefit. It can become second nature very quickly, but the reverse is not true: it is not something that many students will do without modelling and encouragement. Enabling expert learners (perhaps some are better at supporting feedback than other methods) to take a lead will improve the chances of whole-class engagement with an activity likely to produce improved outcomes.

These are the kinds of problem-solving strategies which I'm sure that many of our students can be coached and encouraged to apply, both in class as peer evaluation and at home if more self-reflection is required. Either way, time is needed. One reason that feedback methods too often become half-hearted and tick-box is that not enough time is allocated to insisting on a high level of concentration and effort when completing them. A five-minute starter won't cut it.

4. Expert learners model the journey and gallery critique it

Stop. Flip the whole classroom. Hand over the maps, compass and backpacks to the expert learners. If we have understood and accepted Hattie's three questions (Where am I going? How am I going there? Where to next?), then why not let our expert learners model, explain, support and go over them? Are we scared that they won't understand them? Really?

Expert learner Yolanda can see that a particular unit of geometry is hard, so she shows the class – mid-unit and before any kind of assessment is taken – how she skims the relevant section of the textbook first and then writes down in the back of her exercise book any terms and definitions (e.g. isosceles) which she thinks she will need a reminder for. Then, daringly, she writes out in the front of her book – in spite of having had no specific request to do this by her teacher – the formulae she has already used and is likely to need to know before any test so that she has them in one accessible place.

The class then interrupt and describe what they still find really hard about geometry. Yolanda and Asif, whose skills as a potential expert learner are improving, help the teacher to ensure that each student has written down an area of struggle but also some potential strategies to try. Yolanda shows them how last year's work on basic trigonometry can be really useful as a reminder of how weird and difficult maths can seem at first, but it can then be broken down into a series of intelligible moves. Finally, she reminds the class that they were asked at the start of the year to visit a particular maths website which offers many more examples of calculating angles for students like Asif to practise.

All of this is thrown around the class, adjusted and improved, and then put up on the walls as a gallery critique exercise as big posters or stuck into a book as an excellent exemplar process. David Fawcett (2013) has written a very interesting blog post on how to model and create a culture of critique.

5. The app-liance of science

When I asked my chemistry colleague, Andy Nalty, about apps and web-based learning sites ideal for stretch and challenge, his response was immediate: the Khan Academy, Seneca and YouTube were recommended as free, universal resources that foster self-directed extension work well above and beyond the curriculum. Khan Academy (www.khanacademy.org) makes self-paced practice possible so that students work their way through age-appropriate material individually, in pairs or groups, with you as teacher monitoring their progress. Seneca (www.senecalearning.com) enables homework to be set, marked automatically and monitored by you to inform your planning on the basis of evidence about what has and has not been learned. It also provides a huge pool of resources for students to dip into or study in depth as part of their individual learning journeys. YouTube (www.youtube.co.uk) contains 'walkthrough' resources which offer students instruction, review, self-testing and revision to guide them through units or whole courses. In addition, there are powerful apps such as Showbie (www.showbie.com) and OneNote (www.onenote.com) which make the self-reflective approach outlined in this chapter accessible and powerful.

As a chemistry teacher, Andy was well and truly in his element modelling these platforms to me. Once you have set up a 'classroom' and added assignments and resources to it, your students can annotate tasks which you can see and share with their peers. You can make a short embedded video as you work through a mark scheme, and the students can move through it at their own pace. Alternatively, you can ask an expert learner to take ownership of the task and make the video herself so that her thinking process is made visible to the whole class. Learning about bonding truly has no limits.

Another app, Socrative (https://socrative.com), allows you to ask questions which need short written answers. The class can then vote on which answer they prefer. Andy says: 'You'd be surprised who is best, once they get used to the format. I can anonymise their responses too.' Socrative also has an exit ticket function (see Chapter 6) which means you can plan the next lesson based on what your students actually know about alkali metals and how they react to water, rather than what you think they know.

There is much more to say about the potential that these and other powerful learning platforms offer, but three quick points are paramount in the context of this chapter. Firstly, their content is huge – they are Britannica with bells or Wikipedia with whistles. Secondly, they are founded on the very principle of modelling expertise and becoming an expert learner which this book champions. Thirdly, they can be tailored to meet individual learning needs or the needs of particular 'rooms' within a class. The ability to customise content and improve interactivity means that these technologies are starting to pass some of the tough tests which we, as teachers, rightly apply to any ICT initiative.

6. Video vox pop

In the past, I have been quite sceptical about the benefits of student voice, and part of that reservation derived from seeing it used surreptitiously by an SLT to gather opinion about the department I was leading. I've also worried that student voice is vulnerable to confirmation bias in that it comfortingly tells us what we already suspected about what works or what doesn't, or what we think works in Spanish but not in French. Nevertheless, it may help to gain a sense of how well a policy or practice is working, provided that it is viewed in a critical fashion alongside other evidence or triangulated against other data.

As a G&T coordinator, you know who your highest attaining students are, so a video vox pop can be as simple as a tablet set up in an office or classroom with the students talking to camera. Common sense will tell you how to make this work: I would suggest putting the students in pairs for mutual support, and not having a teacher present. You may want to implement this with another department on a reciprocal basis.

What will you ask about? The more precise and focused the questions, the greater the likelihood of worthwhile responses. Asking for broad-brush comments may trigger the kinds of conversational answers you want, but they may be too challenging or vague; conversely, simple yes/no responses will not be of much value either. Are you interested in the whole school's high-attainer policy and how it works in practice, or do you want the students to suggest new activities or resources? Is the focus on a department or a year group? Will you use a list of common questions or allow free expression, or both?

Technology allows self-review to be instant. Google Forms is one such example, and seems to encourage honest responses. For surveys and quizzes you can gain immediate feedback about how a recent task or assignment has been judged. If your aim as a head of subject, for example, is to monitor and then modify a scheme of work while it is live, Google Forms can provide evidence about what is working, or not working, and why. Your students will be impressed if they see the results of their comments in the classroom the following week. They won't be impressed by a six-week delay in any changes because everything has to be run past the head of faculty or whoever. Can you make a change based on their thoughts which is actioned as quickly as you expect Anna and Maya to respond to your feedback on their *Dr Jekyll and Mr Hyde* essays?

7. Follow my leader

If you were to undertake a pupil pursuit at my school, in one day you could follow a student from feedback via WWW/EBI (Spanish) to self-assessment (maths) to purple pen (in my history lesson) to no marking at all (in the lesson of a geography colleague). This may cause you to throw up your hands in horror or dance with pedagogical delight. Within the remit of whole-school policies and principles of assessment, we allow departments a good deal of leeway to devise strategies which work for them, using their familiarity with the technical demands of their subjects and the complex needs of their students. I should add that these are not even universal practices within a single department. My geography colleague is currently trialling a model of peer and oral evaluation with one Year 9 set by not doing any routine 'tick and flick' marking of classwork or homework. He is judging their attainment by very regular monitoring and testing; his other Year 9 set are a control group. Of course, both classes are subject to the school-wide practice of regular testing and end-of-year exams.

It surprises me that schools don't use their own resources more systematically to find out what works for their high-attaining students. As you follow expert learner Yolanda from lesson to lesson, what you are picking up may have all the limitations of anecdotal evidence, and certainly shouldn't be dignified by the label of research, but it might be a valuable way to devise a series of prompts or cues of your own when you subsequently sit down with your colleagues – and, hopefully, Yolanda – to discuss what your snapshot revealed. I suggest that you layer this up using the task, process, expert model (Strategy 3):

- How did you get better at answering those geometry questions today? Did you and the other students in your class know how to find help for that particular type of question?

- How do you plan to do well in those questions next time in a test, for example? How can you gain an achievement point for effort?

This is perfect material for your next CPD session. Ideally, you will have taken on board an earlier suggestion and ditched at least some of your formal, sit-down-and-listen CPD for more of a coaching model. Either way, 'follow my leader' means asking your colleagues this question: do you understand how the expert learners in your school improve? This big question provides your starting point. I am lucky that my school encourages staff to go into each other's lessons on a reciprocal basis, enabling teachers to track pupil learning across subjects. It's an imperfect system, but without it I wouldn't know about, let alone be able to assess critically, good habits of learning happening under my nose.

Pupil pursuits are expensive in time and difficult to administer. However, many schools still send teachers to distant cities for expensive and time-dear gifted and talented student courses, which, truth be told, often deliver much less – I've been to plenty of them. More able provision does change and schools have a legal duty to remain legally compliant, but I would argue that internal CPD can go a long way to ensuring that you are asking the right questions for your school. The process of arriving at valid answers for your circumstances should be undertaken with the greatest relevance and integrity.

8. Change your lenses

Depth and overview are needed – boreholes *and* big landscapes. This applies to principles of feedback as well as being an important strand of curriculum design and scheme of work construction.

In a Year 8 history lesson, I won't write on the board 'Elizabeth I and marriage', and still less will I ask the class to write down a pointless learning objective along the lines of: 'Aims: to find out why Elizabeth never married'. Rather, I'll encourage the class to help me frame a suitable big question such as, 'Why does it matter that Elizabeth never married?' as an overview enquiry (I'll steer them that way if it's proving difficult). This question will ease them away from the illusion of 'finding out' the answer to a closed question and towards the open issue of how and where Elizabeth fits in, if indeed she does, to a pattern of successful and unsuccessful marriages and successions among Tudor and Stuart rulers. The class will want to know more about her suitors, of course, so we will drill down for depth and look at the Earl of Leicester and the Duke of Alençon and have fun with some speed-dating role play.

If I can use both telescope and microscope in my subject teacher role, I can surely do something similar when it comes to feedback in the end-of-unit assessment. Just as students improve in thinking up and framing interesting enquiry questions, so they will become more accustomed to looking for and measuring a second-order concept such as significance or change and continuity – but only if they practise this and come back to it.

I like the analogy of different lenses or glasses. Microscopes offer varying magnitudes of enlargement, depending on what is needed. The reading glasses we wear to look in detail at a source or text will not work well during a walk in the countryside. Improving self-review skills might be a question of close attention to the detail of a formula or a timeline of dates. Alternatively, expert learners might raise their eyes metaphorically to the second-order concept of causation and assess whether they are evaluating this and not something less important.

Feedback can be micro or macro. How we look at the assessment of a task or process will depend on what we are examining it for: did we get the big picture roughly right using wide-angle lenses because we need to have a destination in sight at least some of the time? How were we with the close-up, precise, small steps or chunks which we need to get right in order to build up to success?

9. Putting it into words

A growing trend among many teachers who are trying to build feedback into their hectic weekly lives is to use oral feedback methods. This includes Ben Newmark (2016), who is reducing the quantity but improving the quality of assessment by developing a portfolio of techniques. He uses verbal feedback for direct instruction and tasks set for improvement, and saves detailed written and verbal feedback for regular assessed tasks. This makes assessment more regular, accurate, clearer and immediate. This approach is wholly to be welcomed for several reasons:

- It reduces a reliance on written feedback alone, which can be counterproductive and one dimensional for pupils who find organising their thoughts on paper difficult.

- It immediately informs planning and makes it more responsive.

- It may help with teacher workload because there is no ridiculous requirement to 'mark' pupil feedback. We truly are in a Kafkaesque world when the SLT assesses our assessment of how well we have assessed how pupils have assessed themselves.

- It develops oracy, and none can doubt the importance of oral fluency in the real world. As Alex Quigley (2012) puts it in an excellent blog post, oral feedback helps to make learning visible – quite literally if you are using one of the cheap visualisers now on the market or discussing a worked example with the class. The mysterious processes involved in how a student produces a very good piece of work can be opened up and dissected.

How can expert learners offer leadership here? There are many oral feedback techniques but here are two that I've used.

Argument tunnel

I saw Leigh Almey demonstrate an argument tunnel at a TeachMeet in Bristol,[2] developing an idea from Phil Beadle (2010). It's brilliant. First of all, the students need to be familiar with a topic and able to understand a good range of divergent views. The more they know, the better the discussion. Equip the class with a list of argument points or pieces of evidence and assign them into two groups, typically for and against. This is vital. They need knowledge and more knowledge in order to have something to argue about. (I've used it with Sir Douglas Haig and his reputation as an incompetent First World War general and the 'butcher of the Somme'.) It's fun to take a straw poll at this stage and record the results, so you can compare it with their views at the end of the session.

The tunnel is formed by lining up the students on chairs facing each other down the classroom. Ask each pair of students to pick a point from a list you have explained and discussed and argue it with their opponent. After a minute or two, on a given signal, one side of the tunnel moves along one chair to face a new partner. Repeat at your discretion. The noise level can get quite high to start with but should then reduce. Now the feedback kicks in. Ask the class which pieces of information or evidence have proved most useful in building an argument, and why.

Next, tell the students to argue the opposite case. Repeat at your discretion. Now more feedback: which student has used evidence most effectively, and why? Which student was most persuasive? Who found that they were changing their mind during the exercise, and why? What are the straw poll results now?

The argument tunnel may sound like an exercise in screaming and chaos, but it can be a powerful way of demonstrating how expert learners think, deploy evidence, persuade and sometimes change their minds. The dialectic and rhetoric involved in selecting evidence, shaping points and responding to counter-evidence represents high-level thinking by every student. This is Martin Robinson's (2013) trivium in action again.

---

2 See https://www.youtube.com/watch?v=aCMvcPPzfQ0 to see an argument tunnel in action.

Think-pair-share

Tom Sherrington is a big advocate of paired discussion and feedback, and his 2012 blog post on think-pair-share outlines why this pedagogical practice trumps the classic 'hands up' approach, if we aspire to check the learning of anything approaching a whole class.

Quite simply, think-pair-share gives pupils time to think – and why not continue in silence after a period of silent reading? Since the context of this chapter is feedback and self-review, it is appropriate for the class to work quietly on their task-process-expert layering of feedback. As the pair work begins, at your signal, encourage listening and shared insight to enrich what has already been written down. The self-review then moves to the whole class, using cold calling, random name pickers or hands down, and an agreed method of noting down fresh points.

Creating a series of safe mini-environments for thinking, discussing, reflecting and sharing in pairs will enrich the quality of responses and facilitate a greater range of responses from more than just the same familiar faces. Moreover, because your sampling of pairs can be random, all the students will need to listen carefully. The aim here is to create high challenge self-review and reflection.

High-attaining students can really lead the way with discussion learning tasks and oral feedback techniques. They can act as expert learners themselves, offering leadership, guidance and support, but they can also be stretched by the particular rhythms and rules of an argument tunnel or think-pair-share.

Expert learners can emerge from unexpected places during oral feedback activities. They may not be the faces and names we would predict and may well not be the highest attaining students in the class when measuring, as we so often do, written performance. Expertise takes many forms and requires much purposeful practice. A little humility along the way is no bad thing.

10. Personalise it

At the risk of aiming for the unattainable, I want to raise the question of whether one-to-one pupil feedback is possible. If it is, it could be transformational. I'm firmly of the belief, perhaps naively, that many students do actually want to hear from us directly, personally and regularly, despite what they may say or how they may act to the contrary. Frequent brief conversations about progress in your subject could be worth a lot of written targets, stamps and stickers. What better way of demonstrating Vic Goddard's (2014) unconditional positive regard than by improving your listening skills, not dominating the conversation and making it instructional?

As discussed above, scripted question prompts may help if one-to-one conversations aren't possible. Doctors sometimes use scripts, especially when training. With scaffolding, the conversation can move on quickly from lower level task- and process-based comments to the higher layers of weighing up and evaluating recent pieces of work or contributions to a discussion, or linking them to what is coming up next.

Student voice really does become powerful when it is one student expressing their thoughts about a recent success directly into the ear of a teacher who is keen to build a relationship of trust and support. Although I've used a medical analogy, it only stretches so far. This is not a patient requiring a repeat prescription – it's a learner on a once-only journey to excellence and beyond.

Journey's end: all change, please

Feedback never really ends. What seems to be the termination of one particular ride or journey is the start of another. To stretch the analogy to breaking point, Anna, Tom and their classmates may have become accustomed to the rollercoaster but there is a monster theme park ride ahead in Chapter 7, where the passengers loop the loop and come full circle. This is often the forgotten part of feedback: it's where it leads to that matters. Where next, and why, having learned what we've learned?

Self-review can subvert the natural order of things. As teachers, we are often so wedded to the ideas of natural ability and genius that we may still believe that high-attaining students will just 'know' how to improve and how to leap from strong Year 10 Robert Louis Stevenson essays to literary criticism of undergraduate level. But if learning per se is a rollercoaster, then so is giving and receiving feedback. 'Fill in this pro forma with some ways you might have improved that essay' will tick the box saying that students should review their work, but by itself it will not take account of the peaks and troughs in progress along the way. What if high-attaining Asif has hit a plateau and doesn't know how to get better? Equally likely, what if he has lost his mojo and can't be bothered to improve?

Further along the learning spectrum, we still have Maya facing that 8/25 with a sinking feeling in her stomach because she is about to compound academic failure, in her eyes, with yet another task at which she won't succeed. Cue big handwriting and small thoughts. In my experience, there is often little correlation, if any, between the ability to self-diagnose and academic attainment. If Maya trusts her talking partner, her table, her class, her teacher and the process (hopefully all of these elements), she will be able to see the rollercoaster ride for what it is and look forward to the next adrenaline rush. That is, with practice and encouragement she can become as good as, or even better than, Asif in responding to feedback in English, which in turn could become an important component in her overall improvement in the subject.

Just because Asif hits a plateau with his English task and his reflections on it, this doesn't mean that he will struggle to self-reflect in the following religious studies lesson, nor that Maya will make the same steps forward that she just has in English. Both students will need to call on the domain-specific feedback strategies relevant to those particular subjects and practise them, just as they will for the core content knowledge and skills germane to each subject.

Intelligence about feedback is malleable. Asif and Maya's religious studies teacher may call this growth mindset or may have big 'positive mental attitude' posters on his classroom walls, whereas their English teacher Mrs Targett may prefer student-generated displays about great poets with some quotations from their work, but this variety could well be beneficial because it emphasises differences in approaches and skills.

Crucially, what the process is called is much less important than what it does. A self-reflective feedback process which is itself self-reviewed – and which acknowledges that feedback needs as much careful thought as the content of a typical lesson – is likely to move learners forward on their journeys in that subject. All hope is not lost for the English teacher collecting in those pro formas. She takes them away and uses them as a springboard to catch Asif at the end of the next lesson with a few suggestions for a route off the plateau and onto higher ground. Feedback takes deliberate practice, like all learning, and that applies to teachers too.

On the feedback rollercoaster

Some students are better at giving feedback to others than they are at receiving it themselves, and vice versa. Wise teachers and learners recognise this. Some will be in the front cars, arms aloft throughout the journey, while others will be happier at the back, and others still won't mind at all as long as they are near their friends. Whatever the seating plan, the aim of the feedback loop is to close the gap between where the student is and where they are meant to be. The loop itself is a thing of beauty and wonder. It is expertly engineered and delivers long lasting and repeated results. It is itself part of the journey.

Some questions to consider

Task layer

- How happy is your department or school with your current feedback methods? What is working well and what could be improved?

Sharing success

- What instances do you already have internally of colleagues using, for example, one-to-one sessions or peer feedback well?

- How far does staff monitoring of feedback match what the students in your department or school are saying in their video vox pops or in a quick Google Form survey?

- Who are the expert learners in each year group?

Process layer

- How do colleagues in your department react to the strategies, ideas and research discussed in this chapter?

- How deeply is feedback built into your curriculum and schemes of work, or is it merely bolted on?

Expert layer

- What are the implications of this chapter for feedback methods in your department or school?

- How can your department dovetail your work with that of a whole-school CPD or coaching programme, and how can you share your struggles, pitfalls and achievements?

- What small, manageable steps could you, as teachers, take to build on current strengths with more purposeful practice in schemes of work and weekly routines?

- What small, manageable steps could you, as teachers, take to build on this further by modelling more expert feedback in front of the students?

The challenge for the teacher creating a self-review framework for Maya's class is to build in sufficient flexibility for all students to be able to generate mental models of improvement. The challenge for Anna, Tom and Asif is to develop the knowledge, skills and trust to use that flexibility. If these two preconditions apply then there is real scope for change. Without them, feedback can become the tick-box exercise learners and teachers too often recognise.

Summary

High-attaining students won't suddenly, or even gradually, become remarkable by spontaneously developing the core skills of self-awareness. Effective feedback needs a coach, a mentor, a teacher or an expert learner to model, monitor and build it. Expert learners can be integral to the process of self-review in our classrooms. They have used their plastic, malleable intelligence to improve their own feedback skills to make learning more conscious and visible to themselves and their peers. They can serve as constant reminders to us that feedback needs to be integral to a curriculum or unit of study, rather than being bolted on to the end of a unit.

What else helps to make feedback effective? It certainly needs to be more than task based if we are aiming to teach to the top and learn to the top. Layering up feedback so that it addresses bigger overview questions designed to offer signposts along students' learning journeys will increase the chances of it being successful. This may require us to look at assessment and data. Are we reducing feedback to a number or grade? Our systems and processes for helping students to improve by evaluating their own work need not be terrifyingly complex. Simple, understandable methods which can be quickly adjusted in the light of professional common sense will work.

The implications of feedback for student and teacher well-being should never be forgotten. Trust and unconditional positive regard will always underpin the potentially painful process of insisting that students take a step back and look at what they've done, before asking the questions which will help them to move forward on their learning journeys.

Chapter 5

Collaborative Learning

Good leadership means leading the way, not hectoring other people to do things your way.

Chris Hadfield, *An Astronaut's Guide to Life on Earth* (2013)

Key themes

- Collaborative learning is the herd of elephants in the room. As teachers of classroom-based subjects, you are probably missing more than a few tricks which colleagues in other departments within your school or college already appreciate – learning is a shared and social process.

- Whether it be in the context of team sports, the Duke of Edinburgh's Award scheme, chess club, junior choir or a hundred other enrichment opportunities and curriculum lessons, the templates already exist within your walls to build exciting collaborative classrooms where roles are more flexible, power is transferred and the snow globe of your classroom is shaken.

- Collaborative learning can help to raise attainment. This is where the case becomes compelling. Research evidence shows that it is at the very least a promising way of making a difference, and inspectors praise it when they see it. It is a good thing and you should do more of it. It does not equate to poor quality group work.

- Collaborative learning uses the power of the class or group to influence behaviour for the better. It is not *the* answer, but it can play a valuable role in creating a culture of working towards a common shared goal.

- Strategies such as flipped learning and co-construction, as well as enrichment opportunities like Model United Nations, help to generate a sense of collective ownership of learning and adventure among pupils. Adventure makes students critical observers and questioners who are pursuing *scientia* (wisdom). That journey may take them into outer space – now that really is exciting!

Adults lead, students learn, students lead

It may seem a radical move to give collaborative learning and teamwork a prominent place in this book. Surely, it is individual students who will need to produce first-rate A level geography fieldwork or master the subjunctive mood in French? Ultimately, in a results-driven education system students take their exams on their own. No amount of team games or collaborative learning is going to help them with their non-calculator maths paper.

My contention is that collaboration helps to raise attainment. It's not simply a desirable, bolt-on extra. The idea is not to sweeten the pill of a hard slog through a unit of particularly difficult material through the promise of some fun work in groups. We're not just going to go outside and do some sketching. If we did, as any teacher knows, it's likely that some children will go off-task because they recognise something so different from the norm when they see it but don't quite know how to respond. Adults, I wager, would be just the same. When we try something once and it doesn't go to plan, it's easy to hold up our hands in mock horror, chalk it down to hard-won professional experience in the School of Hard Knocks and silently pledge, 'Never again!'

However, if shared work becomes the norm, if expectation levels are set high and if patterns of behaviour are well established, then the chances of unwelcome responses will diminish. An alternative response to the unsuccessful lesson is not to swear never to repeat it, but to consider the reasons why it bombed and, in particular, the element most likely to be at the root of the issue – planning. Turning this around, if curriculum planning becomes more collaborative and is constructed with the rigour and care of an A level lesson, then it will be treated with the respect it deserves.

Why collaborative learning matters

Let's start with the main challenge to the ideas underpinning this chapter: behaviour management.

Collaborative learning improves behaviour

Where pupil behaviour acts as a barrier to a learning process in team or group work, then action needs to be taken which is firm, fair and consistent. Whether this behaviour is what is euphemistically called low-level disruption or is more serious, it should trigger a response according to the principles and practices of the school's behaviour policy. As I've already mentioned several times in earlier chapters, specific institutional contexts and solutions which have been considered, reviewed and shared should not be trampled over by outside consultants, authors or Twitter big beasts. The same goes, multiplied by a hundred, for ill-informed businessmen and politicians. Just because they once went to school, it doesn't make them behavioural experts.

Those are my caveats and here are my views – very much within the philosophy and in the context of a pursuit of high attainment and excellence for every student. I have no problem with schools which have resorted to Ready to Learn or similar processes because other approaches have been tried and failed. Some schools are very tough places in which to teach. I've never had to teach in a school like that. Tapping into the latent potential of every student is often impossible when the actions of a minority seriously prejudice the learning of the majority. Nevertheless, for many schools, in my opinion exclusion rooms and similar sanctions are inappropriate and counterproductive. A model based on punishment and 'no excuses' may secure a short-term gain but at too great a cost to the all-important relationships between staff, students and parents which constitute the core culture of the school and on which learning will ultimately depend.

Just as I argue throughout this book that getting the approach to high-attainer provision right underpins everything (e.g. inclusivity, high expectations which get higher all the time, students learning from adults then leading themselves), so I believe that a culture of consistently applying simple behavioural rules and scripts, with specialist support for pupils who refuse to engage, is appropriate in most cases. Children make poor choices, including high-attainers. Some will respond to the sanction and deterrent approach constructively, but others won't. I believe that more children respond more often to approaches based on principles such as restore, redraw and repair. There are creative ways of improving on classroom exclusion which allow teachers, parents and students to think about what has happened and why, without the emotional trauma of blunt instrument sanctions. It's strange how schools (and teachers) packed with outstandingly creative thinking and learning become remarkably fixed mindset about punishment and exclusion.

There is one more piece of evidence which helps to support my view. Pupils with learning needs are overrepresented in exclusion rooms and on exclusion lists. How can that be right? What is this telling us about an inclusive culture which recognises the potential of every learner? Is it really the best we can do to have such children sitting in isolation and writing out lines or copying from pointless laminated sheets? I hope not. This is not excellent educational provision.

Paul Dix's book *When the Adults Change, Everything Changes* (2017) is a singular contribution to this debate. I urge everyone to read it. He has worked with schools and pupils far more challenging than I have known or experienced (at least, since I was at school myself).

In a nutshell, his approach is based on the consistency crucial to any school behaviour management system – but it is a consistency of *adult* attitudes and behaviours. It is built on routines such as meet-and-greet at the classroom door, silence in class at key moments and 'eyes on me'; it is a culture which, in a memorable phrase, 'eats strategy for breakfast' (Dix 2017: 2). Restoring broken relationships with question scripts and, where necessary, adult apologies leads to small steps forward and realistic outcomes. Dix even has a chapter entitled 'Deliberate Botheredness' in which he discusses going over and above with rewards for pupils who exceed behavioural expectations, which is an approach with chimes with my own thoughts on staff and pupil well-being in Chapter 8. Dix's ideas may not work for every school, but to dismiss them without a fair hearing – or, worse still, to lampoon them by comic exaggeration – is to practise precisely the type of closed thinking his book sets out to challenge.

A recent study by Sarah-Jayne Blakemore and her team at University College London lends support to the idea that adolescents are less likely to learn from punishment than reward. Comparing the responses of a group of adults and a group of adolescents to a series of abstract symbols, the study found that both groups were equally good at learning to choose symbols associated with reward, but adolescents were less effective at avoiding symbols associated with punishment (Palminteri et al. 2016). It's a long way from the research lab to a lesson with a low-attaining science set on a Friday afternoon, but as the field of cognitive neuroscience, which until just a few years ago was still in its infancy itself, grows it will have more to tell us about the teenage brain and its workings.

Whether you agree with my own views or not, I hope that they are at least consistent with what I'm arguing about collaboration and positive relationships. I want children to have a say in designing ideal lessons and schemes of work. I want them to take a lead with feedback, as outlined in the previous chapter, having learned about what the research tells us works. I want children to build strong images in their heads of how focused practice in learning and applying formulae or vocabulary or dates or sequences will help them to get a better mark next time. They learn to construct these pictures from adults and successful learners in the classroom. I want children to harness the power of the group or the team for the good of all, because it works and because adults show this all the time. If poor behaviour is stopping any of this from happening, it can be addressed and set right by adults taking the lead to repair the broken relationships with kindness, trust, consistency and clarity. Teacher–student relationships, vague as this is, merit an effect size of 0.72 (Hattie 2012b), which is high (12/150).

Collaborative learning builds trust

Few children really want to be outside the group looking in. The group has the power to isolate and it's traumatic when it happens in schools. But the group also has the influence to help prevent it from happening or to bring it to a sudden end.

If we think back to Chapter 2, where students were asked by Russell Earnshaw to devise their ideal lesson, many of the elements were shared between the students. Even the quieter, more contemplative parts of lessons possess the power of common bonding between learners. Children want to be accepted. They want to learn together. When we sit them in rows too much (I also like teaching in rows – it's the frequency that's the issue here), isolate them or make them feel cut off from others, we sometimes lose the power of common purpose and the strengths of self-regulation.

I learn from the teams that I belong to in my own school. When I rush to a pastoral leader and blurt out my own shallow analysis of a behavioural issue, he may well surprise me with an altogether different assessment of cause and effect. When I reflect on the issue a little later on, I may well conclude that his approach is more forensic and would produce a desirable outcome; just occasionally, I'll consider that I was spot on. Either way, even a hurried chat will stand more chance of leading to effective support for a child than if I hadn't shared it at all. So, the next time it happens, as it surely will, I'll be back.

All learning is collaborative

In a case study of twelve primary and secondary schools based in and around London (Wallace 2007), evidence was found of an impressive array of extra-curricular opportunities, typically between five and ten during the lunch hour and between seven and twenty after school, ranging from creative writing to choirs and table tennis to trampolining. Pupils were found not only to be suggesting such activities but also mentoring and organising them. In many schools, my sense is that sustained, effective teamwork starts outside the classroom door. Why is this? If anything demonstrates the willingness of most students to be brave, versatile and inspiring to themselves and others, it is what they do outside the classroom every week and in some cases much more often.

We think nothing of asking our teenagers to take an extraordinary leap of faith when playing organised games. For example, we expect them to dress up in 'uncool' and at times ridiculous looking kits and uniforms to chase around after a ball, to catch or hit a ball with a stick or bat, to run until it hurts and then quite a lot more when it really hurts. We also expect them to travel long distances to unfamiliar places to play unfamiliar opponents in outdoor environments, and at unpleasant temperatures, and then to be shouted at and jeered at by adult strangers, who should know better, from the touchlines.

All of this is routinely expected for little or no reward; conversely, there is a good chance of ridicule and embarrassment, not to mention pain and injury. My point is that many young people are prepared to push themselves through gymnastics on a Saturday morning or jazz dance on a Tuesday after school (in addition to curriculum PE), where a culture of team-work is absolutely normal and indeed essential for cooperation and group safety.

If students go through all of this because of a cultural convention we label 'games', then they will go through something similar to help them become better learners and foster all-round skills which correspond to those which most parents would like to see their children develop. The same point holds entirely true for drama, the Duke of Edinburgh's Award or a myriad of other organised activities where we ask students to do what they never ordinarily would in our classrooms. It is also in such disciplines that a culture arises of pupil question-ing, adjustment, improvement and performance – precisely some of the qualities we wish to inculcate in more able students if we are to make them remarkable.

Once again, there is no need to reinvent the process of making fire. Collaborative learning is already red hot in schools. Perhaps we just need to ask the PE and games staff to come into our classrooms and set us all alight!

Sport shows how collaborative learning works

Exploring how professional sport operates can be very instructive for schools. We admire football managers with player management skills: they soothe egos, swathe in cotton wool, seamlessly transition into technical adviser and motivator and, yes, sanction when neces-sary, but all with a lightness of touch and a keen awareness of the crucial red line between the dressing room and the outside world. Conversely, managers who put themselves first, moan to the TV cameras about players and allow cliques of more senior (or more expen-sive) players to dominate training create unnecessary obstacles for themselves in terms of getting the best from every team member.

Perhaps you don't follow football or a major team sport but you do enjoy, say, Olympic hockey, team pursuit cycling or Paralympic basketball. The same principle holds – the sum is greater than the parts. Even a star player can't compensate for the absence of a team ethic, whereas teams of allegedly less talented players can outperform more highly thought-of teams because they have a disciplined approach which champions the unglamorous work-off-the-ball approach which so often produces good results.

Emily Diamond is a former pupil from my school. As an international athlete representing Great Britain she won a gold medal in the 4x400 metre relay in the 2016 European Athletics Championships and a bronze medal in the Olympic Games later that year. When Emily came back to school to give a talk, she revealed just how much of an elite athlete's sport is collaborative. She spoke glowingly of 'having my team around me': she uses a physiotherapist, a masseur and a sports psychologist as well as a coach, and she has the emotional and financial support of sponsors. Her presentation perfectly illustrated the iceberg principle – that what you see on the surface of even a single competitor sprinting around a track obscures the mass of support beneath her.

As an experienced athlete, Emily knows what to do day by day, but a coaching model is based less on instruction than on frequent small-scale interventions, tweaks and support, with resilience and motivation to ensure that the mental models of success are still working. If not, they can be changed to accommodate fresh challenges.

There is another aspect to thinking about teamwork which might help to change the way we think about its role in curriculum and lesson planning. Take a look at the Football Association's new coaching standards for youth football.[1] They allow no coaching or instructions from the touchlines – only questions. Sidelines should be silent: parents applaud when either team scores but should not call out. All squad members, including the goalkeeper, must be given time to play in all positions. The rules are part of an agenda designed to encourage respect between players but, equally importantly, between everyone involved in the match – from officials to coaches to grandparents on the touchline. The approach is built around long-term player development, not short-term wins. This is revolutionary thinking. I have attended matches as a 'touchline dad' where the nature of the 'advice' from the sidelines was nothing short of animalistic: 'Crunch him!' 'Get stuck in!' 'Are you blind, ref?' How can our young footballers develop the courage to fail, try again and learn in such a hostile and competitive atmosphere?

At last, we are waking up to the idea that children's sport is different to adult sport. We've long realised that children's learning is different to that of adults, but we remain gripped by the idea and the practice of the teacher-led lesson or interaction. Genuine teamwork, which must start at youth level, aims to promote adaptability to circumstances, self-appraisal, and fast and effective communication on the pitch – where it matters. *Adults lead, students learn, students lead.*

---

1 See www.respectleague.com.

Collaborative learning is necessary in the outside world

The skills of working together are now so important that they have become integral to the way that a number of leading companies are organised. Businesses such as Innocent, Arup and Google have, at least in some instances, abandoned traditional, hierarchical structures with managers working individually in separate offices to achieve a target or solve a problem. Instead, executives and workers sit alongside each other, collaborating in fluid and cooperative teams with a rich and varied input of ideas and solutions. Work *is* teamwork. Problem solving is communal. Input is collective. This is not to deny or sublimate the particular talents of an individual in, for example, manipulating numbers, creating marketing copy or working out engineering solutions to a specified problem, but these skills are part of a bigger whole.

A civil engineer doesn't design a bridge over a motorway by herself. Equally, as teachers (to state the blindingly obvious), we are each part of several overlapping teams and have to juggle our time and energy between them. Now, it's true that almost all professions require many hours of working alone, but for the vast majority of workers it isn't one or the other but both. Whatever the challenges facing our pupils as they work on into the 2070s and 2080s, they will need to spend at least some of their daily lives with others in a team with a shared purpose.

To be honest, this argument persuades me the least. I think that working in groups is a skill to learn because it's a great skill to learn, not for any utilitarian purpose it may or may not have in the future. If it has that result, then that's a bonus.

The research evidence says that collaborative learning matters a lot

Still not convinced? There's one more argument which persuaded me that collaborative work more than earns its place in a book about raising attainment levels for all pupils. It's the research evidence drawn up by the EEF.

The EEF has looked at various interventions used in schools to raise pupil attainment, including smaller class sizes, investment in ICT and many others.[2] When measuring cost per

---

2 See https://educationendowmentfoundation.org.uk/evidence-summaries/teaching-learning-toolkit.

pupil against effect size, assessed in terms of months of learning gained, the interventions found to be the most promising for raising attainment were:

Metacognition and self-regulation: +7 months (discussed in Chapter 3)

Feedback: +8 months (discussed in Chapter 4)

Collaborative learning: +5 months

To put the numbers of months of learning gained into context, collaborative learning matches homework in secondary schools and comfortably beats reducing class sizes (+3) or teaching assistants (+1). I doubt if many schools plan to stop setting homework (or home learning as it is becoming known) in the near future, but how many are choosing to overlook the equal benefits to be gained from collaborative learning?

Famously, John Hattie's team at the University of Melbourne has looked at interventions, identifying outcomes and calculating average effect sizes by comparison of groups or comparisons over time. Hattie (2009, 2012b) reports consistently high effect sizes from interventions such as reciprocal teaching, feedback, providing formative evaluation to teachers, teacher credibility in the eyes of students and student expectations. Leaving to one side for a moment the important reservations which Dylan Wiliam (2016: 96–98) and others have about the suitability of meta-analysis for summarising the effectiveness of different approaches to students' learning, we can take Hattie's dictum of 'know thy impact' at face value: whatever we do, we should know why we are doing it and how to make it better.

Dylan Wiliam (2016: 64) observes that 'Research will never be able to tell teachers what to do, because the contexts in which teachers work are so variable. What research can do is to identify which directions are likely to be the most profitable avenues for teachers to explore.' So the question is whether collaborative learning really stands up to close scrutiny. Do examples from national and international sport and the findings of educational research fit together to create a model that will help us in the classroom?

Nine strategies for effective teamwork in the classroom (and two for outside it)

1. Think workload, save time

Effective teamwork in the classroom begins with adults modelling excellent time management. If your school or college wants to move away from putting red pen marks on every page of an exercise book or folder and a mark on every piece of work – because you are convinced that there are better ways to offer feedback involving students doing most of the work – then help is at hand. Joe Kirby's excellent blog post 'Marking is a Hornet' (2015) sets out in detail how Michaela School saves thousands of hours of marking time by asking pupils, for example, to self-evaluate their paragraphs using subject keyword checklists or to use whole-class oral feedback on a task, perhaps with a visualiser. The onus is on pupil self-improvement and a collective sense of working for better outcomes. The benefits for teacher workload and well-being don't need to be spelled out. This is collaborative learning in the sense of overlapping teams: each classroom is a team, not a collection of individuals; each classroom is part of a bigger team who share common values and methods of working.

2. Make feedback collaborative

Perhaps you remain sceptical about what collaborative methods can do to raise attainment and improve outcomes for all the students in your class, including the high attainers. Will they really help you to achieve classroom excellence on Monday morning? There may be a way to secure the best of both worlds by adapting classically high scoring interventions, such as feedback and metacognition, to whole-class learning.

You can save time and workload by summarising some of the task- and process-level feedback on a single slide or handout. For example, wizard Bristol teacher Richard Kennett (@kenradical) has adopted some smart ways of giving whole-class feedback to his A level sets which address strengths and weaknesses in a clear and robust fashion. This means that he only has to make the feedback effort once, instead of a dozen times, leaving him free to do what Hattie and others counsel: offer one-to-one student support to check that it is being internalised and acted on effectively. The feedback is collective and collaborative because all the students can see common comments and work together in response. This is so much better than a dozen heads glancing at marks and largely ignoring a set of teacher comments, however beautifully crafted.

Feedback can be just as powerful as an intervention when it takes place as a group or team activity. The sense of collaboration between individuals can stimulate high-attaining students to greater heights because they see excellent examples from their peers and join in constructive criticism of a worked example or model answer.

Metacognitive methods are enhanced when set within a context wider than simply an individual learner. Indeed, it may be that the very success of such techniques depends on their application to a whole class, year group or school, not just their enthusiastic adoption by a particular teacher. Group and teamwork, using metacognition to help, are entirely appropriate to stretching and challenging your students. This awareness can be collective. One of the key elements of Carol Dweck's (2012) work on growth mindset is that it can, and perhaps should, occur within large organisations, not just at a personal level. Dweck found that an individual learner might see themselves as having a low ability and fixed mindset in maths but a high ability and growth mindset in athletics, for example.

3. Get in touch with your inner astronaut

'Who do I want sitting next to me in the rocket ship?' Commander Chris Hadfield, the most celebrated astronaut of our time, took part in a 2017 BBC Two series entitled *Astronauts: Do You Have What it Takes?* The premise was that from over 3,000 applicants, twelve had been shortlisted, and from among these men and women one would be selected to bear Chris Hadfield's endorsement when the next round of astronaut selection by the European Space Agency began.

The series gave the candidates many chances to test their individual mental and physical abilities (the shortlisted dozen included men and women with multiple degrees and very impressive physical achievements to their names) in a demanding round of tests and scenarios, but this was not all that Hadfield and his fellow appraisers were evaluating. The candidates were challenged to demonstrate a model of leadership and teamwork which was not all about 'me first'. It showed itself when one contender helped a struggling fellow competitor to complete a swim, even though it meant coming in last herself. It showed itself by contestants allocating very clear targets in a team task involving a complex underwater survey of a laboratory and by responding collectively to life-or-death decisions in a simulated emergency scenario.

Astronaut recruitment is about selecting the best of the best – no surprises there. But 'best' did not fit the classic spaceman-hero model. Major Tom is nothing without Ground Control. There are at this very moment six men and women on the International Space Station, circling the Earth at 17,000 mph. What keeps them in orbit is that particular combination of innate and acquired, painstakingly gained and trained qualities which maintain teamwork above any notion of individual glory. Remarkable women and men are made, not born.

Ask your students to research and present an example of effective teamwork in action: from Formula 1 mechanics carrying out a pit stop under extreme time pressure, to a surgical procedure or a technical rehearsal for a play. What makes good teamwork, and why – and, crucially, why does it apply inside the classroom and not just on the games field or in a specialist setting in the outside world? What are the obvious qualities of a team (e.g. the surgeons and nurses must communicate clearly with each other)? What are more disguised (e.g. the process knowledge needed to anticipate the next stage of the sequence or the next prompt)?

Tim Peake is a pilot, scientist and astronaut. His mindset is that of an individual very willing to be trained. He and his international astronaut colleagues are not gifted individuals, programmed by their DNA to be winners. Excellent learners, which is what astronauts-in-selection have to be, became remarkable learners because they need to acquire and retain vast amounts of domain-specific knowledge. Crews are all delivered to and from the Space Station in a Russian-built Soyuz spacecraft, so astronauts need to learn to read Russian; not just tourist pleasantries but the lexis of control and navigation systems. Two degrees are not enough without some linguistic homework.

So, doctors are really scientists, filled with biochemistry; astronauts are scientists and engineers in disguise, topped up with Russian; English teachers are historians and English literature students first and foremost, with pedagogy and acting skills thrown in. Once we can remind ourselves and demonstrate to students that learning is a complex, lifelong enterprise carried out by groups of interesting and interested people, we are making strides towards a better vision of what education can be about.

4. Bring in your teamwork guru

When did you last invite into your department or faculty the teacher with the most expertise at your school in getting the best out of a group of students? You know who it is. When did they last observe a lesson in your subject? When did they last see you on your home patch?

Invite into your lesson or department the teamwork guru from your school or college. Give them a clear brief to comment on examples of learning groups or clusters: this could include the nuts-and-bolts of how staff use whole-class learning and how and why they transition into and out of groups for questioning, feedback or other tasks. They might also address the wider culture of group work in your department, from gender relations (do girls stick together?) to monitoring behaviour in groups (do the boys mess around?). The point I'm making is that if there is research indicating that good teamwork in the classroom can raise attainment, and there is, then it makes sense to draw on the existing expertise within your institution to share and build on what is already there, rather than bringing in an outside consultant with all the costs and additional background briefing work this would involve.

Perhaps we are sceptical about models drawn from sport or the creative arts and would prefer to consider examples from other walks of professional life. But wherever we turn, the central importance of team skills are apparent. Doctors, nurses, chefs, lawyers, civil servants, web designers, engineers, events managers – they all allow scope for individual talents and flair, but always within the context of a unit, crew or team. Even the ultimate schoolchild hero, the astronaut, turns out to be one just component of a much bigger machine.

5. Take a learning walk outside your comfort zone

As we've seen, classroom teachers have a lot to learn from PE and games colleagues, for whom team and group work is not an occasional fad or a tick-box for a lesson observation but their daily professional practice. The same applies to dance and drama teachers and many others. When I 'learning walked' a dance lesson a while ago, I was struck not by how different the activities and challenges of the session were to my own history lessons but how similar. Clear signposts, the modelling of a skill or problem, practising it, assessing the learning partway through, repeating, monitoring knowledge and skill acquisition, and then reassessing at the end — it all corresponded well. There were differences, of course (not least the relentless pace necessitated by the need to get changed quickly at the end of the lesson), but I saw my Year 8s in a different context, much to my benefit.

To reiterate, there are colleagues in every school with skills in pair work, group work, team-work and leadership which they may well take entirely for granted. This includes using those talents themselves but also recognising and fostering them in others, both students and staff. This is why the coaching model is transferable across schools. If it works effectively for an Olympic athlete, Duke of Edinburgh's Award expeditions and Year 7 netball, then it can most certainly be effective in improving the daily practice of classroom teachers. The coaching model is built on trust, manageable aims, repetition, revisiting, repetition, more trust, deliberate practice, repetition, modelling success, success. Repeat. In other words, lots of small, low-key, low-stakes interventions rather than big-bang, CPD-style initiatives whose impact lasts a week. Maximum.

6. An inspector calls

The EEF is pretty vague about what collaborative learning actually looks like in practice.[3] When compared to other interventions it is difficult to avoid generalities. It may be a good thing, but how do I describe it to my sceptical line manager?

Perhaps that is the beauty of this approach as well as its beast. Teachers are so wonderfully imaginative that they are more than capable of getting the gist of an idea and running with

---

3 See https://educationendowmentfoundation.org.uk/evidence-summaries/teaching-learning-toolkit/collaborative-learning/.

it; not everything has to be prescribed to the nth degree. Refreshingly, this seems to be the view of at least some Ofsted inspectors who made comments during 2017 about what they had seen. After all, we can't have it both ways: damning Ofsted when they seem to favour a particular approach or learning method, yet criticising them when it might look as if anything goes. The following comments come from reports on schools rated outstanding; I have no knowledge of or connection with any of them.

School A:

The most able pupils also do very well. The open-ended nature of the work pupils do and their eagerness to succeed, combined with high levels of staff challenge, mean that there is no 'ceiling' to the standards that pupils can reach. A group of most-able Year 9 pupils spoke to inspectors with real enthusiasm about their study of three sciences and the ways it could enable them to follow routes to become doctors or vets.

School B:

Interesting resources and excellent planning and seating arrangements so that pupils work well together – concepts introduced at the right level, with clear explanations and deep exploration of pupils' understanding – effective evaluation of pupils' progress to spot where intervention is needed – helpful guidance for pupils, often during lessons, on how they could improve – teaching assistants who know the pupils really well and therefore give them the right level of support – 'learn by doing, not just copying stuff', as one pupil contributed when discussing lessons that they enjoy.

School C:

Leaders rightly recognise the importance of raising pupils' aspirations, providing them with inspirational role models – often former pupils – to stimulate their ambition and focus on achieving their best. Events such as prize-giving and award assemblies enable pupils to celebrate their own and others' achievements. The weekly Top Table is a marvellous opportunity for nominated pupils to have a formal lunch together in recognition of their accomplishments, developing valuable social skills and experiences and often sharing the event with invited guests.

School D:

Pupils read widely and often. Opportunities for reading are rich across the curriculum. Pupils talk openly about their reading and confidently read aloud in class. Many take part in an extra-curricular reading circle, where they have the opportunity to read alongside others and discuss what they are reading. Pupils use the library frequently and are proud of their literacy developments.

School E:

Staff very regularly check on the progress that pupils are making to gauge how well they are doing, identify who may be falling behind and to help inform next steps in teaching and learning. Staff assure the accuracy of their assessments by sharing and regularly testing their judgements with other members of staff. In addition, the school has strong links with the local teaching alliance, Partners in Learning. Colleagues from this partnership regularly meet with staff to check the accuracy of their assessments. As a result of these stringent processes, the school's assessments of pupils' progress are accurate. This is borne out by inspection evidence.

A quick sample of these Ofsted inspection reports on outstanding schools shows an interesting selection of teamwork activities and collaborative learning in action. School B has clearly tried out some different seating arrangements to facilitate learning, and is praised for its use of feedback from teaching assistants and, by implication, from the pupils themselves so they understand how to make progress. This is effectively DIRT and metacognition in practice. School D earns plaudits for not just encouraging reading, as any school prospectus or mission statement would claim, but for building in discussion time and encouraging a sense of developing literacy among the pupils. Reading time is so often a simple but overlooked way of challenging pupils to expand their vocabulary and cultural capital.

Students at School A have a vision from Year 9 about where their science learning (as opposed to teaching) might take them, and surely there is a link between this inspection comment and the preceding one about open-ended tasks and high levels of teacher challenge. Speaking of which, another way in which these reports acknowledge the use and benefits of collaborative learning relates to school staff. I am struck by the way in which School E staff subject their assessments to scrutiny within a teaching alliance – and, presumably, students are aware that this process of staff peer learning and support is going on. Further collaboration is apparent at School C, where staff and students celebrate high achievement in a distinctive fashion entirely suited to their shared learning environment, adding the extra element of inviting former pupils back into the school.

There are common threads here: high-attaining students (what Ofsted calls most able students) are being challenged in some of our best schools right now in ways we might reasonably expect as professional teachers. Grandmothers and eggs may come into our minds. High aspirations, open questions, a positive learning environment, committed and knowledgeable teaching staff – these are among the most common terms on the flip chart for any CPD session on stretching our bright students. But without being overly prescriptive about it, and with an open mind about how this might be achieved, Ofsted has fulfilled its statutory obligation to comment on provision for more able students by identifying ways in which these schools go further than simply satisfying a tick-box list for the gifted and talented. Collaborative learning offers just such an opportunity for every school to demonstrate its individuality, using what it already has rather than starting from scratch.

7. The flipped school

The idea of the flipped classroom is well-embedded in our pedagogy. Essentially, the traditional teacher-led lesson, which is strong on chalk and talk or which features a detailed PowerPoint, is replaced by student presentations and activities based on homework and research carried out ahead of the lesson. Students teach and teachers act as mentors – it's a fine model on which to build.

What matters is allowing multiple opportunities for students to lead the lesson and improve. Ron Berger's (2003) celebrated gallery critique methods can be fruitfully adapted here to offer informed, balanced and fair criticism with a view to improvement. Not only are the students responsible for producing resources and leading the lesson, but they are critical friends finding common interest (their collective learning) in making the next lesson better for all. Flipping the learning casts the teacher in a different role as facilitator and mentor, offering advice and encouragement but limiting their interventions to a minimum (perhaps using simple prompt or cue cards).

Let's apply a multiplier effect here: the flipped classroom can become a template for collaborative learning throughout the school. Increasingly on Twitter I'm seeing some ambitious claims that schools and colleges make for themselves as #family or #community. Mission statement fantasy or practical reality? The following strategies, which extend the idea of the flipped classroom, may help to provide an answer.

Governors as learners, students as teachers, then a flip

How interesting would it be to give high-attaining students a chance to explain their recent work in maths to governors in the classroom? How compelling might it be for governors to talk about how maths has affected their lives? Governors give up their time freely to schools, and it is excellent that they do, but at times it is the legal and regulatory frameworks in which schools operate which take their energy. Valuable as their contributions in this area can be, it may not be what they had in mind when accepting an invitation to serve a school community. Getting them involved in classrooms may offer a better learning experience all round.

Former students as learners, students as teachers, then a flip

Former students are a massively underused resource. Year 18 or Year 25 students (as we might term them for fun) are often fascinating for current pupils and this can feed into effective collaborative learning, embodying as they do both continuity and change. Former students might enjoy seeing how apps are used on tablet computers in schools and, in turn, can offer mentoring advice in breakout sessions about work and university opportunities.

Teachers as learners, teachers as teachers

It's called a TeachMeet, of course, and their spread has been one of the most joyous and exciting developments in education in recent years. TeachMeets or BrewEds just go to show that learning is naturally collaborative and rarely unproductive. I've helped to organise one in Bristol attended by teachers from across the South West (Pedagoo South West 2014) and I've organised in-school TeachEats featuring doughnuts. Having INSET from your own colleagues makes it inexpensive, relevant and automatically appropriate to your students. What's not to like?

SLT as teachers, teachers joining the SLT

Flipped schools – and every school – should have a head who teaches. Tom Sherrington (2013) is absolutely right about this, and he put his neck on the line by teaching a GCSE physics class at King Edward VI Grammar School, in Chelmsford while a head. He did it using co-construction (see Chapter 7) – even braver and more commendable. Teachers being co-opted onto the SLT for a term or a year offers an unmatched opportunity to gain experience in areas of decision making normally out of sight.

Parents as learners, pupils as mentors

The idea of parents taking a course and learning something new or something they have always wanted to study while being helped by professional learners (i.e. their children) has much to commend it. Perhaps technology could lend a hand here, given that it is not possible to allow parents into classrooms. There is something instinctively right about parents and children learning together, but perhaps homework help is as far as this idea can run at the moment.

Pupils as coaches, coaches as mentors

Rachel Jones (2015) is a big advocate of pupils sharing work inside and outside the classroom via online portfolios and blogs. The digital classroom allows young people to try out different roles as learners, coaches and mentors with other classes or other schools using Skype or Google Hangouts. What better way to build citizenship skills and to encourage global awareness?

Outside speakers as resources, pupils and teachers as learners

Would you like to have Jonathan Phillips, Professor of Crusading History at Royal Holloway, University of London in your classroom? Would it be exciting to have your Year 7s ask him about why people went on Crusade, or whether the eleventh century Islamic world has relevance to the situation in the Middle East today? Skype is the not-so-new piece of software which makes this direct interaction between leading university experts and you and your students possible.

The benefits are obvious, not the least among them that a barrier to learning is removed on both sides: the time and expense of a visit in person are eliminated and the commitment to the learning of all students and staff remains. The collaborative learning comes not just from the fact that a university academic is addressing staff and students; the shared interest in learning and the bridge between universities and schools is invaluable. Skype can open doors.

8. Model United Nations

If you are looking for a low-cost, unbeatable activity which will challenge all your students to improve a range of their skills, then look no further. If you have never walked into a sports hall or assembly hall filled with 300 students listening to each other and debating, while also regulating themselves, with a few staff observing from the sidelines (if they are not in the staffroom catching up on marking and preparation) then educationally you haven't lived. Yet.

The big idea

Model United Nations (MUN) is a role play based on the United Nations in Geneva. Committees of delegates represent their chosen countries' views on a range of topical subjects, typically in a security council, environment committee, disarmament committee, human rights committee and so on. There are rules of procedure to learn which look formidable but can be picked up rapidly.

Cost

You need nothing more than some sheets of paper with the names of the countries written on them. If you have a little money to spend you can buy flags and button badges with the United Nations logo on them; you can print out national flags or what we call 'Toblerones' (triangular country identifiers made from card which delegates place in front of them). If you have more to spend, there are MUN schools meetings across the UK within a day's travelling distance. If you have even more to spend, there are international MUNs at The Hague, Paris and New York, among hundreds of others, to which some British schools travel every year.

Resources

Delegates need to research their countries' positions on various issues: where does the Democratic Republic of the Congo stand on deforestation? What is Kazakhstan's stance on female genital mutilation? The Internet is the first port of call for many. Access to broadsheet newspapers and periodicals such as *The Economist*, either online or as hard copies, is useful. The quality and depth of the research makes a real difference to the standard of the arguments produced, so this is a good moment to insist on high expectations and going further than the most obvious websites. Knowledge and cultural capital are at a premium.

Skills

The three stages of MUN can be treated as formally or as informally as suits your school. The first stage is resolution writing, next comes lobbying, and the third and final stage is public speaking. This approach chimes well with the views expressed by Martin Robinson in *Trivium 21c* (2013). Robinson argues that all schools today have much to learn from the classical curriculum of rhetoric, grammar and logic, which can be readily updated to provide a twenty-first century framework for learning. Foremost among these skills are the formulation and expression of a clear line of thinking and speaking. What better medium than MUN? Likewise, debating has much to offer in terms of the acquisition and cultivation of these core skills.

Hundreds of thousands of young people across the world in schools, colleges and universities love MUN. In some cases, they master the requisite skills to the extent of becoming committee chairs or General Assembly chairs; they attend multiple conferences and carry on with the activity at university. MUN combines elements of the individual and the team. Pursuing learning and loving wisdom for their own sake is at the heart of scholarship, philosophy and genuine learning. We do ourselves and our students a disservice if we devalue reading, researching, arguing and debating in the pursuit of 'relevance' or immediate practical value.

MUN shares many of the characteristics of games and team sports: travelling, a dress code (smart clothing) and the risk of failure – of saying something unintentional or making a mess of a speech. It appeals to pupils' sense of wanting to make the world a better place, even if just by talking. Success at MUN is defined by having an amendment or a resolution passed, but this can only be done by a group of students acting together. However able, no single delegate can achieve MUN success without the support of others.

If you need a clincher for debating, for MUN or for any similar exercise that challenges your brightest students, it comes from the notion that fluency in speech often translates into fluency on paper. By fostering and developing rhetorical skills – offering a view and defending it or challenging a view and knocking it down – students (and teachers) enhance their abilities to critique a poem or learn not to take a historical source at face value. They become polished in prose, concise in criticism and exact in explanation.

The point about the benefits of clear thinking both in speech and in writing is important. I've missed a few opportunities when students have said to me, 'Sir, we'd love to see you and Miss X go head to head in a history debate.' I should take up the chance. Modelling skills means practising what we preach. I now tackle five-minute essay plans when my students do and try to write a PEE paragraph while they do the same. Sometimes I impress myself but more often I am daunted by what they can achieve, especially under timed conditions. Part of scaffolding to the top is showing students what 'the top' looks like, which, for better or worse, is often us. How can we expect our students to be remarkable if we are not trying to be remarkable ourselves?

9. Higher Project Qualification and Extended Project Qualification

During the last few years, many schools have adopted either the Higher Project Qualification (HPQ) or Extended Project Qualification (EPQ) in order to offer another dimension of learning to students. They both share common elements:

- The area of interest is chosen by the student.

- The student goes through formative stages not dissimilar to those for the MUN activity: planning the project, researching it and writing it up.

- The student then has to present their findings to an audience of peers and teachers.

- The final assessment grade is dependent, in part, on how and why the project changed as it developed.

The strategy here is to look at your curriculum planning to see whether you currently offer a comparable opportunity offering similar benefits for your students. Interest in and demand for the HPQ at Key Stage 3 and EPQ at Key Stage 4 bears testimony to the timelessness of such skills and their continued relevance to our students. The assessment objective which carries double the marks of the others is 'Develop and Realise', with extra credits for problem solving and for changes to or development of the initial project plan. The awarding authorities also recognise a variety of assessment outcomes – for example, alongside the written report, the EPQ can be assessed as a live performance or artefact.

The HPQ and EPQ also enable students to undertake a group project. This may not be teamwork in the classic sense, but there is a stronger requirement for students to work effectively with others and for mid-project and end-of-project review than in more traditional qualifications and forms of assessment. They offer breadth and allow students to explore a passion or interest they may have had since primary school or a creative pursuit which they follow outside school.

Here are two extra opportunities for collaborative learning outside the classroom.

10. Low ropes

Some schools have access to a low ropes facility. Ropes are tied horizontally between trees or other supports, with the lower rope being about a metre above the ground and a higher rope at about chest height. The elevation provides a sufficient amount of challenge without danger – this is not an assault course. Students are put into teams and told they have to cross the ropes and reach the safety of tree platforms without touching the ground. Each stage is graded in difficulty to present varying degrees of challenge. There are many variations in the layout of courses and the challenges set to cross them – for example, carrying plastic cups of water without spilling any.

What do students learn from this activity? The four-letter word which looms large at every stage is, once again, plan. Without a plan to cross the obstacle, one or two individuals may reach a platform but the team won't. The instructor can introduce the idea of planning at an early stage – as part of a safety briefing, for example – or he or she can allow the idea of planning to emerge from the students themselves as their frustrations mount. What matters is that the idea of needing a plan A and a plan B is paramount.

High-attaining students are often unpractised in this kind of applied intelligence. Classically they are the pioneers and lone wolves – drawing that map more accurately than others in their class, remembering those Spanish verb endings every time, working through the maths problems in the textbook seemingly effortlessly, getting to the end of the chapter before the others. What these students may not find so easy is working with others to achieve a desired outcome, particularly one where success or failure is so palpable. This is not to suggest that high-attaining pupils don't contribute to drama productions or the like, where the stakes can be very high, because clearly that does happen. But rope work and practical activities of the kind I'm describing can present a distinctive set of challenges which quite literally stretch pupils, even if they are in groups of similarly able peers. If anything, this makes it even harder: falling off a ridiculously low rope or not getting to the next 'easy' platform teaches mutual dependence in a very particular way.

There are hundreds of team-building games and activities that can be adapted for your students. They can form part of a PSHE or gifted and talented programme or be offered as occasional form periods or lunchtime activities. Frequency and repetition are the key to success: doing these activities as a one-off is great in its own right, but practising variations of them several times leads to learning.

11. Massive open online courses

Massive open online courses (MOOCs) are online courses open to students from around the world. They offer a large number of students the opportunity to study high quality courses online with prestigious universities, in many cases free of charge.[4]

MOOCs may offer some interesting opportunities for your high-attaining students, who can sample a course without committing to a formal qualification. They usually offer assessment through peer review and group collaboration or automated feedback in the form of computer-marked tests. Inevitably, it is that great success story of British education, the Open University, which is leading the way in Britain with its FutureLearn project, which has millions of students signed up to study courses from forty universities. From liver disease to First World War aviation, from dentistry to Shakespeare and from computer coding to the Higgs boson, new courses are emerging all the time.

---

4 For more on MOOCs visit www.coursera.org or www.futurelearn.com.

Is this teamwork? Perhaps not as we might normally think about it, but that's the whole point: MOOCs use blogs and 'live' interaction with peers and tutors, and that's teamwork of a different kind. A child aged 11 in 2019 will be retiring in around 2089. She may then want to pick up a course on Andy Warhol or linguistics as part of lifelong learning which will take her into the 2090s or 2100s. I don't know what the world of learning or work will look like in the twenty-second century, but the more creativity we can accustom our students to in the here and now, the better prepared they will be for whatever lies ahead.

Some questions to consider

Make it excellent

- How could you instantly improve one of the suggested strategies in this chapter?
- What does excellent collaborative learning currently look like in your subject?
- Why does collaborative learning matter in your subject?
- How might whole-class feedback help your students to become expert learners?

Share the load

- How might the benefits of collaborative learning improve behaviour and build trust in your school?
- How could collaborative learning reduce teacher workload in your subject?

Beyond the classroom

- How might collaborative learning extend outside your classroom? Who are the teamwork gurus in your school or college, and how could your department use their expertise?
- How could collaborative learning extend to, for example, your former students or to current governors or parents?

Summary

Whether we label it teamwork, group activities or collaborative learning, the case I've tried to make in this chapter is that learning is a shared and social process. Home learning programmes may be effective and appropriate for some, but one of the reasons they don't work for many students and parents is that they can't replicate the benefits of learning with peers. Whatever our views on the ideal class size, the sheer enforced togetherness of adolescent learning is a feature to turn to our advantage and exploit. Lessons, clubs, enrichment activities and fieldwork can become exciting collaborative activities when a critical mass of students and staff decide to make inclusive work routine rather than exceptional.

Classroom practitioners can learn lessons from the games field and the lunchtime club: what is appropriate to the one is not out of place in the other, because they are linked by a shared purpose that is universal to all schools. The power of a table of learners is equal to the power of a whole class which is equal to the power of a basketball team: it represents the collective ethos of the entire school community. Pupils see this daily because we expect it of them daily as they transition from one space and role to another, but do we see it as teachers? Schools which have integrated collaborative learning into their core purpose and practice understand that a collective desire to get a result – to raise performance, to improve, to move forward – is one of the most powerful forces at their disposal. They understand that in order to improve any aspect of school life, from behaviour to attainment, pupils need to see and understand the benefits of the group ethos, both individually and collectively. The strength of this force to shape mindsets, rein in off-task activities and attitudes, and influence positive thinking should not be dismissed lightly.

This need not take money. There is in-house expertise within many schools and colleges and across MATs which can be drawn on to show how coaching and flipping roles can be transformed from discrete activities, often considered suitable only for the games pitch or drama studio, and brought inside for common benefit. Educational research highlights the promise which such activities hold for improving behaviour and attainment. Astronauts are the ultimate team players, not heroic and exceptional individuals. They are the ultimate trainees – made, not born.

Chapter 6

Questioning

The point of the question is to teach rather than to test. The successful teacher's question is precisely one that can be answered, not one that can't be.

Michael Marland, *The Craft of the Classroom* (1975)

Key themes

- Questioning techniques can be modelled, explained and taken on board so they become second nature to expert learners, just as they are to teachers. Expert learners have questioning in their toolkit of study skills.

- Some students may be more intelligent than others, but any student can ask and answer a good question. Deliberate practice in questioning and a mental representation of success can be acquired by any student.

- Intelligence in the devising, framing, asking and answering of questions is malleable and something which all schools can help students to improve.

- Purposeful practice is an integral part of improving questioning skills. Praising effort and helping to build resilience and motivation will be as key to improving the quality and quantity of student questions as they are to feedback or any other part of school life.

- Some types of questioning may be more effective in helping a learner to reach for the top on her learning journey, just as they are for the teacher teaching to the top on his.

My learning journey through this chapter

This chapter focuses on the importance of questioning by students as a bedrock of provision for high-attaining students. The toolbox of questioning is explored and suggestions made about some practical skills which will encourage a depth of response and a thoughtfulness of response.

My own learning journey through this chapter started off promisingly enough in my mind with a series of observations about the significance of questioning in the classroom. This almost went without saying. It is so much of teachers' stock-in-trade that it would seem odd to ignore it. If pupils are going to make the journey from able to remarkable, then advice on helping them along the journey was only reasonable, I suggested to myself, and there wasn't a great deal out there on questioning strategies for high-attaining students.

As I laboured my way through a draft, I took my own advice and started to question myself. I was perfectly entitled to share some thoughts on hinge questions, ABC questioning and so on, because I genuinely use those techniques in my teaching and they are relevant to this book. But I was in danger of adding nothing to what is already available. Doug Lemov's Teach Like a Champion books are a hands-on, inspiring port of call for anyone wanting to brush up on or acquire skills such as 'cold calling'. Shaun Allison and Andy Tharby's (2015) deservedly popular *Making Every Lesson Count* has a fine chapter on questioning in which a number of methods are described and assessed, and spin-off volumes relate these habits to individual subjects. There are many other books and blogs which offer truly creative and insightful ideas on questioning.

Instead, my self-questioning has led to another approach. I'm putting expert learners at the heart of the story in the form of our emerging expert learners, Anna and Tom. I'm still going to be referring to some of the methods explained and advocated by Alex Quigley (2013), Doug Lemov (2010) and others, however; what interests me is the part that questioning plays in learners' lives, and what part it could play. My own learning journey is now student led, as they take me around my school and show me what questioning really looks like. You are welcome aboard.

So many questions, so little time

Teachers are well aware that there is a plethora of information available about teaching and questioning. There are famous taxonomies of questioning, such as Bloom's taxonomy, which set out in detail the aims and purposes of questioning as a pedagogical and learning device:

- To check pupil knowledge.

- To test understanding.

- To assess progress or performance.

- As a lesson starter, to recap where we are.

- In a plenary, to assess what we did and where we've got to.

Questioning can be Socratic, pupil led, peer to peer, oral, written, spoken and recorded. In sum, there are a thousand variations on the theme of questioning, and they stand as a monument to educators' professional determination and resourcefulness in finding ways to understand and explain an issue for the benefit of young people.

So, which of these countless methods might best serve to create more high-attaining students in the classroom? Which ones will generate increasing oral confidence for pupils whose home backgrounds may not encourage this? How does questioning help to boost intelligence and take more pupils from able to remarkable?

Why questioning matters for high-attaining students

Research evidence tells us that questioning matters

There is quite a lot of disparity amid the evidence about the extent of the impact of effective questioning on pupil outcomes, but there does seem to be a consensus that it makes a desirable difference. Hattie's *Visible Learning for Teachers* (2012b) gives what is simply listed as 'questioning' an effect size of 0.49 (53/150) but 'classroom discussion', which could hardly take place or be effective without good questioning, ranks 7/150 with an effect size of 0.82. In 2018, 'questioning' had slipped down a notch in the league table on his website and 'classroom discussion' had disappeared. However, 'self-verbalization and self-questioning' had retained their consistent place high up in the table at 0.64, putting it among the top twenty influences on achievement.[1]

Barak Rosenshine's estimable 'Principles of Instruction' (2012) confirms that questions help students to connect new material to prior learning. However, he refers only briefly to the practice of students developing questions from stems provided to them in order to ask questions of each other – something I will develop below.

According to Hattie (2012b: 73), 'The most important task is for teachers to listen.' The reason he wants teachers to talk less is to enable productive talking about learning. Citing research from Walter Parker (2006), he argues that listening:

- Requires respect for students' views but also an evaluation of those views.

- Allows for the sharing of genuine depth of thinking and processing in our questioning.

- Informs students and teachers alike about what the student brings to the learning.

- Informs the teacher about the gap between where the student is and where he or she needs to be.

Hattie also summarises research from Mikhail Bakhtin (1981) and Robin Alexander (2008) on the difference between 'monologic' and 'dialogic' teacher talk. Monologic talk by teachers transmits knowledge and uses questioning largely to check responses and the acquisition of knowledge. Recapitulations and reformulations of answers tend to loom large in this style of questioning. Dialogic talk helps students to share and build meaning collaboratively, and students ask more questions than teachers. Dialogue is seen as a tool for learning because learning is collective and reciprocal, linking to the themes in the previous chapter on collaborative learning. Teachers learn by listening to students think out loud.

Hattie argues that these methods 'have a powerful effect on student involvement and learning' (2012b: 74). He goes as far as suggesting that monologic talk may cause less damage to brighter students than to the struggling and disengaged (2012b: 163), which I would question within the context of this book. If high-attaining students are not able to contribute fully to a lesson or sequence of lessons, then not only are their own abilities capped but so are the beneficial spin-offs to the whole class. However, as Hattie acknowledges, it is not necessarily the case that less teacher talk, more student talk and more listening lead to improved outcomes. More research is needed about the type of talk in each case and, crucially, about the reactions to both the talk and the listening as formative feedback.

---

1 See https://visible-learning.org/hattie-ranking-influences-effect-sizes-learning-achievement/.

We need a grammar of questioning to improve attainment

Many books (including this one), blogs, websites and speakers talk by necessity about generic skills such as feedback and questioning. We have to generalise to a broad readership, and fair enough. However, talk of generic skills risks a return to the 'key skills' idea in the first incarnation of the national curriculum, where politicians and businesspeople decided that what young people needed was the application of number or communication or working with others. There was even a key skill called 'improving own learning and performance'. Good luck with unpacking that one.

The point I'm making here is that for learners' questioning and listening skills to improve in, say, geography, students need domain-specific geography practice – there is a specific grammar of questioning which is particular to each subject. With lots of prompting and practice, high-attaining geographers should be able to see the relevance and applicability of what they have done in a medical geography unit on the spread of disease in sub-Saharan Africa to their work on epidemiology in biology, and vice versa, but such connections and parallels will not be automatic and routine. Indeed, the inability of learners to transfer knowledge and skills across the curriculum is a repeated complaint among teachers. Daisy Christodoulou (2017: 29–54) has made this an area of particular expertise. Her forensic analysis of why 'generic skills' approaches founder has explained why well-meaning, established classroom practice often produces disappointing outcomes. In fact, breaking down skills into chunks (which may not resemble the final outcome) and isolating and offering repeated practice in weaker areas provides a better chance of bringing about those desirable changes in long-term memory which constitute learning.

Don't assume that high-attaining students are automatically good questioners

High-attaining students like Asif and Yolanda may be no more adept at learning to ask questions about learning than other students. They are not automatically expert learners in feedback, oracy or anything else in the learner's toolkit – at least, not until they have tried and applied it. Expert questioners are just that, whatever their prior level of attainment, and they earn their kudos by having a good mental model of what successful learner questioning looks like, by having motivation and resilience and by practice. As a teacher, I know that it is sometimes the middle or low-attaining student who seems to specialise in the offbeat, hard-to-answer question which offers intrigue and perhaps a degree of cheekiness. Wherever this facility and self-confidence have come from, they offer a resource from which every pupil in the class can share and benefit.

Purposeful practice is needed for every different learner questioning technique. Just as the raw PGCE student gets it wrong and faces a sea of eager hands, confusedly and repeatedly taking refuge in accepting answers from the same few reliable faces, so our learners will need ample and repeated chances to improve what they do.

Questioning allows us to start from what high-attaining students know

Dylan Wiliam is fond of a particular response when questioned about formative assessment, quoting David Ausubel's suggestion that 'the most important factor influencing learning is what the learner already knows ... ascertain this and teach accordingly' (Wiliam 2011: 1; see also Ausubel 1968). There can, of course, be quite a large gap in perception and reality between this and the assumptions I make about what my students know as I walk into a lesson. As I set sail with my starter, urging and prompting my class to keep up, enjoy the journey and even take time to look at the seascape, some pupils may already be reaching for the lifebelts or baling out. A friendly colleague or coach might gently suggest that in my next lesson I could ditch the lesson-by-numbers starter hook, since the students already find the topic we are studying genuinely interesting, and instead initiate a dialogue about where we are, what has been tricky and what is straightforward, and perhaps throw in a low-stakes quiz as a bit of back-up so I'm not just taking students' word for it.

There are two benefits to this approach. Firstly, questioning in these ways throws up centre stage a number of issues which might otherwise disappear in the general busy-ness of the lesson: mistakes, errors in sequencing, misunderstandings – all too important to leave to a plenary and not its purpose. The dialogic approach may not always succeed, but it can help to transform 'I don't get this' to 'I'm still not 100% but I think it's getting clearer.'

Secondly, questioning by self-review makes feedback more effective. One of the criticisms of feedback as a general means of improving learning outcomes is that there is a lack of focus on responses to it. More attention is paid in schools to pen colours, stamps, triple impact marking and the like than to the ways in which students absorb and respond to what they are being told about how to make good work better and very good work excellent.

Self-review and self-reflection is, again, not a study habit or skill automatically poured into the mouths of more able students soon after birth. These are acquired abilities, fostered by teachers and peers alike and capable of being shared, improved and built on for the benefit of every learner in the class. This may literally take the form of a dialogue with other learners or may be an internal conversation. Mental representations of success at self-review come from deliberate practice rather than one-off, hit-or-miss interventions in a single lesson.

Questioning helps to make learning visible

Young people have remarkably few examples of good questioning available to them. If you think for a moment about popular culture and the media, where will they see evidence of effective questioning at work? Perhaps in popular detective programmes such as *Sherlock* or legal dramas and films. In both cases, these highly scripted performances are designed to lead to a climax of success (or failure) as Sherlock Holmes deduces that the client before him is a dog-loving bachelor recently returned from Switzerland to resume a banking career. Even more improbably, in a courtroom drama the brilliant prosecuting QC leads a helpless defendant to a crushing admission of guilt through a series of leading questions delivered with rhetorical gusto.

Popular culture often depicts expert questioning as akin to or a component of natural genius. It is as logical as it is effortless as it is successful. Contradictions, non-sequiturs, fallacies and straw men are seldom shown and explored. Questioning as a group or team activity is rare. Detectives are allowed to appear in pairs, but one is usually the dumber foil of the other and tolerated only to shine yet more light on the virtuosity of the main protagonist, classically Watson to Holmes or Lewis to Morse.

Politicians, likewise, set poor examples for young people. Evasion and obfuscation are the hallmarks of too many of their answers. Scientists discover, engineers create and great thinkers just think. We picture Newton in the orchard 'discovering' gravity or James Dyson seeing an industrial vacuum and inventing the bag-less vacuum cleaner, ignoring the years of thinking and struggle by Newton and the 5,000 prototypes that Dyson needed.

In real life, and I bow to the expertise of my barrister son, questions by lawyers are often procedural and technical. They establish times, locations and sequences of events. Questions link together events and people as part of an explanatory framework for a jury or magistrate; they also serve the purpose of raising doubts and discrepancies for a jury to consider. This is too dull and long-winded for film or TV, but it works. The same painstaking qualities characterise questions by detectives. Scientists typically test a hypothesis through a series of small-scale questions, procedures and observations and publish their results as part of a collaborative team.

A great deal of questioning skill and fluency is therefore invisible. We can't readily see into the mind of the person asking the questions and nor can we discern their real motive in asking that particular question – to clarify? To reveal an inconsistency? To set a trap? There may be an end product, such as a piece in a newspaper, a laboratory report or scientific paper, but the processes that produced it can't easily be observed or replicated. Can this process become more visible so that more learners become expert questioners?

Twelve strategies to build effective questioning with high-attaining students

1. Desert Island Discs

Some of the more intelligent, visible questioning is carried out by another group of people who, like journalists, lawyers and detectives, depend on it for their livelihood – by which I mean radio and television presenters. Their habits may give us some clues as to how we might make questioning more visible to our students so they can use it every day in lessons. After all, radio interviewers are invisible to listeners so their questioning has to be effective.

Desert Island Discs is a celebrated and long-lived format which has become a classic of radio. The presenter asks their guest to select eight pieces of music, a book and a luxury item to have with them on their mythical desert island. What will they choose, and why? Why does the programme work so well and what lessons does this have for us?

Ask the students to review an extract from a past episode. What makes it work?

- The types of questions asked – what are they, and what is the purpose of each one?

- The way the questions are triggers to enable the guest to unveil a sequence of events about their life and work.

- The use of declarative statements: 'Tell us about your second piece of music and why you chose it.'

- The way the interview is shaped and guided rather than rigorously controlled and closely scripted. There remains an ad hoc feel, with the conversational journey depending on the answers given.

- The relationship between presenter and guest – what adjectives would describe it?

- The amount of research the presenter carries out before she formulates her questions and meets her guest.

Showing Tom and Anna how to decode effective questions is a powerful step towards them being able to do the same thing themselves. An immediate and formative follow-up is to ask them to conduct some mini-interviews with staff, asking them about just one or two pieces of music. Decoding, assessing, weighing, internalising and then producing effective questioning is going to stretch and challenge every student.

Perhaps students have never heard (or heard of) *Desert Island Discs*. There's an ancillary challenge: download an episode for them and encourage the students to practise their listening skills. Podcasts have proved an unexpectedly popular medium with young people, so here is a chance to build on that starting point.

2. The Graham Norton Show

If we compare *Desert Island Discs* to a celebrity chat show, such as the *Graham Norton Show*, there are more similarities than differences. Unlike a radio programme, most students will at least have seen a trailer for this or similar talk shows.

Ask Anna and Tom to act as producers for next week's episode:

- Who will you invite to appear, and why?

- What fact-finding will you do as a researcher, and what research must a host do themselves so they have the knowledge needed to make a flowing conversation more likely?

- What questions will you prepare about each guest for Graham's question cards? Explain why you think those questions will produce good responses for the live audience and viewers. How will you avoid the obvious pitfalls – that an actress only wants to talk about her new film or a celebrity insists on talking over and stealing the limelight from the other guests?

Strip away the showbiz and the razzmatazz and it is clear that any chat show host who is going to survive and be successful (many haven't) must be very good at asking the right questions. Many of the characteristics of *Desert Island Discs* still apply, despite the palpable differences. Each presenter is adept at putting his guests at ease, at teasing out something below the surface, at drawing inferences from a statement or an omission, at switching the subject matter and the mood from the serious to the light-hearted and back again, at making a celebrity feel so relaxed in front of the studio audience and the millions watching at home that they (sometimes) share thoughts well beyond their stated purpose of shamelessly promoting their latest film.

Encouraging learners to appreciate the role of knowledge is crucial. Hard, accurate factual detail about film and book titles, dates, a guest's biography and achievements is vital to avoid embarrassment. This is why researchers are listed in the programme credits. Anna and Tom can well imagine and role play the squirming, the shock and the social media reaction if Graham forgets a name or puts his foot in his mouth about a sensitive relationship.

3. Make listening visible

Given Graham Nuthall's (2007) observations about the poor quality and negligible quantity of teacher listening in many lessons, perhaps we should take active steps to work with our classes to encourage this skill in them and us. This can constitute another good example of collaborative learning.

An obvious choice to make listening visible is to use a poem. I love Robert Frost's definition of poetry as 'language under pressure'. Every word has to earn its keep; nothing is superfluous. Listening skills will be at a premium. Many students won't have them, yet. This may well include some high-attaining students who may be much more familiar with reading. They too face a challenge.

Role cards can work well here:

- Interrogator – listen with a view to asking a question to the reader at the end of the poem.

- Empathiser – take a sympathetic view of the poet's aims and try to understand what he or she is saying.

- Positive critic – explain to your group why you think this poem works well.

- Negative critic – explain to your group why you think this poem doesn't work well.

- Connector – link this poem to others you have read on this theme or by this writer.

- Sharer – your listening will be targeted at explaining to others what you like or don't like about this poem.

- Silent listener – only when pressed by a sharer will your thoughts be known because you have concentrated so hard on listening to every word.

In this way, intelligent, visible listening and questioning is available and accessible. I would be surprised if most teachers can't read through these role cards listing the characteristics of good and effective questioning and immediately think of a few current or past students who could do as good a job as many TV and radio stars. These are our expert learners. If a few can do it, why can't all our students? They don't need the larger-than-life personality of a Jonathan Ross or the journalistic pedigree of a David Dimbleby, so that is not a barrier. What they do need is to have the invisible thought processes of the barrister, detective or engineer made transparent so they can add them to their repertoire of skills. The skill set helps to produce the personality, not the other way around.

Questioning and listening skills will need to be modelled, shared, practised and improved if they are to play any part in our lessons. But we need not strip out all the romance and fun from questioning. Oracy can be practised and enjoyed in a hundred different ways – and as long as the students are aware of what they are doing and why, they will still be learning. Theme park hairs-on-the-back-of-the-neck will never be too far away from a lively discussion, debate or mock trial. These are memorable experiences for many students.

4. Textbook questioning

Writing textbooks is difficult – such a lot of information has to go into so few pages. As with poetry, words need to be chosen carefully, along with photographs, graphs, tables, glossaries and much more. Unfortunately, the quality of the questions in many textbooks is not as high as the accompanying text. It's as if the questions have been added as an afterthought by a hard-pressed author to meet a strict deadline. As teachers we sometimes have to supplement or replace them with something better. Can Anna and Tom do it themselves?

Have a look at the quality of the questions on the next worksheet or in the next textbook you use. How many of those questions could your class have come up with, if guided and prompted? Here's the chance to find out: set them that very exercise. How could and should the questions be improved:

- For their meaning?

- For the stretch and challenge they offer high-attaining students?

- For the way they structure questioning from, for example, comprehension to analysis?

- For their connections to apps and websites which could enrich how they are answered?

Make the task more meaningful by revising your worksheet or textbook double-spread with much improved questions before their eyes for next year's class. Then show it being stored on a learning platform such as OneNote.

5. Film critic

Every teacher wishes to avoid a class passively viewing a video clip or DVD. The lesson has been carefully planned to include the excerpt, which has been chosen for its appropriateness and relevance to the scheme of work – and yet a nagging doubt persists that the effort will not be reciprocated. 'What might the students have gained from watching this clip that they might not have learned from another source?' is the kindest way a coach or critical friend might review the choice of material. More unkindly, as the voice in your head may chastise you, a critic might ask if the class has just switched off for ten minutes. All that effort, so little outcome.

Try the textbook questioning exercise with a video clip. Depending on the class and the complexity of the clip, allow them to watch it through once with a view to preparing questions for a repeat showing. What kinds of questions will be appropriate to the aims of the lesson, and why?

Tom's group might begin this task by treating it as a classic gap-fill exercise: using low-order questions, they may simply ask for the number of Spanish ships in the Armada which was mentioned in the clip. But with whole-class feedback from Maya, Yolanda and their table, shared by the teacher, the group might quickly model more expert questioning about attitudes and beliefs – for example, moving on much further in their thinking than searching for a literal 'right answer'. They might consider how the Spanish crew were feeling about their failure to rendezvous with the Duke of Parma or to what extent the historian's view about why the Armada failed was persuasive.

Deliberate, purposeful practice in identifying and then asking and answering different types and orders of questions helps students to make progress by demonstrating the purpose of questions – for information, for modelling, as discussion prompts, to check simple understanding, for sequencing, for research and so on. They will learn to apply a grammar and terminology of questioning which is nuanced and sophisticated. Student viewers can become student critics. Expert questioners are made, not born.

6. So what?

'So what?' is a rhetorical device for encouraging logical sequencing and explanation. It may sound rude, but the key is to establish the ground rules and to have the whole class comfortable with it before you try it in earnest. When they understand why you are deploying a particular tool from your toolkit of questioning skills, there is more of a chance of an empathetic and meaningful response.

Tom offers an all too brief answer to your open-ended question on euthanasia. You ask, 'So what?' This forces him to build on what he's said, to amplify, support and focus it for the benefit of the class and their own thinking processes. After a while, only 'So ...?' is needed, because the class knows where you are going.

'So what?' can be hugely enjoyable and frustrating at the same time. The technique can also be reversed, so that you can be explaining a problem or story and the students set you the same challenge. Thinking on your feet in this way involves you directly in the learning process and raises the bar for everyone. All the students raise their expectations when they see their teachers on the spot.

7. Little, big, meta

The 'little, big, meta' method has been well known to history teachers for many years, and is a useful addition to the toolbox of questions we are encouraging learners to deploy.

For example, we are studying the Black Death in the fourteenth century.

Little questions

- How many priests died as a result of the plague?

- What were living conditions like in towns at this time?

- What do sources from the time tell us about possible causes of the plague?

Little questions can normally be responded to with a direct answer based on research. They are useful as building blocks within a specific grammar or taxonomy of questioning and allow for some difference of opinion, but they too often characterise low-quality worksheets and textbooks. We can go much further with ...

Big questions

- Why did some people at the time blame miasma/God/the Jews for the plague?

- Why did the Black Death affect the religious beliefs of ordinary people in the fourteenth century?

Domain-specific knowledge is needed to provide persuasive answers to these questions, which layer up the understanding from the foundations already established.

Meta questions

- Why does it matter whether we study the Black Death?

- Why does the Black Death still feature so prominently in the popular imagination today and in school textbooks about the Middle Ages?

- How can we claim to know anything about ordinary people's attitudes in the fourteenth century?

Little questions shelter under the umbrella of their bigger cousins and may help to provide evidence for answering big questions. Meta questions are the glass-covered walkway we take with an open mind: they protect us but we can see through them to the blue sky beyond. They set the fundamental 'why' challenges which we all ask from time to time, and prompt us to justify and contextualise rather than provide a definitive, evidence-based answer.

Expert learners can become expert questioners by seeing, understanding and then deploying a similar taxonomy of questions themselves. It can be invigorating to ask students to discuss and then write down on sticky notes the issues they wish to resolve at the start of a new unit of work. They can become skilled setters and decoders of questions, if we give them the opportunity.

Who is to say that the students won't come up with more intriguing or difficult questions than those in your scheme of work? In turn, this will generate shared research and investigation processes which flow naturally between teacher and students. Who specialises in those really tricksy, mind-bending problems that Google can never answer? Who is adept at drilling down into the assumptions underpinning a seemingly simple question? Which table can come up with a progressive series of questions for next year's class?

Purposeful practice will improve the use of this questioning model, as with all questioning techniques. Middle-attainer Tom will need to work on details at the micro level to add more weight to his responses rather than jumping straight to answering or creating meta questions. Meanwhile, Anna is working hard to become an expert learner with questioning excellence in her toolkit by addressing with rigour all types of questioning her teacher throws at her (including 'So what?'). She is improving her own classroom craft by taking nothing for granted.

8. Hinge and brackets

Hinge questions and agree, build, challenge (ABC) questioning are powerful strategies which can be bracketed together in the arsenal of the teacher keen to improve the listening and response techniques of the class.

Hinge questions

Hinge questions allow you to test understanding at a key moment in the lesson. This might be twenty or thirty minutes into a sixty-minute lesson, but it can come at any point. Are they 'getting it'? Has your explanation worked thus far? Is the skill being learned? Has understanding moved on during this lesson or across a sequence of lessons? Responses gathered from monitoring at this point will allow you to assess the nature and pace of the next stages – fast forward, rewind, pause, tweak and so on.

Careful planning is usually required to ensure that hinge questions neatly fit into a sequence of learning. However, the questions can also be improvised, which I've found to be more to my liking. You know by instinct and experience when you've arrived at a crunch point in the lesson (or sequence of lessons) and that it is the appropriate moment for a hinge question. If at this point you have a set of green (or mostly green) traffic lights, thumbs up or sticky notes on the wall in the right place, then you have a benchmark. You also have the means to identify and support those not quite grasping or applying the concept or skill, yet. Expert learners can be deployed post-hinge to support any students finding the task or exercise more difficult.

Hinge questioning can be difficult to get right. A good way forward, which I haven't yet tried, is to use multiple choice questions to tease out misunderstandings and confirm knowledge.

ABC questions

Alex Quigley (2013) has generously blogged about this style of questioning, which you can readily adapt to your classroom practice as I have mine.

A (agree). You are interested in the ethical issues surrounding euthanasia and Anna gives you her view in response to an open question which emerges as part of a discussion. Following the ground rules you have already established, you move to the side or back of the classroom (or sit down) and 'ABC' the issue. I have found that this gives a very clear visual signal to the class that I am now handing over the flow of the lesson to them. Asif agrees with Anna but doesn't move the discussion on much further, so you ask for more ideas. In this variation on ABC, I'm encouraging Asif to pass the metaphorical basketball to another student.

B (build). Yolanda has another angle on the debate, while not disagreeing with Anna's stance. She is able to build the discussion and take it further, adding another example or using 'because'. As part of the ABC convention we've built up, she won't be able to pass the basketball without 'because'.

C (challenge). Maya has not been at all persuaded by what she has heard and takes a different line. This gives the class a range of views, which is precisely what you had hoped for, plus this pupil-led approach has required minimal direction from you. Having set up the ground rules or conventions, your students know exactly what to do.

ABC questioning puts a premium on listening skills – sometimes the forgotten angle of questioning. In order to know what Yolanda's stance is, the whole class has to listen. This is particularly the case if the ABC questioning is supported by a basketball technique (although there are many possible variations) because the students don't know if they might be chosen next by the speaker. It leaves no hiding place and raises the bar for all.

Liar, liar

For a further twist, encourage your students to counter-argue their own genuine positions – that really is moving them on. The ancient skill of rhetoric requires the development of logical skills of argument. Many humanities GCSE mark schemes require a set formulation of a balanced argument. A high-level response might require agreement with an assertion in a question balanced against a challenge to it. For the highest level, a mark scheme may require a supported judgement to explain why one position is stronger than another. This is challenging work which requires deliberate practice. What better practice than by encouraging lying? As I say to my students, there is no lie detector test as you leave the exam room or an examiner exclaiming, 'You don't really believe that the United States caused the Cold War! Fail that exam!' *Teachers lie, students learn, students lie.*

It took well into university before the truth of this dawned on me. If the evidence leads you in a particular way and you have a body of knowledge to support the view, then argue it, even if you don't in your heart believe it – you don't have to. Modelling response techniques to students and letting them experiment with them raises the standard for everyone. They need not wait until university to realise that rhetorical skills have no ceiling.

Exit tickets

Many teachers use exit tickets to check understanding during a plenary or as the pupils leave the classroom, perhaps in the form of a quick question-and-answer exercise or as a sticky note response to a series of questions. This has been the limit of my own practice. Harry Fletcher-Wood and other leading practitioners have opened up many more possibilities for the humble exit ticket: according to Fletcher-Wood (2016), 'introducing exit tickets may be the most powerful change a teacher can make'. What better way to find out if what you have taught has been learnt?

Our professional practice becomes more evidence based, and immediate, if we plan the next lesson or sequence of lessons based on the students' exit ticket responses. The opportunity then arises in the next lesson to deploy our expert learners or those who have understood the task to support those who have not, among many other possibilities. Questioning as a form of diagnosis and remedy has much to commend it.

9. Question time

We've all taught classes where a few dominant voices and raised hands control the ebb and flow of the questioning. These well-meaning students set the tone for the lesson and, if I'm being honest, they are sometimes a blessing because their enthusiasm and commitment is so worthy and they act as a catalyst to others. But we also know that the price for this is too often under-engagement and under-achievement elsewhere and a lack of parity of provision.

Here are a couple of ways to influence not only the quantity of classroom questioning but also to raise its quality for all:

- Giving out 'answer tickets' means that each student has only, say, three opportunities that lesson to answer a teacher-led question (tweaks can be made to encourage and support pair or group work by suspending the rule for these activities). This will encourage learners to ration their answers and/or use up their three cards for fear of whatever minor sanction you've put in place for not using them. The aim here is to increase the number of expert learners.

- 'Question tickets' can be used in the same way to foster question asking. The sooner such techniques are embedded at the start of an academic year, the better, so that minimal effort is needed thereafter in applying the method. However mechanical these methods might seem at first, they soon become second nature. Are question tickets relevant to high-attainer provision? Of course. How will we attain any sense of Anna's acuity or Maya's imaginativeness unless we hear from them, regularly and on their own terms, not yours? I've deliberately chosen female students here because, in my experience, it is girls who lose out (but not always) when dominant boys capture the attention of the teacher and the class.

  Issue question tickets of three different colours: one for closed questions, one for bigger and more open questions and one for meta questions. Your own context and knowledge of your classroom will determine who gets what, in what combination and for what purpose – but it will be fun and interesting.

  What does an excellent question in your lesson look like? Great question! Do your students know? If they cannot recognise excellence in questioning, then they are leaving it up to you and playing 'guess what's in Miss's mind'. If students' desks are not already awash with question and answer cards or tickets, you could hand one out when you hear a question which qualifies or, better still, model how the students could use one of three already on their desk – for example, using a ticket exclusively when they think of a 'meta' question. The possibilities are endless. It will help to put examples of excellent questions on the classroom walls.

10. Closed all hours

Closed questions have had a bad press for a long time. PGCE students are warned of the perils of playing 'guess what's in my mind?' with a class by asking impossibly narrow and specific questions. Dylan Wiliam (2009) has urged us to move on from 'ping pong' call and response questioning to something more closely resembling basketball than table tennis, with questions flowing and listening skills being put to good use – more in line with the dialogic model than the monologic. It is vital to pause. It is absolutely vital to pause before expecting a response.

It would be churlish to take issue with this advice. Questions that produce a simple right or wrong answer may be evidence of little more than effective recall or general knowledge, and demonstrate nothing by way of learning or progress. But not so fast. Do closed questions have a valuable role to play? Yes. Should *all* whole-class questioning be open ended, encouraging a wide variety of responses and admitting no definitive answer? No. As always, it's a matter of degree. A lesson or unit of lessons that consisted only of open or closed questions would be both immensely tedious and hugely frustrating. A questioning dialogue needs a balance of question types, some of which might be justifiably closed. Dropping in a closed question at the start, end or hinge point of a lesson tells me as a teacher what hasn't been understood and influences my planning from that moment.

'In which century did the Black Death take place, Tom?' If neither Tom nor his peers can get this right, some relearning and consolidation needs to happen before we can move on to thinking about the long-term impact of population decline on the medieval rural economy – because, of course, we have high expectations of these Year 8 pupils.

11. Multiple choice revived

Intriguingly, another form of questioning which has recently started to come back in from the cold (as I'm suggesting needs to happen for closed questions) is multiple choice questions. Once banished to the outer limits of respectability as the province of town centre questionnaire fillers and American university application forms, the multiple choice pro forma is back in the toolkit of techniques thanks to the work of Daisy Christodoulou (2017) and others.

'Thirteenth, fourteenth or seventeenth century, Tom?' As a diagnostic tool, we can see the power of this method for Tom and his class. If a majority claim that the Black Death happened in the seventeenth century, they may just be guessing and pick the outlier date because it looks most likely. But they may also be thinking legitimately about the Great

Plague in London and other cities in the 1660s which some of them may have studied at primary school. If so – and your own dialogue with the class will establish this – it is an interesting starting point and will help the class to build an overview of medicine through time, which could extend into outbreaks of cholera in nineteenth-century London. Not a bad outcome from a simple incorrect multiple choice answer.

If Tom plumps for the thirteenth century, this exposes a limited understanding of how centuries are labelled in many European countries (although not in Italy). This is never a bad topic to recap and consolidate at Key Stage 3. If Tom opts for the fourteenth century, we have some evidence that he knows that the 1340s was the right decade and that this is in the fourteenth century. We may wish to triangulate this against other evidence, but it is a good starting point.

The common criticism of multiple choice questions is that they simply give students the answer and encourage guesswork. But there is good statistical evidence that multiple choice questions are reliable and robust (Christodoulou 2017). A well-constructed set of questions with more than one plausible 'right' answer can be a powerful diagnostic tool, and one that should be welcome in any teacher's toolbox if raising attainment is the goal. Some A level science courses now deploy multiple choice questions as an integral assessment method.

12. Philosophy in schools: primary schools lead the way

Adam Barber is the inspirational head teacher of Henleaze Junior School in Bristol. A qualified architect and a musician, he teaches philosophy as a springboard for higher level thinking. He is convinced that the school curriculum, even for busy Year 6 pupils taking SATs, needs to offer some big questions and shared discussion about the types of moral and ethical issues which will confront them on their individual and collective learning journeys. It strikes me as odd that when my son was at this very primary school there was a lunchtime Philosophy Club once a week, but that many secondary schools don't offer something similar.

There is nothing new about philosophical stretch and challenge – the Philosophy for Children (P4C) movement has been around for a long time.[2] There can be no better way of encouraging big thinking about our school curriculums than by adopting a philosophical

---

2 For more information visit www.sapere.org.uk, www.philosophyforschools.co.uk or www.p4c.com.

approach to all learning. The EEF has conducted the first efficacy trial of a P4C model in primary schools, which was evaluated by the University of Durham. They report that:

> Year 4 and 5 pupils doing Philosophy for Children made about two months' additional progress in Key Stage 2 maths and reading compared with other pupils. ...
>
> Teachers and pupils generally reported that P4C had a positive influence on the wider outcomes such as pupils' confidence to speak, listening skills, and self-esteem. (Education Endowment Foundation 2018c: 1, 3)

These results have 'moderate security' and further evaluation is required before the EEF can be certain that such projects could be successfully replicated across other schools. But the fact that the EEF is prepared to look at this idea and fund it is promising.

My school's philosophy, religion and ethics department has a display which reminds students of the differences between straw man arguments, ad hominem arguments and many others. This display could be put up in any staffroom because its relevance is universal. An approach to all subjects which questions, takes little for granted and adopts a diagnostic perspective is exactly what we wish to inculcate in our young people.

Philosophy encourages a critical and discerning look at the world, and the rational pursuit of enquiry questions. There is no arcane body of knowledge that you need as a 15-year-old, or even a 9-year-old, in order to adopt such an approach, which makes it all the more attractive as a proposition. Observing students engaged in a structured philosophical debate can be empowering. Television has all but given up on serious debating and the exchange of ideas, which means it is down to us as adults to model to our students the kind of respectful academic discussion which is needed. A 'question club' or Philosothon can work well because there are rules of engagement and a structure which students can work within.

The Philosothon is an international movement which started in Australia and has been pioneered in the South West of England. A series of competitive challenges take place in rounds within a framework which deliberately mixes up year groups (Years 9–13). The students will need prior practice within lessons or as a regular lunchtime or after-school activity if they are to enter the competition fully prepared, but this is no different to netball practice or preparation for a chess tournament. The obstacles to schools engaging more with moral, ethical and philosophical debates are often more imagined than real.

Teachers with specialist knowledge and libraries full of the collected works of Aristotle and Plato can sometimes be more of a hindrance than a help. What counts more is a willingness to give free rein to the enthusiasm and intellectual creativity of our young people. The

Philosothon sets a premium on respecting the arguments of others, building logical points and a collective, reasoned response to points raised by supporters of, and challengers to, a student's line of argument. Successful contributions build on the arguments of others within the context of a 'community of enquiry'.

I first came across the idea of a community of enquiry in Peter Fisher's *Thinking Through History* (2002). He includes an exercise which invites pupils to engage with a rich story from the past – in the example demonstrated, the suffering of a family during the Anglo-Scottish border wars in the sixteenth century, chosen for its local relevance to the school. Once the context has been well understood, the pupils can practise and develop skills such as speculating, summarising, empathy, reasoning and self-correcting, not to mention question framing of their own. Explaining, sharing, critiquing and listening to the views of others with the teacher as facilitator or observer can be liberating.

Alternatively, try a question club. This requires nothing more than an interested teacher and some keen students. Our version runs for half an hour once a week at lunchtime and is Year 12 led. No pre-existing knowledge is needed. The aims are to encourage participation for all, adventurous questioning and answering and the fostering of listening skills – the often underplayed aspect of questioning as a technique. Biscuits help to generate the right atmosphere.

You haven't mentioned differentiation

As a term, differentiation is deeply scary – it has the slipperiness of a fish. Ask any three teachers about differentiation and two will admit they don't do enough of it. The third will be lying.

I have deliberately chosen not to isolate differentiation in its own chapter because the more it is seen as integral to questioning (and vice versa) and regarded as part and parcel of our normal daily practice, the less reason we have to worry about it. My point here is that questioning strategies provide a genuine and considered response when a head of subject or SLT member asks about the ways we differentiate in our daily practice.

Differentiation by questioning

- Expert questioners can lead the way. They may be Anna and Tom, not Asif and Yolanda, so not necessarily the most high-attaining students in a class, but they will have a knack for formulating and pursuing a question. They are on the path to becoming expert learners, not just able but remarkable. They might use some of the role cards we encountered earlier in this chapter to allocate a focus to each listener. They may be smart in teasing out from the class what would constitute little, big and meta questions and in helping to decide which ones are worth answering.

- DIRT is another opportunity to direct different levels of questions to a student and for the other students to do the same as self-reflection, according to how well they have or haven't completed a task.

- Market stall exercises offer further differentiation by questioning: students rotate around 'stalls' in the classroom and ask questions of the expert stallholder before returning 'home' to teach the rest of their table. Questioning, listening, summarising and explaining are skills that need regular, focused and deliberate practice.

- Question time: asking very good students to formulate their own questions to provide insight into an issue can be rewarding. We have to understand a subject well before we can take it apart for questioning.

- Dialogic marking provides differentiation by questioning because the attention is one to one, positive and directed.

- A well-timed hinge question – or any other valid class check method – will tell you who is struggling, who is coping and who is mastering today's material.

Differentiation works best when it slips in seamlessly alongside other good learning and teaching practices, not when it is isolated in lesson planning as a clunky extra.

Some questions to consider

Student voice

- What are your high-attaining students saying about how effectively questioning works in lessons? Credible recent evidence via tablet computer feedback, SurveyMonkey or student voice will count for more than anecdote or hunch.

- Does your department's policy on questioning match what your students say works for them? (You do have a policy on questioning, don't you?)

Questioning your questioning

- Is questioning in your department as varied as other learning methods or is it basically all done in the same way? Consistency may be desirable for comparative purposes but variety is appropriate too. Match the method to the task.

- Is formulating and answering questions an integral part of your habits of teaching and learning (e.g. via hinge questions)? If it's a bolt-on, however skilfully done, it will not work as well.

Developing expert questioners

- Can you honestly say that you take as much time in questioning your very best students as your other students? It's a myth to think that for some reason high attainers won't benefit from questions that stretch them, and us, but this is a skill to be learned.

- Can you honestly say that questioning helps your students to improve (e.g. by modelling the process of deploying different types of questions for different purposes)? Even with your best students, you may end up summarising what they did or didn't do well.

- Do the expert questioners in your classes take a lead in classroom dialogues? Students become expert questioners and can model their skills to others.

- Is questioning an integrated part of your teaching and learning, so the students have a chance to come back to a task and improve it? Spacing or interleaving learning with review and revisiting is part of the feedback and questioning cycle.

- Would a coach or a critical friend visiting your lessons see questioning as part of a dialogue or a monologue? Consider the research findings on the benefits of building such dialogues.

- Has your department and school given you the time necessary to embed good habits in questioning? Any adjustment in teaching strategies takes time, coaching, revisiting and support in order to be effective.

Summary

When done well questioning puts the students in charge. Expert questioners become polished and adept through practice. 'Mistakes' carried out in an environment which is supportive and non-judgemental don't have the crushing impact on self-esteem which real mistakes do. Expert questioners might not be the highest attaining pupils in the school but they should certainly be among the most valued, and not just in semi-public events such as debating.

It is in the classroom where speaking and listening skills are acquired, perhaps from peers more than teachers, who can therefore enable and facilitate rather than lead. Questions help to locate and maintain Anna and Tom in the Goldilocks struggle zone – out of their comfort zone but not into the zone of impossibility, yet. A lot of good questioning happens in schools, but I suspect that it isn't shared consistently. Students can become expert viewers of video clips. They can become film critics. They can be question creators, not just answerers. They can even become expert liars.

Questioning requires thinking, which is why we admire radio and TV presenters and barristers because they can do it under intense public scrutiny. Thinking leads to more thinking. Thinking up questions in a class discussion makes a more critical and questioning approach on paper almost inevitable. Unless we build in opportunities in lessons to develop question asking, listening and answering techniques, how can we legitimately expect such skills to be demonstrated in essays or EPQs? Practising, modelling, repeating, embedding, challenging – these are the questioning techniques which students should be using and testing every week in our schools.

Good questioning translates mission statement wishful thinking into actual thinking. It is at the heart of excellent provision for all our students. Questioning propels students along their learning journeys from good to able to remarkable.

Chapter 7

The Learning Rollercoaster

Learning is a change in long-term memory.

Daniel Willingham, *Why Don't Students Like School?* (2009)

Key themes

- If you look carefully at how students learn, the process is more akin to a rollercoaster ride than a learning curve or staircase. Rollercoaster rides are thrilling and take students to the top, but we should prepare well for the journey's climbs and dips.

- Myths in education can be as powerful and entrenched as they are in history.

- Expert revision methods which use research evidence from cognitive science can help provide the scaffolding for every learner to aim high. We can close the knowing–doing gap in this area more easily and effectively than in many others.

Progress for our students rarely follows a straight line. The learning of high-attaining students is often irregular and episodic and accompanied by minor setbacks and reversals. Improved learning, knowledge acquisition, skill mastery and progress can coexist with moments or longer periods of difficulty, incomprehension and limited improvement. This can apply within a single lesson, across a sequence of lessons or across a whole term. There may not be a perfect analogy to describe this pattern, but the learning curve is frequently used in the literature and in common parlance.

The myth of the learning curve

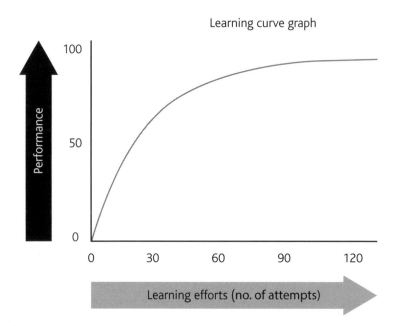

Learning curve graph

We say, 'It's a learning curve, all right!' when we describe a new process or skill we want to master. The phrase is perfectly acceptable in everyday speech, but when used in education does it really help us to understand how best to make more able students into remarkable ones? My contention is that it does not.

The learning curve is usually depicted as being neat and regular. Sometimes it is not even a curve but a 45 degree diagonal line. Learning isn't often like that. As teachers, we know that smooth, controlled advances by an individual pupil, let alone a whole class, are the exception rather than the rule. When we check students' understanding mid-lesson with simple red, amber or green traffic light cards, or ask for a quick visual thumbs up/thumbs level/ thumbs down, or use mini-whiteboards to demonstrate understanding, we find disparities and difference.

The seductive smoothness and predictability of the learning curve resembles the automatic gearbox of a luxury saloon, with effortless engineering facilitating outstanding forward motion. What you and I may be facing in the real world may resemble more stick shift clunkiness, gearbox grinding and the occasional stall. Even the students able and willing to get into top gear may find the shift from second to third tricky. If you think about your own learning you may concur. Did you pass all your exams? How easy was the learning when you tried that Spanish evening class a couple of years ago? How straightforward was it to explain to the family the rules of that new board game acquired last Christmas?

The contention of this chapter is that if we want to support *all* our students on the journey from able to remarkable, it is vital that we understand the nature of the journey ahead and help them to prepare for the difficulties they will undoubtedly encounter. Even, and perhaps especially, those who make it look easy. If we just assume that our more able learners will cope inherently with setbacks and the occasional judder of the clutch, then we are doing them, the learners around them and ourselves a disservice. They have much to explain and model to us and their peers about what is hard for them and why. Successful journeys require planning and review. Successful journeys need flexibility as circumstances change en route.

A case study from history: the learning staircase

Historians writing about the First World War have faced particular challenges. For every successful advance against German forces on the Western Front there were defeats and setbacks. Indeed, the whole history of the Great War, at least from the British perspective, has been characterised as a series of defeats and disasters, the names of which are seared into the national consciousness: the Somme, Gallipoli, Passchendaele. British soldiers have been labelled as 'lions led by donkeys' and their generals as butchers and bunglers.

No serious historian of the First World War holds such views today. Of the many problems which devotees of the traditional thesis have to resolve is how such ineptitude actually led to an Allied victory. Even the fiercest critics of British generalship cannot deny that fact. About as far as the case goes is that it must have been a victory inspired or led by the Americans or that the Germans just collapsed.

When military historians (such as my friend Peter Hart, oral historian at the Imperial War Museum) started to look at these arguments in detail, they were able to reassess them using the most powerful medium of all – evidence. The copious archival evidence of officer review, reflection and innovation in the wake of each major attack, or the evidence that when American troops first entered the war they typically made many of the same mistakes as their British counterparts (Hart 2009: ch. 12). The analogy which some historians have adopted to explain how and why the Allied troops made progress is 'the learning staircase'. A breakthrough was made using a particular method, such as 'bite and hold': think of this as the riser. Then there might follow a period of consolidation as the method was more widely adopted, or may not have succeeded elsewhere, or was refined, before another advance was made: this equates to the tread or flat part of the stair.

However, parallel to the British/Allied learning staircase, German generals were artfully constructing their own. They too had brilliant engineers making their own advances and improvements, some of which cancelled out or succeeded against those of their enemy. And so the war went on, with each side trying ever faster to build a dominant 'staircase' to overtop the other.

The staircase idea is a useful and powerful explanatory metaphor for shedding light on learning in the classroom. We can appreciate the idea of movement upwards and the arrival at a plateau before a further advance is made. However, whether we envision a staircase or an escalator, the metaphor doesn't fully capture the sheer variability in the scale or speed of progress – particularly not the scale. When we picture a staircase, the treads are evenly spaced and it moves you upwards. Learning simply isn't like that most of the time.

An alternative: the learning rollercoaster

The rollercoaster is arguably a more potent and persuasive point of comparison. With the rollercoaster we can see that:

- Forward momentum is possible in spite of severe and repeated dips.

- Dips can be sharp or prolonged or sharp and prolonged.

- Progress can be simultaneously fast and exciting and scary.

- Even though we may expect the unexpected, the precise nature of the unexpected will be by definition unknown and uncontrollable.

Returning briefly to the Great War, some historians now appreciate that, for the participants in the fighting, especially the senior officers responsible for the strategy of the war, the learning rollercoaster was viscerally real. Dips in the ride meant thousands of casualties because of an Axis rollercoaster advance or an unexpected setback in planning or coordination. Lest this may seem to trivialise the Western Front offensive by comparing it to a theme park ride, it is clear from Field Marshal Sir Douglas Haig's (2006) war diaries and letters that he understood better than anyone, certainly the politicians who criticised him so vocally, that this was a war of attrition in which huge numbers of casualties were unavoidable.

The rollercoaster may be a useful learning tool in visualising how surprising and unexpected a chain of events may be. From the viewpoint of the spring of 1918, it would have been astonishing to millions of people that the war could end in a ceasefire and Allied victory in November of that year. There were confident predictions from the time that the terrible slaughter would be brought to an end by a simultaneous Allied advance in the spring of 1919. Unexpected advances in how quickly soldiers and airmen were able to apply new techniques (the 'all arms battle'), learned by harsh and bitter experience on the learning rollercoaster, helped to bring the Great War to the 11 November armistice (Hart 2008: 2–6 and ch. 1).

The power of myths in education and in history

One of the reasons I have dwelt on this apparent tangent of the Great War is because it enshrines so many ideas that are hard to challenge, let alone displace, such is their hold on the popular imagination. Education, like military history, seems peculiarly vulnerable not just to passing fads and quick-fix solutions but also to deeply entrenched ideas. There is a long and depressing list of beliefs and practices which are passionately upheld and widely implemented without any sound research evidence to uphold them.

They include:

- Pupils should be taught according to their preferred learning style.
- Every lesson should involve some group work or similar activities.
- Tablet computers and laptops improve results.
- Writing lesson objectives on the board and target grades in books boosts results.

- Brain myths: people are left-brained or right-brained because the left hemisphere favours logical, analytical thinking and the right creative, intuitive and emotional thinking.

For the Great War, a parallel list of myths might encompass:

- Brave Tommies were led by incompetent generals: 'lions led by donkeys'.
- Incompetent generals refused to use new technology such as machine guns and tanks.
- Haig was simply a butcher.
- The French army was cowardly and incompetent, while the German and American armies were well-equipped and highly competent.

We need evidence, not fairy tales. There is no credible, substantive evidence that we will make our students brighter by teaching them according to their preferred learning style or that they will work harder if we put up hortatory posters in our classrooms. There is no evidence that we remember 80% of what we teach others but only 10% of what we read. And yet these beliefs are hard to shake. On a parallel plane, the *Blackadder* view of the Great War's generals, brilliantly written and performed comedy though it is, is not supported by officer casualty figures and detailed archival research.

The obvious implication of the rollercoaster is that our students' performances will dip and peak. Do we have the flexibility in our testing and assessment mechanisms to cope with this? If we demand that our high-attaining students are always in the top 5% for class or year group attainment, as many gifted and talented schemes do, then we may protect the integrity of an academic league table but we may impose unrealistic pressures on individual students.

Do we offer pastoral support to those who take a rollercoaster dip? This is a decision for individual schools. My ideal would be to see students coming in and out of high-attainer programmes if they cannot manage the admirable consistency that a few do manage, but in practice it is difficult to administer repeated movement in and out of a particular cohort. More importantly, high-attaining students need just as much pastoral care as others. Kicking them off a school's gifted and talented programme may well damage their self-esteem irreparably.

This rollercoaster performance may be nothing more than an effective man-made mimic for a natural and organic process of knowledge acquisition followed by a period of resting and consolidation, or of falling back into familiar habits and knowledge before a fresh advance can be attempted. We learn effectively by breaking work into chunks, testing and retesting frequently, and adding the unfamiliar and unexpected to a framework of the known and anticipated. Unlike the falsely consistent progress associated with the classic learning curve, a natural cycle which incorporates periods of review, reflection and consolidation may just feel more right for learner and teacher. Our well-being may demand that the bone-shaking gravity defiance of that first meeting with the subjunctive mood in French ('Hang on – we have a subjunctive in English? I've been speaking English for seventeen years and I never knew that!') might require an interval of careful revision of other tenses before moving on – the equivalent of a quiet cup of tea in the theme park cafe before the next ride.

Rollercoasters take us to the top

Rollercoasters are inherently frightening. We fear the shockingly fast descents and crazy cornering and worry instinctively about the consequences if something goes wrong. And yet … we love the fleeting views from the top, the element of risk and the sense of adventure. Our logic tells us that we are safe, whatever our emotions may urge to the contrary. High-attainer provision should offer a fusion of raw feelings and powerful thinking to capitalise on the adventure that the rollercoaster offers. Dips and troughs are expected and prepared for because the students are working in struggle zones where the next concept, skill or piece of valuable knowledge will add to and build on what is already there without it seeming like a bolt-on extra. The rollercoaster is an ambitious ride but teamwork and a supportive learning atmosphere can encourage all to participate. It requires mental and emotional scaffolding to get there, and a mental model of success to continue, but the view from 'the top' is thrilling for all learners.

The top means just that. Reaching it cannot be left to happenstance. I've already argued that an innate ability in maths or a natural facility with languages – familiar everyday constructs in the media, at home and in the staffroom – are chimerical. We need such cultural constructs to explain success and failure, but too often in education this has meant an attachment to 'gifted' and 'talented' as explanatory tools. Better explanations of academic success can be found and should be at our fingertips. Not just hard work – if only it were that simple! Hard work of the right 'deliberate practice' kind, expertly guided and targeted at the struggle zone and with a real sense of a learning journey being undertaken, map in hand and direction of travel clear. These and other attributes will trump random and hopeful wandering every time.

From able to remarkable: scaffolding to the top

A very uplifting and positive feature of the research evidence on learning, memory and metacognition is that the learning process is not fixed. As our students become better learners, and better at learning about how they learn and why, some of the scaffolding we have used to help them get to the top can be removed. They can take genuine, verifiable steps to becoming self-actualised, independent learners – that goal of every school and college in the country. The process of planning, modelling, monitoring and reflecting becomes as automatic as a chess opening. It no longer sits in working memory causing overload but has become a chunk of learned and rapidly retrievable knowledge embedded in long-term memory.

Expert performance depends in part on a very large collection of these chunks, arranged in a sequence or framework which works because retrieval is assured. Once accumulated, the high-attaining student can really start to push against the boundaries of the subject. They come to resent the artificial confines of specifications and ask bigger questions than their course can accommodate. Some students should be designing the next generation of rollercoasters.

The problem is that we may not be providing the means for our high-attaining students to move up to the next level. They may not wish to go there – students like their comfort zones as much as we do. They may deny that there is any more they can do to pass their maths GCSE with a grade 9, since they already know that they can and the accuracy of grade predictions is very high. Nevertheless, it is our duty and responsibility to point out where their learning and abilities could take them. Isn't that what we are in our jobs to do?

Revision strategies

If we want our students to learn, including our more able cohort, we should test them more often. David Didau (2013a) is fond of quoting the following principle: which learning method works best?

1. Study study study study – test

2. Study study study test – test

3. Study study test test – test

4. Study test test test – test

Drawing on the work of Robert Bjork[1] and other psychologists, Didau points out that without frequent factual recall of what we've recently acquired, the information journey from Tom's working memory to his long-term memory won't be made. That's why the final method listed is the most effective when followed by a further assessment. We need to give Tom's memory the best chance of learning the biology of plant reproduction so that it becomes available for instant recall. Memory loss without recall is as high as 90%, as we all remember from Ebbinghaus' forgetting curve, so much of the time we are spending in the classroom is effectively wasted unless we actively do something to address this. Older readers may use their memories at this point to recall that there were a number of revision and study aids available in the 1970s which made pretty much the same point – for example, the SQ3R method (discussed in detail on pages 190–191).

The standard response of colleagues is to admit that while there may be something in the research, they are blowed if they are going to turn their lessons and departments into a testing factory. And quite right too. No one is advocating a return to Gradgrindian fact learning of the entirely pointless kind that so traumatised Louisa, Sissy and Bitzer, and which *Hard Times* parodies so expertly. The problem is that the Dickensian caricature of Mr M'Choakumchild 'murdering the innocents' has become almost too successful. Like the *Oh! What a Lovely War* and *Blackadder* view of the Great War, the opinions we have acquired as a society from brilliant works of fiction and popular entertainment are now regarded as unshakeable fact. People become very defensive indeed when challenged about them.

The power of song and story

Ironically, the very methods which have worked so well to embed entertaining fictions from Charles Dickens and Richard Curtis and Ben Elton in our collective minds as 'truth' show perfectly their power and effectiveness: simple stories effectively told, memorable characters, humour, drama, poetry, song, repetition. Pop song lyricists have always known this too.

It is time to claim back some of these processes now that we have cognitive science to explain to us just why these methods work as well as they do. We don't despise friends and colleagues who can recite a poem from memory, who can speak Spanish well or who can remember a common maths formula without having to look it up. So why do we seemingly disdain chanting, singing or formulae learning in the classroom when it clearly serves a direct and immediate purpose? Even if we were so adept and accomplished as a society at producing hundreds of thousands of creative, resourceful learners capable of problem

---

1 See https://bjorklab.psych.ucla.edu/.

solving and analytical thinking on the scale of Stephen Hawking or Marie Curie (which currently we are not), then we might look down our educational beaks at too great an emphasis on knowledge acquisition. Except that we wouldn't, because you can't have too much emphasis on knowledge acquisition. It isn't binary – knowledge or skills. It's a false dichotomy.

The paradox is that more frequent mini-testing saves time and acts formatively, not just summatively. The app Socrative offers an example of how this works. Once a test has been created (which can readily be shared across a department and saved), it can be fun to do for the pupils, takes little time and can be carried out at high speed. The results appear in a spreadsheet on the teacher's screen and she can see at once which areas have been comfortably internalised and which need more attention – for example, Maya's need to revise irregular verb endings is evidenced and can be fed into a reporting process and acted upon.

Ten strategies to ride the rollercoaster of revision

1. Space it out

There are a number of books and articles which explain brilliantly, using research from studies in behavioural psychology, why cramming or 'massed practice' is ineffective as a revision process for all our learners. It doesn't offer enough time for information to be absorbed efficiently into long-term memory for efficient retrieval, for which the brain needs several spaced opportunities. Spaced or distributed learning, typically offering three or four opportunities to come back to the revision material in different ways, is much more likely to be effective (Wiliam, 2018: chs 9 and 10). Curiously, students know this full well when they play a video game or practise for a piano grade: they may not realise that what they are doing is distributed or spaced practice but that is effectively what is leading to improvements. Buried within a now famous research paper from Kirschner et al. (2006: 77) lies the following gem: 'The aim of all instruction is to alter long-term memory. If nothing has changed in long-term memory, nothing has been learned.'

2. Practice testing

Self-testing – using cover and check, notes or practice answers – is one of the most effective strategies for improving students' learning. Knowledge organisers provide an adept way for students to learn the essential information they need for each topic because they must compress all the information onto one side of A3 or A4: important vocabulary and terminology, characters in a play, tools and equipment and their roles, plot summaries, sequences for an experiment – the list goes on. Knowledge organisers are a staple of revision and test preparation, but they can also form the basis for a cover lesson if the pupils are challenged to learn or improve or remodel in another format a section of their organiser.

There are many variations on the related method of look-cover-say-write-check, but all these techniques are founded on the principle of giving the infinite long-term memory more opportunities to take over the burden of remembering knowledge from the overburdened and fixed-capacity working memory. John Dunlosky (2013) tells us that we now have over 100 years of research confirming this. Do we intend to wait another century before we start doing it in schools?

3. Memorable T-shirts

The ultimate fashion accessory! I bought cheap T-shirts online (or you can ask students to bring in an old plain one) and invited my Year 11 students to write some memorable learning on them using fabric marker pens – such as periodic table symbols or verbs taking *être*. The process of selecting and deploying the chosen information accurately is integral to the task. Some of my students surprised me by walking around the school at lunchtime wearing the T-shirts they had made in class, which created an instant talking point. More importantly, they wore them at home. This is a one-off, fun task – ideal for the Instagram generation.

4. Rudeness in Roman Rooms

Tony Buzan wrote a number of popular books in the 1970s and 1980s about memory learning methods. In *Use Your Memory* (1986) he describes the Roman Room System. The Romans used a technique of imagining and memorising the layout of a typical house with furnishings and everyday objects. To each item in each room, they would assign the information or knowledge they wanted to learn. The vital next step is to forge a link with that item, so this chair connects with that line of poetry and that candlestick with the following line. This can be done with exaggeration, making the chair tiny or gigantic or turning it into a floating raft with the poet clinging on to it while reciting her verse.

The system sounds daft but it has worked for thousands of years. The imagination runs riot, and the more ridiculous or rude the associations, the more they are likely to stick. Your students, if they are like mine, should have no difficulties. This method can be used to memorise 100 pieces of information, and one of the beauties of it is that, once the layout of the house and the furniture has been decided by the learner, they can use it as a template for different subjects.

This is an absolutely classic example of scaffolding to the top and teaching to the top: why should we shy away from teaching such methods? All students can benefit, and our high attainers or expert learners can provide a lead. Without such methods, how can we reasonably expect our students to improve – by osmosis, with maturity?

5. App-solutely fabulous

Quizlet (https://quizlet.com) and Kahoot! (https://kahoot.com) are deservedly popular free apps which encourage pupils to create and share revision aids, such as electronic flashcards and quizzes for self-testing. They offer instant retrieval practice in electronic form.

Improving educational technology can help us to go much further. Apps such as Socrative (https://socrative.com) offer multiple choice questions, and this is apposite because many A level science papers now include a whole unit of such questions requiring, for example, that a calculation is performed and the only right answer out of four is chosen. Expert learners can take centre stage here. My chemistry colleague, Andy, can ask Yolanda to model to the class her thinking process when eliminating possible responses using the screen recording function in OneNote (www.onenote.com) or an app such as Explain Everything (https://explaineverything.com) or ShowMe (www.showme.com). A self-made video can capture the learning for self-testing or revision. Alternatively, he can ask Asif and Maya to take photographs of a distillation process in action, label the colour changes on a diagram and then embed them in OneNote for revision. This is dual coding in action.

One of the many advantages of this approach is that it doesn't isolate revision and testing as separate processes to be forced on recalcitrant students at the end of a unit or year of work. Rather, self-testing and self-actualised learning are happening within a 'routine' lesson which is personalised to a class – and which may be dangerously close to fun.

6. Fakebook

Russel Tarr has created a website (www.classtools.net) full of brilliant resources, including Fakebook, where students create a Facebook-style page for a famous person or historical figure they have studied. This is an active method of transforming information into one of the best forms of story – biography. The site's countdown timer uses various TV theme tunes which you can play in class to set the context for revision games or activities.

Hawaii Five-0? The Avengers? The resources are there. Translating facts from a textbook to a 'connect wall' or creating an individual version of 'fling the teacher!' involves thinking: the selection and deployment of information, the assessment of appropriateness, debate and discussion, a notion of importance and significance. This is game playing, but not as we know it.

7. Mind maps

Mind maps are familiar to most teachers but they come with health warnings. The first is that not all students like them and/or learn from them, so they will appeal to some and not others. Secondly, thinking about and then selecting data is often not sufficiently ruthless – so too much text makes its way into the diagram, making it crowded and confusing. This is another instance where we can scaffold to the top. If we want the task to be done well, it can't be left to chance: model concise, colourful and effective examples and make pupils repeat poorly executed work until it is excellent. It is a skill to create effective, summarising mind maps, and it requires practice and repetition.

8. Flashcards

Flashcards are simple and familiar. I'm a big fan because I've rarely come across a student who disdains them. Indeed, whenever I've given out commercially produced sets to low-attaining students, everyone else in the class (including the high attainers) has looked on enviously and insisted on having some too. Professional sets come in bright wrappers with pre-punched cards and shiny rings to keep them together, but my pupils are just as happy with improvised index cards in pale colours. As with previous techniques, the trick for the learner lies in the apposite selection and deployment of key information: which kinds of erosion in geography do I know from general knowledge or common sense, and which have particular names and characteristics which require active learning? Pupil and class-made sets also work very well.

9. Top Trumps

Top Trumps appeal to the inner nerd in all of us. Who says it isn't cool to know stuff? When he was 9, my son could tell you the engine size, brake horsepower and acceleration times to 60 mph of any supercar you could mention. His primary school had a Top Trumps club, so there was competition to learn more stuff.

Why do these methods work? Quite apart from the inherent joy of knowing things, which is never to be underestimated, Top Trumps (and flashcards) trade giving for taking. The cards take time and effort to create, categorise and compile before they give out their payback of repeated recall. No self-respecting geek would put credibility in a method which seemingly required no effort at all. It is in the categorising and crafting that the long-term memory has a chance to get to work. As Maya works her way through the pH scale for acids and alkalis and the neutralisation of salts, she is asking herself: what goes where, and why? How should I select, deploy, classify and condense the information? And when they revise together, how has Anna done it (because Top Trumps is a game, after all)?

10. Gamble aware

Students love rolling dice, either physically or electronically. Put up a grid of twelve pictures on the screen and ask students in pairs or groups to roll the dice. The number will correspond to an image they have to identify and then connect to another image. This can be easily modified into twelve maths formulae due to feature in a test soon, twelve verbs needing accurate verb endings, twelve terms used in poetry analysis that you want to check for familiarity and so on.

SQ3R reading method and Cornell note-taking

SQ3R is another example of the more traditional methods I advocate as still relevant to learners today. Its origins go back to the US educationalist Francis Robinson in the 1940s, but I first came across it in the 1980s via a paperback copy of *Learn How to Study* by Derek Rowntree (1970). Similarly, Cornell note-taking has been around for a long time in several different guises. The longevity of these methods is testimony to their success, but also to the truth of the adage that there is nothing new under the sun. Study systems for learning are as old as humanity.

These two examples long pre-date what we now know about the brain from neuroscience and cognitive psychology: their originators had neither the benefit of blood flow scans and brain autopsies nor a large body of experiential evidence on working memory and cognitive load. Yet these techniques can be adapted to schools and colleges today. As long as the core principles – largely based on what we might now term spaced learning or interleaved learning and retrieval practice – are kept intact, the capacity for modification of these methods is endless.

Neither method will work without practice and then more practice. Neither method will work without it having been modelled successfully. Neither method will work without careful thought about the motivations needed to begin and continue using it. But these methods are not fads. They really do work.

SQ3R

SQ3R is a reading strategy formed from its letters: *survey*, *question*, *read*, *recall* (or summarise) and *review*. This is how it works:

Step 1: Survey (before you read properly)

Skim through the chapter looking for the shape of the piece: title, subheadings, captions, introductory and concluding paragraphs.

Step 2: Question (while you are surveying)

Turn the title and/or subheadings into questions. Ask yourself: 'How does this chapter relate to the work we are doing in class?' and 'What do I already know about this subject?' Look for answers to these questions as you survey. The question stage builds on survey by encouraging active questioning and the idea of a dialogue with the chapter or article.

Step 3: Read (this should be the third step in the process, not the first, as students commonly suppose)

Read only a section at a time and summarise after each section. Reduce your speed for difficult passages. Stop and reread parts which are unclear. The survey and question stages should already have alerted you to the key areas which you should read and focus on; conversely, other areas can be read through more quickly.

Stage 4: Recall/summarise (after you've read a section)

Ask yourself questions in your head about what you have just read or summarise it in *your own words* – this is vital. Underline or note down important points you've just read.

Stage 5: Review (the crucial part of the SQ3R process)

Day 1: After you have read and summarised the entire chapter, think of some questions you have raised and answered or partly answered. If you took notes while summarising, write down questions about the notes you have taken (see 'Cornell notes' on page 193 for a method of doing this).

Day 2: Skim the text and/or your folder to reacquaint yourself with important points from the text. Ask yourself key questions in your head about what you've read. Recite or write down the answers from memory. Use mnemonics for material which needs to be memorised. Make flashcards for those questions which give you difficulty.

Day 7: Alternate between your flashcards and notes and test yourself (orally or in writing) on the questions you have formulated. Make a table of contents – list all the topics and sub-topics you need to know from the chapter. From the table of contents, make a summary sheet or mind map. Recite the information orally and in your own words as you devise the summary sheet/mind map.

Payback time now begins. Because you have now consolidated all the information you need for this chapter, you need only periodically review the summary sheet/mind map so that at test time you will not have to cram.

Described in this way, SQ3R may seem boring and tick-box. Who would want to through so many stages to learn displacement reactions in chemistry, kidney function in biology or glacial erosion terms in geography? In practice, such methods can become quick, automatic and easily completed. They may be 'old school' but they work, and today we have the cognitive science to explain why. Compared to the Morris Minor methods that some of my students have used – at times involving nothing more than a set of highlighter pens applied liberally to everything in sight, textbooks included – SQ3R represents a veritable Rolls Royce of learning.

Cornell note-taking

In the 1960s, Cornell University advocated the use of a note-taking method for its students which tried to turn them into more active learners.[2] It became well known and appeared in a number of psychology textbooks and student revision aids, which is probably where I first came across it. After several half-hearted efforts, I decided to give it a proper try a

---

2 I must credit the influential history teacher and author, Dale Banham, for reawakening my interest in how Cornell note-taking might work with students (see Banham and Hall 2016).

couple of years ago. In previous attempts I had used it purely as a revision method, which can work but is not ideal; introducing a new method of learning at revision time is too little and too late.

Traditional linear notes

Yolanda shows me her folder full of A level history notes. They are neat, well-ordered, dated and fully headed/subheaded. My handouts and practice papers are interleaved nicely. Her parents could take pride in such diligent presentation. These notes would surely pass muster in any school tracking exercise or inspection. She could talk about her work in a follow-up interview and, more importantly, she believes her notes will act as a good foundation for the forthcoming exams. Classic linear note-taking of this kind has underpinned hundreds of thousands of hours of routine classroom learning and homework in a range of subjects. It is not for me to say that this method doesn't work for Yolanda and many other students. However, research into the rollercoaster of learning and study methods has been extensive and has produced too many consistent results for us to think that we can ignore it completely.

The problems with traditional linear notes include:

- They are often a dumping ground for all the information covered on the course, with little discrimination between the vital and the peripheral.

- They make no provision for reflection or review but flatter with neat presentation – a poor proxy for learning.

- Even Yolanda might admit (diligent student that she is) that the sheer quantity of notes in her folder is off-putting. It's not a ring binder; it's a lever arch file.

- Students commonly don't feel great ownership of 'their' notes because they are all too aware that the rest of the class have got the same handouts and materials. This doesn't encourage them to develop an individual mental model of success for their revision.

Cornell notes

Cornell notes try to address these shortcomings. There are many examples and tweaks available, and students can easily create their own versions suitable for your learning environment and subject. What they all have in common is:

- A central section of every page where the routine note-making occurs, but in a more compressed and selective form than might naturally occur to students. This will need to be explicitly modelled and taught to your students.

- A horizontal space at the bottom of the page for reviewing the notes and topic. This stage is undertaken a week after the original notes are made. This is where the Cornell method connects to the revision and memory methods discussed above. In order to help expedite the transfer of information from working memory to long-term memory, the review phase is a vital active learning process which helps to cancel out the worst impact of high memory loss associated with the rapid intake of lots of information, which is what characterises the school day.

- A vertical column to the left of the page is for questions which arise as the student is making notes. How does the learning hook into what they already know? (What does consubstantiation mean, and how does it differ from transubstantiation?) These queries can be followed up in class or at home.

- Alternatively, a student may cover up the note-taking column and use the question or cue column to the left to prompt reflection and review.

- A separate log sheet can be used to record additional reading, viewing and listening undertaken as homework.

A folder of Cornell notes will be much slimmer and more focused than a traditional folder. It may well be more colourful and visually appealing, with more sketches, diagrams, arrows, formulae and flowcharts. It will not contain mass highlighting because, by definition, everything in these notes is of equal importance. The ephemeral and contextual has been cut out.

One of the many advantages of the Cornell method for high-attaining students is that it can itself be part of a bigger strategy of focused learning. It has all the advantages of many of the methods proposed in this book: it excludes no one and sets high expectations for all. For example, we are often frustrated when our students don't read around the subject. We stress the importance of this with UCAS applications in mind. We tell them how competitive university entry is and how a genuine interest in reading outside the curriculum will help their learning and boost their prospects. And then we leave them to it. Parents often don't feel able to help with specialist knowledge about which books or journal articles will help. The same applies to films and DVDs. We know that we don't have time in lessons to show the students all the visual material we would like, so directed viewing lists allow this work to be done in study periods or at home.

Cornell notes allow students to log what they've read or watched as an integral part of the review and feedback process. So, having done some reading and note-taking at home, Asif completes his Cornell log sheet, which doesn't take long. It records what he has read, how long he has spent doing it and what he found useful or not so useful about the resource he was using. Later that week, he watches a recommended film from his directed viewing list and records it on his viewing log. These log sheets then form the basis of one-to-one feedback sessions with his teacher which are scheduled regularly (how often is for your department to decide).

This is the chance to offer the one-to-one feedback which I suggested (in Chapter 4) was best practice. As the term goes on, you are into 'looping the loop' sessions as you review Asif's progress and he becomes aware of his successes and shortcomings in specific, targeted terms. Is he regularly reviewing past topics to keep them in his memory? Any doubts about the veracity of the logging process can be confirmed or denied by regular testing. Is he moving to the next level by finding relevant materials not on your recommended reading or directed viewing lists?

But what happens if Asif's routine work is half-hearted and there is no real engagement with the Cornell process? At the workshop I attended, Dale Banham was clear: Asif would not be entitled to a one-to-one feedback session unless and until he had made good his obligations. Doubtless parents would have been fully informed. (I haven't adopted Dale's method of withdrawing feedback, but I do hold it in reserve as a possible strategy with a difficult student or situation.) I have found with my own students that about two-thirds of them engaged well with the Cornell process I've outlined. Some of the note-taking was superb: it was concise, intelligent and targeted at the question or topic rather than resembling a personalised copy of the textbook they were using.

The review session is what turns the Cornell process into something special and really helps students to make progress, whether they are low, middle or high attainers. It allows you to direct your recommended reading and skill refining to the needs of the student because their logs contain a good summary of where they are. You can see precisely what the next stage should be and engage at first hand, via their logs and personal contact, in dialogue which will help them to tackle the next peak on the rollercoaster.

I am not claiming that Cornell note-taking will work for every student, and it is no more the magic formula to make our able students remarkable than any other. What it does do is to distil many of the themes of this book, and that is why I am using it right now. One size doesn't fit all, but I tell any students who are unwilling to undertake it that they need to show me in other ways that they are fulfilling all my expectations and achieving what I think is their potential. I haven't tried it with year groups below the sixth form, but I see no reason why it wouldn't work there too. After all, there is a pretty good argument that if we want to teach our students good study skills for the sixth form and university, then we need to start in Year 7.

If I may make a special plea for the humanities subjects at A level, it is not uncommon for a student who starts the year with indifferent grades and prospects to become much more highly motivated and to improve their grades as issues click and ownership of key knowledge transfers from teacher and textbook to student consciousness. The step up from GCSE to A level is one of those crucial moments when we, as teachers, must remove any barriers to the top and open up the possibility of very high grades to every student, whatever their past experience in the subject or related subjects. Introducing the Cornell method, if it has not been introduced already, can provide this scaffolding to the top at a formative moment.

Co-construction

Having read Tom Sherrington's (2013) blog post on co-construction, I decided to give this a go as one of my professional targets a couple of years ago. I chose a typical class of Year 9s and away I went. To start at the end of the story, the median percentage mark for this set in the end-of-year exam was 64%; my parallel class of Year 9s who were taught in a more conventional fashion scored 65%. Given that there are so many variables these figures have no research validity whatsoever, but I can say, hand on heart, that the students suffered no disadvantage from my experiment. Would I do it again? Reader, I'm repeating it this very year.

I presented some of my thoughts on co-construction in a blog post (Massey 2014) and at a TeachMeet in Bristol. From those points, I would emphasise that:

- Co-construction does stretch high-attaining students.

- It encourages variety in activity in lessons and in outcome.

- It requires collaborative learning.

- Lessons are less predictable, therefore the students won't always know what to expect as they walk in.

- Students take more responsibility for their learning – we are modelling and practising independent learning, not just putting it in a mission statement or on a website.

- It's not a quick and easy method – it probably takes a bit more teacher time and more energy, certainly first time through.

What is co-construction?

Co-construction is a form of flipped learning where students have a big say in what topics are studied and how they are studied. In my case, I gave them fixed points – namely, the common topics they had to cover and the assessments they had to take in parallel with the rest of the year group. These were non-negotiable. In-between, there was ample freedom to spend more or less time on a topic than usual or to choose topics that I might not have normally considered. This is therefore a very flexible interpretation of a scheme of work. We had to study the Industrial Revolution, Bristol and the slave trade and the First World War, but how we did so was a matter of agreement.

The learning rollercoaster was much in evidence. The students were put into groups, at first chosen by me but subsequently by them. Teamwork skills came more naturally to some groups than others, so this was a constant challenge. There were downs as well as ups. The groups were given responsibility for teaching parts of lessons. This went from bad to worse to better to slightly worse to really very well indeed.

Year 9 co-construction rollercoaster

What I assumed	What actually happened?	Did learning happen?
Year 9 would set a range of tasks in their mini-lessons.	They didn't – beyond reading and simple question and answer activities.	The best group raised the bar for the others and showed them how to build in more activities.
They would set interesting homework.	They set boring homework based on routine textbook exercises.	We discussed a variety of outcomes and by the end of the year they were model making, game making, poem writing and so on. It took deliberate reflection and review before we could all agree about what was wrong and how to put it right.

What I assumed	What actually happened?	Did learning happen?
All students would be involved in a lesson because they knew how it felt to be missed out.	They weren't – a few loud voices dominated.	Learning management improved and more pupils were chosen more often once they'd had some chances to improve. This again required active self-review in order to arrive at better solutions.
Behaviour management might need a lot of help from me.	It didn't – the respect they automatically granted each other was palpable.	We were able to focus on learning. Wow!
Lesson planning would need help.	It did.	Sophisticated lesson plans from more able students stretched and challenged all the others to try for a similar structure and standard. They had to ride the rollercoaster of experience in order to produce better lessons.
Peer marking would be difficult.	It wasn't hard to set up but it was hard to get them to use a full scale rather than clustering to the middle. Marking was ungenerous!	It didn't make a massive difference but it helped to maintain the ethos of pupil-led learning.

Why does co-construction add remarkability?

How can students understand how learning works unless we let them practise some techniques? Ordinarily, teachers might let them have a go at standing at the front and 'delivering' part of a lesson once in a while. They may flourish or crash or, in most cases, the result will be mixed. By building in regular and routine opportunities for control and ownership of the material, the students improve. They begin to take topics in unexpected directions – for example, drawing a parallel between the problems faced by nineteenth-century railway builders encountering opposition from a number of groups to similar issues raised by the proposed HS2 rail link.

Co-construction adds student voice to every lesson rather than just allowing them to fill in a survey once a year. It tests a range of skills and demands participation. The teacher's role is to mentor, suggest, act as a resource and, at times, to teach – this is collaborative learning, not time for teacher marking or email checking. In my case this needed a few changes in mindset. I would not claim for a moment that my students achieved as much as Tom Sherrington's IGCSE physics class, which had some specialist ICT/blog groups and organising groups within it. I proposed these, but they didn't take off with this particular class. With another class they might, or they might if I had set about it in a different way. The learning rollercoaster applies to teachers too.

Nevertheless, I respectfully submit that my Year 9 had a more diverse and challenging experience than they might otherwise have had, and that the raised expectations were, at least in part, of their own making and direction. This gives me the confidence to be able to recommend co-construction. I was providing the scaffolding but the building work in the best moments of the process was taken over by the students. They were scaffolding to the top as a self-build project. This was their grand design – individual and imperfect but memorable.

From able to remarkable via the rollercoaster

Cornell note-taking, SQ3R and co-construction (or flipped learning) all have in common the simple beauty of built-in self-review. Integral to each process is the seemingly hard task of forcing learners to ask questions about what they know and how they know it, how well they understand a topic and what they still need to work on. This is metacognition in action.

The reward for the effort put into these processes is exponential. Having grasped Cornell note-taking, it becomes second nature and it seems strange and self-limiting not to do it. Similarly, to go back now to some of my older assessment processes and to ignore the gains I think my students have experienced from DIRT time would seem perverse. My own rollercoaster ride as a teacher has at times given me vertigo. I've had to grit my teeth as Year 9's work on the railways hit the buffers with a dull PowerPoint which the group recited while staring at the screen. But how could it be otherwise unless and until they had ridden the rollercoaster and listened to peer and teacher advice?

Deliberate practice and mental representations of success produced better and more ambitious class and homework eventually, and that's what matters. My class reached the same destination as the rest of the year group via a few more dead ends and derailments, but by the end their awareness of themselves as learners was first class, not standard.

Some questions to consider

The rollercoaster of learning

- Can you think of examples of how learning might resemble a rollercoaster in your subject?

- What are the powerful learning myths which instantly come to mind when you consider learning in your subject?

- How might your department provide scaffolding to the top in one of your typical schemes of work?

Memory matters

- How have you incorporated low-stakes quizzing and spaced learning into your lessons?

- Have you explained to students how learning corresponds to a change in long-term memory – and have your expert learners modelled this to others?

- How are you helping your students to avoid overloading their working memories?

- Does your department or school explicitly teach and model memory techniques?

Note-able changes

- Do you or your expert learners explain and model efficient note-taking methods?

- Is co-construction or a similar strategy something your department would consider trying?

Summary

If we reflect on our own learning over the years, we may have constructed our own mythology about how we did literally no work all year for *that* exam but still got away with it, or how Mr Collins was a rubbish teacher and the whole class had to resit chemistry. Stories are powerful explanatory tools and live long in individual and collective memories. But they are not unchallengeable: there is usually scope for more than a single reading.

When we consider how the students we teach typically learn, we see a pattern more akin to a rollercoaster than a learning curve or a staircase. Progress, if it can be measured at all, seems fragmentary and episodic. Accepting this diversity in learning is part of understanding how to support it and move it on. The knowing–doing gap is nowhere more capable of being closed than in the field of memory and revision. Revision methods are plentiful and as old as the hills, but some have been proven to work better than others for pupils at every level of attainment.

If students want to improve they need to develop deliberate practice skills in the classroom, and at home, which will keep them in their struggle zone. This includes revision habits based on spaced learning, which will ideally become second nature as a result of the low-stakes quizzing and spaced testing they have shared with teachers in lessons. They need to know what success looks like and have a mental model of how to acquire and recall the knowledge and skills they need.

Refreshingly, research evidence indicates that these processes are not elitist or pie in the sky, but democratic and open to all learners and educators. Everyone can win because SQ3R and Cornell note-taking strip away the mystique of effective learning: it's not derived from innate processing power or genetic advantage but from the habits and rituals embedded in having learned how to learn, recall, review and revise successfully. In the same way, pure memory techniques, such as the Roman Room System, help to scaffold learning to the top and are as powerful when practised in the classroom regularly as they are at home during revision time or study leave. Understanding the learning rollercoaster may be another small contribution towards closing the excellence gap in schools.

Part 3:

Excellence for All

Chapter 8

Well-being

Students, Teachers and Parents

When I tell people I study the adolescent brain, the immediate response is often a joke – something along the lines of: 'What? *Teenagers have brains?*'

Sarah-Jayne Blakemore, *Inventing Ourselves: The Secret Life of the Teenage Brain* (2018)

Key themes

- Teacher mental health has suffered as a consequence of, among much else, the relentless revolution in public exam provision of recent years, so a coach or mentor scheme running parallel to appraisal may be helpful.

- Teaching high-attaining students can be stressful and can bring particular pressures to bear on colleagues. Schools and departments should think carefully about the impact on teachers of decisions about the staffing of high-attaining sets.

- Some high-attaining children will feel under great stress to maintain their place in the hierarchy of a high-attainer programme or similar.

- The adolescent brain is undergoing rapid physical changes leading to results which we should understand and celebrate, not condemn as aberrations.

Botheredness

I once attended an after-school winter CPD session at my school which all staff were 'strongly encouraged' to attend. It was led by an external provider whose company made some pretty ambitious claims about offering world-class trainers. You can probably draw in your head an emoji showing the feelings I had when I went into the session. I've been around long enough to have a bullshit radar so finely tuned that no stealth aircraft can get past it. I think I even sat in the front row so I could truly relish this twilight box of delights, the better to report them to disbelieving family and friends later on.

Not for the first time, I was proved wrong within three minutes. After five minutes I was moving around the room shaking hands with colleagues (part of the activity) and after forty-five I was heading home ready to enthuse about what I'd heard. The session was delivered to a large group of expert teachers by someone who hadn't been in a classroom for a long time but who knew his stuff anyway.[1] The takeaway message was simple: be yourself. Show a bit more of yourself to your pupils and good things will happen.

To some of my fellow staff this was a gentle reminder and a return to familiar ground. To me it was something of a revelation. I am the kind of teacher who won't naturally let a lot out in terms of emotions and who I am, give or take the odd rant about politics or football (Luton Town, since I'm in the mood). I've had extra buttons sewn into my suits, that's how buttoned up I am.

So, did this change me overnight? No, but I've thought about it a lot since and it has had the effect of a slow release fertiliser in a plant pot: a small dose, as and when needed, will remind Mr Buttons that children will hardly think any less of a teacher who lets go a little more often. I think I have warmth and sensitivity, but you have to get through that tough outer shell first before you reach the liquid centre. Just like one of Nina Jackson's sherbet lemons. As she says, 'Getting through the hard shell makes going in search of the fizzy centre that much more satisfying' (Jackson 2015: 1).

The approach of the legendary 'Ninja' and other hugely personable teachers intrigues me. Nina is hugely committed to the well-being of every student and teacher lucky enough to meet her. Hywel Roberts is another.[2] Amjad Ali yet another.[3] If you attend one of their CPD sessions or read their tweets and blogs, you are just astounded by the level of emotional intelligence and inspiration they offer. Hywel is 'bothered' and wants to inculcate more of a sense of 'botheredness'. This term has been used recently by Paul Dix in *When the Adults Change, Everything Changes* in a chapter entitled 'Deliberate Botheredness' (2017: ch. 3). If we want to build positive relationships with students, it means taking care of the small interactions and building trust on a drip-feed basis rather than through grand gestures or policy initiatives. We need the consistency and the kindness, the routines and the rituals if we are to improve the well-being of every pupil.

---

1 The session was delivered by Chris Atkinson at Elysian Training in Bristol: https://uk.linkedin.com/in/chrisatkinson.
2 See www.createlearninspire.co.uk.
3 See www.trythisteaching.com.

Nina, Amjad, Hywel and others had worked this out years before 'well-being' became a buzzword. Now, thankfully, they are not lone pioneers but leaders of a choir of educational professionals dedicated to raising awareness of, and generating responses to, the mental health issues facing schools today. This means offering solutions and not just diagnosing problems.

Where's the research?

Looking after the well-being of teachers has at last become an issue recognised by politicians, teaching unions and school leaders. Teachers have also become creative in looking after each other with campaigns such as #teacherfiveaday. We've slowly acknowledged the importance of sleep, exercise, a healthy diet and downtime from work emails and social media in the holidays. Hurrah! Ross Morrison McGill (2014) was among the first to champion this cause with a five-point plan for teacher well-being, and more recently Andrew Cowley has produced *The Wellbeing Toolkit* (2019), offering a comprehensive plan for embedding mutual support into the culture of a school. Jill Berry (2018) has always offered words of wisdom on the particular strains of being a school leader and the need for work–life balance within a school year and across a career.

However, I've seen very little about the particular pressures brought about by teaching high-attaining students. Is it special pleading to claim that there might be unique challenges in teaching them? Is it a case of dreaming up solutions to an issue that doesn't really exist to say that all this focus on stretch and challenge risks stretching staff too far? I don't think so. I am not building a case here for the idea that teachers of high-attaining pupils face more problems than, say, the teachers of children with special learning needs, or that they face more severe problems. Not at all. It's just that from my own anecdotal observations and experience in more than twenty-five years of teaching, more than from anything I've read, I have the sense that teaching bright kids can be tough.

- Self-esteem can take a battering when pupils know more than us and can do more with it, faster.

- PGCE students and recently qualified teachers can feel especially vulnerable when pupils show or even brag about just how good they are at something.

- When high attainers can draw, execute a dance move, design a circuit board or produce a line of program code more quickly and creatively than us, we face a challenge.

- A teacher's sense of professional worth can be undermined when her head of subject organises the timetable allocations for the following year and that top set class has been moved to someone else.

- A head of subject's sense of professional worth can be challenged when her head teacher looks at Progress 8 figures and interprets the data to mean a lack of teaching to the top and an insufficient culture within the department of high expectations.

- Parents can be pretty blunt at times in questioning teacher competence at parents' evenings. The message may be overt or covert but the meaning is clear: 'Yolanda is very bright. Are you up to the job of teaching her?'

Teacher well-being

If learning is a rollercoaster, as I've suggested, then the same model applies to teachers' emotional well-being as we navigate the multiple demands of teaching high-attaining children. As we monitor their pastoral care, we need to keep an eye on our own thermostat settings. It may help to untangle two threads here: firstly, is there a substantive issue with stretch and challenge, and, secondly, is there a perception of inadequacy?

If the head teacher or head of subject has identified a genuine issue with teaching to the top in our classes, then it can be addressed using, among others, some of the ideas in this book. Schools should be able to remedy the problem using small steps, manageable goals and plenty of support from colleagues. Departmental and school policies will be a starting point, but a school (or chain of schools) should be capable of going well beyond these to use the resources and expertise of a G&T lead or deputy head academic. If he or she has been observing lessons and monitoring high-attainer provision across departments, as I've suggested should be the core of such posts, then practical advice and strategies can be provided according to the school's needs and circumstances.

If the issues are more to do with perception, this can be no less powerful and all-encompassing for the individual concerned. It may be that these concerns combine with more substantive issues to produce a perfect storm of doubt and confusion in the teacher's mind. This can be intensified when we are faced by a cluster or a whole class of pupils who don't seem able or willing to be satisfied with the quality of our explanations and believe they need more.

We hear a good deal in the media about teachers leaving the profession because of workload and marking issues. I believe this may also mask the fact that poor classroom behaviour and weak school behaviour management systems are causing some teachers to leave. I wonder how many teachers also quit because they feel that the academic pressures of teaching are beyond them. The relentless revolution of education is not slowing down. I have rarely had a year without having to teach new material for a GCSE or A level class, let alone at Key Stage 3. Curriculum 2000, the introduction and then removal of AS examinations, strengthened GCSE courses – it's the intensity of change that is sapping as well as the frequency.

Teacher recruitment and retention too often founders on the rocks of phrases such as, 'I came into the profession because I loved my subject, but I can't stand how it's now taught.' If pupils need purposeful practice and mental models of success, as I've suggested in this book, so do the hard-pressed adults in the room. We can only be change agents when we are mentally fit and well.

Ross Morrison McGill has an extensive online presence via Twitter and a popular blog as well as being a regular speaker at teacher CPD events. He campaigns for reductions to teacher workload and improvements to teacher well-being from a position of being well-informed about what is happening 'at the chalkface' (McGill 2014). Some teachers may recoil at the prospect of reading about attrition rates in the profession and the excessive workloads endured by colleagues in other schools, but others will feel informed and empowered to campaign for beneficial changes in their own schools and colleges.

As always, the context of your own school or college will largely determine your choices about how to respond to these very real pressures. I would also recommend reading Nina Jackson's *Sherbet Lemons* (2015: esp. ch. 21) in which she offers advice about what to do when confronted by a difficult line manager. Some of her points have a direct bearing on teaching high-attaining pupils.

Here are some suggested self-care strategies: look out for others and look after yourself.

- Your head of department or line manager should be the first port of call. They will be able to help you and will value your honesty. It would be unusual if they hadn't themselves experienced something similar when starting off in the profession, or even more recently if they've had to teach a new course or an existing course for the first time. They will also be the primary point of contact if a complaint is made by a parent or pupil or if a query is raised by the SLT.

- A wise colleague at my school has recently started offering a ten-minute, once-a-week lunchtime 'switch-off' mindfulness session requiring nothing more than a quiet room and some chairs.

- Some schools have introduced staff coaches or mentors (also called buddies) to provide non-judgemental support for a variety of situations. This is quite separate from the appraisal or line manager structure and can be supplementary or an alternative. What matters is that institutions find pathways to show that they value and can nurture teachers through demanding academic challenges. I'm happy for my GP to refer me to a specialist, so I'm happy for my line manager to suggest the right person for my issue.

- Use every available additional school resource to help you. Many schools now have a counsellor or a dedicated teacher who has had welfare training appropriate to a school setting. Well-being is no longer a Cinderella issue. Teaching unions can also help and can provide access to experienced professional advisers, literature and courses.

- Use your expert learners. Flipping the classroom and recasting yourself as a learner alongside your equivalents – Anna, Maya and Yolanda – can help. You're a science graduate and you love your subject, but, wow, there is an awful lot of it. Moreover, it keeps changing. There was a lot of emphasis a few years ago on science and the environment, which I gather has changed more recently. I've taught goodness knows how many AS history units which are now themselves part of history. Pupils will understand this if it is explained to them. Learning a new unit can become more of a co-constructed journey rather than a make-or-break Arctic expedition if all students, including expert learners, are prepared to help. No one has any interest in anyone failing here. *Adults lead, students learn, students lead, adults learn.*

- Managing expectations to a realistic level is essential. I've referred in this book to Year 12s and 13s who outgrow their maths teachers in terms of what they can do, to languages students who as native speakers can outstrip their teachers and to history students who have made connections and shown powers of analysis greater than my own. Their top is already undergraduate top and perhaps beyond. I've learned to accept this as normal, even though it can still be difficult. My own expectations of what I can offer have to be realistic. I still read specialist books to improve my knowledge, as well as introductory books when I find (as I still do even after many years) that I'm being asked to teach a topic I've never taught before.

- Remember that our students want us to succeed. Rarely have I met arrogance or complacency among students who have gone well beyond the normal ability range and confines of the subject. If anything, they are often deeply appreciative of our knowledge of past papers, mark schemes and course structures, which means they can avoid the pitfalls of the examination process. They understand our worries and self-doubts and want to be part of the solution, not the problem.

I hope that none of this sounds patronising or glib. Irrefutably, every teacher well-being strategy which works should be lauded to the skies – it may also work with high-attaining children. After all, such children are no different to the rest of us in many ways. I'm simply, and I hope gently, edging towards a few thoughts in response to what I've seen, which is colleagues being daunted and upset by an individual or a group of students who already understand the material and don't feel challenged by what is happening in their classroom.

I've had a case recently: a Scholar told me that Mr X's explanations in a subject were no good and that the class were struggling. When Mr X added to the basics with further explanation in a bid to make it clearer, the class lost sight of the basics. I went to the head of department, who in turn asked me for advice. I suggested categorically not taking sides but supporting the colleague with coaching and lesson visitations (short, focused visits to help with an agreed issue), while offering the students reassurance that they were not missing out and that they would benefit from the department's handouts and resources shared across the year group. This was an agreed strategy, together with lunchtime help sessions from the head of department. The situation isn't ideal but it is not being swept aside – and it continues as I write. For me, the well-being of this colleague is no more or less vital than that of the students. If he becomes ill and needs a period of recovery, or even leaves the school, this will tell me that our pastoral support for staff has failed.

High-attaining student well-being

Teachers are high-attaining students. Once the clever kids and now the clever adults, it logically follows that their empathy should be that of the insider and fellow traveller who has been there and done that. But life is nothing like so straightforward and simple. There may be all kinds of reasons why they see adolescents as different and challenging – one being that they sometimes are.

The simple message here is that high-attaining pupils need as much pastoral care as any other student. They don't deserve more 'because they are cleverer'. Nor will they flourish without any such care 'because they are cleverer'. Clever kids are sometimes stereotyped as robots, effortlessly devouring homework and lessons without it seeming to cause them too much stress. The idea that learning is effortless for them (it isn't) then helps to feed the belief that they won't need any extra pastoral support, which is just as well because it's in short supply and we can now direct it towards those who really need it. Alternatively, they are so highly strung as 'genius' musicians or Oxbridge types that without the school's tender loving care they might wither and fade.

If we are encouraging every pupil to learn to the top and to undertake their learning journey with all the rollercoaster risks I have outlined, then inevitably this will be accompanied by periods of difficulty and failure. Since expert learners are made, not born, it's natural that they will take wrong turnings and hit dead ends, whether that's 8/25 or 23/25 for an essay – the failure is in the eye of the beholder. Scaffolding and support systems may vary but they have to be there.

Some more able children will feel particular pressures which they are very adept at hiding. Being on the gifted and talented register may be a mixed blessing: it may induce feelings of great parental pride at family gatherings, while simultaneously inducing fear and guilt at the prospect of the forthcoming mock exams. The burden of being expected to perform to a very high level all the time should never be underestimated. Bland statements from teachers or well-intended posters in the corridor about 'failure making us stronger' cut little ice with a 14-year-old high attainer who has just messed up a science test big time, or at least feels as if he has. This lack of objectivity is integral to the way in which some high attainers quickly lose self-esteem. What does it matter if Asif is reassured by his teachers that he is in the top 10% nationally for maths if the rollercoaster of learning has brought him to a low point with the news that Yolanda has secured a higher test mark? Or if the top 10% does not equate with his own, or perhaps his parents', perceptions of where he should be, which is actually much higher?

What is needed is praise, not platitudes; warmth and trust tempered by realism, not Christmas cracker homilies. Good relationships between learners and staff who are 'bothered' help to smooth out some of the dips and troughs of the rollercoaster, so that the climb to the top can begin again. Schools are full of brilliant mentors, heads of year and heads of house who know all this and much more. Understanding the specific stresses bearing down on children expected to be at the top of their year group, especially when the latest data drop circulates instantly to parent as well as staff inboxes, is always part of the remit.

It's the biology, stupid!

Social attitudes need to catch up with the science. Adolescents set off on their long, rollercoaster learning journeys to the cacophonous accompaniment of vast hormonal changes in their bodies. We've understood this for a while – it's certainly there in the folklore and in the way we speak about teenagers, with many jokes at their expense about mood swings and poor communication. As Sarah-Jayne Blakemore (2018: 2) affirms, adolescence is not an aberration but is a crucial stage in how all of us become both individuals and social human beings.

What is less understood is that teenage brains are undergoing equally remarkable physical changes which neuroscientists are only just starting to comprehend and explain to teachers. Our children need help from the adults in the room, who in turn need help from scientists in the lab. It's arriving. We now know that certain parts of the brain don't stop developing in childhood but continue to change throughout adolescence. We've all heard of synapses in the brain, but who knew that there is an astonishing automatic process of self-review going on in the adolescent prefrontal cortex? Synapses that are needed in order to respond to a teen's individual environment – their home and social life, nutrition and so on – are kept and even strengthened, while those that are not needed are pruned away.

Synaptic pruning may sound like extreme gardening, but it is more akin to fine tuning a radio to lock into the strongest signal from a transmitter, except that there are multiple transmitters from diet and exercise, education and culture. The adolescent brain is therefore physically quite distinctive from a child's or an adult's brain. Since the prefrontal cortex is responsible for, among other cognitive functions, risk-taking, decision making, planning, social interaction and self-awareness, we can see the immediate relevance to our classrooms – because this is where the adolescent brain is undergoing some of its biggest changes. According to Blakemore, teenagers should be encouraged to take the right kind of risks, so neural plasticity has implications for curriculum planning and what we do in the classroom. The adolescent brain is hard-wiring itself to experience the educational risks of the rollercoaster.

How a school counsellor can help

I was reminded of the perils of adolescence after a recent session with my Year 10 Scholars. With the full support of the assistant head of well-being, I asked the school counsellor, Niki, to come in and talk to them all together. I wanted to know more about any particular difficulties they felt. After all, they had been chosen either for their exceptional all-round academic abilities or for their skills in sport, art, dance, drama or music. There were about thirty pupils in the room.

Niki asked them what they thought were the positives and negatives about their roles as Scholars. She also asked about two sets of stresses: from within themselves and from outside (e.g. school, peers, family). They wrote this down on sticky notes which she then collated. Common among the pressures from within that the pupils noted down were wanting to 'do well' and 'be the best' as a matter of personal pride. Some pupils had a 'furiously driven work ethic', in Niki's words, which meant they were trying not to disappoint parents and prove their worth to the rest of the school community. A separate category of pressures came from those around the pupils, recorded as a pressure to perform well in sport and be the best in the team, to know everything in academic terms and never make mistakes.

It was humbling. This was only one year group from across the school, but if it is even partly representative of other Scholar groups then it gives my school plenty to think about in terms of the pressures bearing down on a lot of high-achieving pupils. I don't want students to be 'constantly revising' as one said, any more than games colleagues will want to learn that at least one sports Scholar feels that they have to 'carry the team'.

This whole exercise was a salutary one for me about the very fine line between legitimate stretch and challenge on the one hand and unacceptable pressures on teenagers on the other. If learning is a rollercoaster and a difficult journey at the best of times, is my role to speed up the carriages and steepen the drops? I think not. As an immediate response, we decided to circulate these findings to parents for information and comment.

Niki also asked the Year 10 Scholars what they did to relax. Three categories of activities were identified: the first was social activities for de-stressing – most frequently mentioned were meeting friends and food. The second was physical activities, such as sport and sleeping. Thirdly, activities for emotional de-stressing were dominated by music and television. Interestingly, there were isolated mentions of gaming, gardening, Taekwondo, animal welfare and breathing deeply – clearly, some high-attaining students find individual and distinctive ways of coping with the pressures attendant on outstanding performance.

Here is our school counsellor's professional advice, which we sent to the pupils who had taken part and their parents:

> Please give yourself enough rest and relaxation time each day/week/month and use it to de-stress in a healthy way that works for you.

> For more ideas about de-stressing please check out the link below:

> https://www.psychologytoday.com/gb/blog/teen-angst/201411/top-10-stress-busters-teens

> My personal favourite is to find something really funny to watch and laugh the stress away.

Parent well-being

Parent well-being is another subject which I've seen very little written about. Specifically, what I mean here is whether schools and colleges can, or should, take at least basic steps to support high-attaining students outside the classroom. One relevant benchmark is learning support pupils. Schools will routinely keep parents well informed about the progress of such pupils and may call them in regularly to ensure that schools and families liaise effectively. Students with education, health and care plans must by law have an annual review, necessitating evidence from and consultation with parents.

So what about high-attaining pupils? Should they be treated in exactly the same way as other students or differently? If so, why? Is there more that parents of high-attaining students should know in order to support their children? Niki and I thought that there was following the session with our Year 10 Scholars, so we sent out the findings to them and invited comments. I'm pleased with this as a process of closing the circle: pupil–school–parent. The message we want to convey home is that if our sample of high-attainer provision is at all reliable and indicative, then pupils already feel plenty of stress without adding more of it at home.

High-attaining students in my school need their parents to know that they are brilliant time managers. They juggle huge commitments of classwork, enrichment, sport and house activities, not to mention lunchtime clubs. Oh, I forgot to include year group assemblies and other ad hoc meetings. Now I've forgotten to include being a teenager and peer pressure. What they need from home is reassurance, consistency, routine and, of course, love.

Some parents will be experiencing corresponding work and family pressures themselves. A minority will not respond or will not be interested, but I think that many will find this approach informative. Niki's point as a professional therapist is just to 'big up the love'. Clever kids need as much tender loving care as every other child. But here's the big but – in many cases, they don't need as much external pressure as some other children. It's already within them, mostly for better and perhaps a little for worse. They know about deliberate purposeful practice and they have in their heads mental representations of success. They know how much work they need to do, for which subjects and at which precise moments (which may emphatically not include mock exams). They will sometimes get it wrong, but a lot of the time they won't. As John Holt says in the epigraph to Chapter 2, if we trust children they will get it right. It's all we need to do, but it's a very hard thing to do.

Interestingly, the research evidence is just starting to catch up with the implications of how changing technology can help schools to involve parents about learning and progress in school. What are children learning? When are tests upcoming? Has homework been submitted on time?

A recent EEF project investigated using text message prompts to improve parental engagement and pupil attainment. It found a small positive impact on maths attainment and on decreasing absenteeism. Because sending texts is cheap, the intervention was deemed 'highly cost-effective'. The study found that 'the vast majority of parents were accepting of the programme, including the content, frequency and timing of texts' (Education Endowment Foundation 2018f: 3). Clearly, one study featuring twenty-nine schools is hardly definitive, and strictly speaking parent well-being was not what the project was about. However, many schools worry a lot about closing the circle to involve parents more in students' learning.

It is likely that as society moves to more instant and informal means of communication, then schools and parents will follow suit. Whatever platform is chosen, the evaluation criteria will need to be much broader than simply cost-effectiveness. It would be hugely counter-productive for the well-being of teachers, parents and pupils if the benefits of texting home about student attendance or learning were to be outweighed by a feeling for all parties of being in an unremitting electronic loop. Safeguards have been put in place in many schools in the form of carefully considered policies about, for example, how parents and teachers communicate and what is a reasonable expectation for how, and how quickly, a response should be received. Supporting parents is vital in closing the attainment gap in schools, but the quickest and easiest form of communication between home and school is just one small aspect of the bigger picture of parent well-being.

Well-being and behaviour management

It goes without saying that a school where behaviour management is inconsistent will face more difficulties with the well-being of staff and students. It is the consistency of the response to common challenges facing schools – from banter to swearing to mobile phone policy – which is so important. Schools rely on everyone knowing what to do, how to do it and when, so the power of practised good habits and scripts should never be underestimated. Whatever choices a school makes about its responses to bullying, sexting or other behavioural issues, it is with the certain knowledge that there is an impact on learning, attainment and well-being for the whole community.

As I observed back in Chapter 2, I want children to have a say in designing ideal lessons and schemes of work. I want them to take a lead with feedback on their own work. They should learn how to build strong images in their heads of how deliberate practice in learning and applying formulae or vocabulary will help them to get a better mark next time. They learn to construct these pictures from adults and expert learners whose modelling becomes infectious. *Adults lead, students learn, students lead.*

So how do these two points connect? There is a lot of agreement that consistency of application should be at the heart of any approach to behaviour management. If students can learn, practise and then lead on excellent questioning strategies and memory techniques, improved note-taking, enhanced feedback skills and so on, they can certainly do the same with their attitudes towards each other. Harnessing the power of the group should be part of whatever behaviour policy a school decides to implement. Instead of yet another top-down initiative, we should be making mutual respect more consensual and 'bottom up' because students are at the heart of it from the outset. If we don't think they are capable of improving classroom relationships, then why would we think they are capable of learning complex subjects in a short time frame?

Perhaps schools have something to learn from nudge theory (Thaler and Sunstein 2009). This branch of behavioural science works by influencing the behaviour and decisions of groups and individuals through positive reinforcement and small, often indirect, changes to the environment. Putting fruit on the school lunch counter rather than banning chips outright is often cited as an obvious example. Moving a small proportion of lessons into a different space, because the students agree that it's more than worthwhile for their learning, is another. Holding a door open as pupils enter the classroom is polite and welcoming, as well as being a nudge towards respectful behaviour, while propping the door open with one foot in the corridor and one in the classroom is a nudge towards staff monitoring of corridor and communal space during transition time. Nudges from teachers have a multiplier effect: they signal respect to a class which they carry with them into every lesson that day. Challenging the students', and your own, status quo with positive nudges may be cumulatively powerful for well-being as well as behaviour.

This was precisely the advice offered by headmaster and educationalist Michael Marland back in 1975, in a now little-used primer called *The Craft of the Classroom*:

> In this position you can greet each pupil or bunch of pupils as they arrive, and direct them to their first activity. As each passes you, it is possible to put in a personal word to many of them. Private jokes, reminders, enquiries, warnings, encouragement can all be easily fitted in. You have combined efficient supervision with warm personal relationships. Naturally, you will not want to be nailed to that door jamb for life, but you will find it about the best reception position. (Marland 1975: 46)

Still not convinced? One of my justifications for giving students more of a say in how lessons are planned and delivered (e.g. co-construction), how spaces within a school are used or how consistency in behaviour management is achieved (rather than simply wished for) is that teenagers are essentially social animals. Friendship and peer influence are hugely important to them – they want to understand the mental states of those around them. Secondary school is the time to get this right. These are the characteristics which already help to make most schools work, most of the time. If this were not the case, and teenagers truly were the feral, self-obsessed individuals they are sometimes depicted to be by unthinking adults, then schools simply could not function. We can harness this need for friendship and peer respect to even greater good.

Within these broad generalisations about adolescent sociability, there are major differences between individuals, as we all know as parents and teachers. The developing field of neuroscience goes some way to explaining why this might be the case. Magnetic resonance imaging (MRI) scans of adolescent brains conducted by Sarah-Jayne Blakemore (2018) and her team show that, by the age of 14, in many cases the limbic system (which is associated with reward seeking) is already mature and sensitive to the 'kick' from the reward of risk-taking. By contrast, the prefrontal cortex, which controls impulse and inhibits risk-taking, is far from mature and will in many cases continue to develop into early adulthood. Intriguingly, within the averages, the research team found unexpectedly large individual differences in how both parts of the brain develop. As Blakemore (2018: 139) wryly notes, 'there's no such thing as an average teenager'.

Some teenagers may be more susceptible to greater risk-taking than others, therefore, with all the wider social implications this has both within and outside schools. For that reason, we all need to understand better the physical changes taking place in the adolescent brain. We saw in Chapter 5, in the study by Palminteri et al. (2016), that adults are better than

12- to 17-year-olds at learning to avoid punishment (losing money), but that both groups are equally good at choosing symbols associated with gaining money. To extrapolate from this that adolescents tend to be influenced more by reward than punishment may seem naive or far-fetched. But there is other evidence, too, which suggests that a here-and-now consequence with wider consequences for the group, rather than just an individual, may tap into teenage mentality. To an adult it may seem obvious to design an anti-smoking campaign for schools by emphasising the risks of lung disease and cancer, or to base it on the underhand tactics used by tobacco companies to sell their products to underage smokers. On the contrary, one study found that it was the issues of second-hand smoke and the smoker as a negative role model which resonated most with young people, perhaps because they frame smokers in a broader social context: the harm to one is a harm to all (Pechmann and Reibling 2000).

Guerrilla questioning

We want students to take risks in the classroom, but for their own well-being these need to be the right kind of risks. I'm partial to guerrilla questioning: I will say to students, 'In your next lesson, ask Miss something really tricky.' When they ask for an example, I say, 'How about, "Miss, how do we know this?" or simply "Why?"' The beauty of role play, debate, argument tunnels and the like is that they encourage and foster risk-taking, especially if repeated and practised. Healthy, controlled risk-taking is beneficial for adolescent well-being – how else can young people be exposed to what is happening in their brains? Schools offer safe, social spaces which are ideal for immediate reward and huge amounts of immediate praise when students get it right, which they do most of the time, because their brains predispose them to do so. When they get it wrong, as inevitably they will, the consequence needs to be similarly immediate, proportionate and measured.

Since there is nothing more interesting to most teenagers than what is going on in their own heads, explaining the science of brain development is not a bad place to start, preferably to a whole year group rather than just to those who have made inappropriate choices. In this way, we are tackling the causes of anger and distress rather than mopping up after the consequences. We are also harnessing the power of the group to increase understanding about why things happen in schools as they do. Well-being starts with understanding. Teenage well-being needs even more understanding.

The secret love of September: teachers as change agents

As teachers, our role in the process of generating and fostering positive attitudes towards learning in classrooms is vital. We set the tone. We identify the strategies. We fix what isn't working. We lead our students on their learning journeys – those magical mystery tours happening simultaneously at slightly different paces in thirty adolescent brains and bodies. We lead on unconditional positive regard for every student. Crucially, we are change agents. 'Botheredness' is our core business.

A secret: teachers love September. Ignore the groans and grumbles about the end of the holidays, back to the grindstone, freedom binned for another year. Cast aside the cynicism, my own included, about the endless CPD meetings which accompany the start of a school year. Autumn offers renewal as the leaves start to fall. There is a fresh opportunity to be a change agent with our classes.

So, you're taking over a Year 11 class from Mr Tonks who taught them last year. In a quick Q&A you establish that Mr Tonks was terrible. No, wait a minute, he was great. Hang on, some students can barely remember him but, yeah, he was strict. He never looked at their notes. He kept asking them pointless questions but rarely marked their work. They never had fun debates in a lesson (Asif and Maya spell this out very clearly) and they certainly didn't cover the topics. When you ask them about what Mr Tonks explicitly talked through with you in a departmental heads-up back in the summer term, they will admit to none of it – apart from the boring League of Nations which they studied for at least a month (but please don't ask us about it now, Sir).

By October, if not before, as a change agent you will have built on all the positivity hiding behind that teenage bravura. Lo and behold, Mr Tonks didn't take in routine classroom notes because he didn't need to: his assessment strategy was judiciously focused on low-stakes quizzing and the regular oral testing of knowledge, saving homework and deliberate practice for bigger tasks. Wise Mr Tonks had actually fostered a range of oral, knowledge organising and testing skills so subtly that some students had barely noticed it was happening.

We routinely take student perceptions with a pinch of salt, quite rightly in this instance, but whether we like what we hear or don't, we have the capacity – indeed the need – to change it. Too long on one particular topic? Let's up the pace, and you can convince me as your new teacher that we can all cope. Not enough discussion, debate and controversy? We can change that. Asif and Maya, let's set up a mock League of Nations to recap and consolidate that month of hard work. And away we go.

The secret love of September: pupils as change agents

A secret: pupils love September. At least, a lot of them do. A fresh start to a new academic year offers new opportunities with a new teacher and classmates. Students love to be change agents. If Asif and Maya can come up with all these great ideas about how last year's lessons with Mr Tonks could have been better, and should have been better, they can do the same for this week's sessions with you. They can be change agents, if we let them. They can harness all their abilities as expert questioners, collaborative learners and feedback specialists – in other words, as expert learners – to help you generate the changes in attitudes to learning and behaviour that you want to see in your classroom. Their neural plasticity comes to the fore.

This is where behaviour management becomes critical. In practice, is your school's behaviour management an obstacle to improved outcomes by high-attaining students? If so, those students cannot help you to raise the bar for everyone. If your school is going to harness the learning power of your high-attaining students, there needs to be a positive learning environment where geek is chic and clever is cool. Otherwise, negative peer pressure will militate against your best efforts to foster learning at the highest level.

Persistent, low-level name calling or other forms of bullying will drive a stagecoach and horses through your best intentions to raise achievement and attainment. Off-task behaviour is very difficult to prevent unless students themselves accept that, for most of the time at least, they are on an interesting learning journey and decline to buy into such behaviour. A whole-school approach which is consistent and which works will allow students to be a bit nerdy in your lesson without taking a verbal or physical beating for it in the corridor later.

I know that this all sounds naive and idealistic. Guilty as charged. But even if you know in your heart of hearts that all is not well at a whole-school level, your classroom is still the space that you can control and none of us can abnegate responsibility for the behaviour management within it. Students know that every teacher and class are different and will adjust to your standards as they come through the door, which is where you stand to greet and dismiss them, whatever is happening outside.

If I want Maya in Year 11 to make sophisticated points in defence of the League of Nations in the 1920s, she will do so with my encouragement to aim for the top, but she needs to feel safe, encouraged and supported, not only by Asif but by the whole class. This scaffolding links the learning about refugee agencies and international migration, which Maya will need to know and be able to explain on the one hand, to the emotional support which Asif and the others can give her on the other. They are not separate: the framework which helps to improve aspiration is all-encompassing and comprehensive. Change agents have no boundaries and don't separate out the academic from the pastoral. Care is care. Maya and Asif can be change agents, just as I can, only a bit different and undoubtedly much cooler. My students will listen and respond to Asif and Maya differently to how they respond to me, and for some, their points will stick much better.

Summary

Teachers and counsellors who offer warmth and humanity are priceless. Hell, this maxim even applies to outside speakers who may, on occasion, knock us cold with their insight and the long-term resonance of their ideas. It is vital that schools pay attention to the well-being of their high-attaining pupils and to the well-being of the colleagues who teach them. Parents also need to come into this loop, for their attitudes and values transmit directly into the physically transforming adolescent brains of their children, just as ours do as teachers. Making those messages harmonious and coordinated seems to make sense.

High-attaining pupils deserve our pastoral care, not least because they may feel additional pressure from the public roles they hold as beacons and badge wearers, prefects and expert learners. Teachers charged with leading and monitoring the learning journeys of these more able children may also feel additional pressures as they share the rollercoaster ride. 'Both-eredness' is a collective responsibility and not the sole remit of the school counsellor or well-being lead.

Chapter 9

Renaissance Scholars for the Twenty-First Century

When [her children] grow older and have some understanding, she will want them to be apprised of practical matters, government and everything princes should know about ... This lady will pay close attention to the behaviour and wisdom of the teacher and others who come in contact with her children. She will have them removed if they are not good and replace them with others.

Christine de Pizan, *The Treasure of the City of Ladies* (2003 [1405])

Key themes

- Expert learners build a list of qualities which help to take them on a learning journey from able to remarkable. You need not look to television or film for idealised portraits of what remarkable students might look like. They look just like your current classes.

- Expert learners are not necessarily those who acquire, or who will acquire, the best exam grades. Education is about ideas and visions, not just outcomes. Whatever their differences in intelligence, all pupils have the potential to become remarkable in terms of their knowledge, attitudes, skills and aspirations.

- Expert learners create great chains of remarkability in their schools. High-attaining pupils become remarkable when we let go and allow them to be so.

- Expert learners are renaissance scholars worthy of comparison with their illustrious forebears.

Who are our remarkable young people?

To many of us, remarkable young people are the ones we see on television performing amazing feats of mental arithmetic, spelling impossible words at spelling bees or competing in 'child genius' competitions. The media shorthand for such children is 'genius' because it's too complicated to explain properly that intelligence is malleable and plastic, and that it manifests in many different ways, some of which we are still struggling to understand. It's too worthy to talk about spaced and interleaved learning, and definitely too boring to outline mental models of success and the need for hours of purposeful practice. So child genius it is then, reinforcing stereotypes about mini-Mozarts and small-scale Stephen Hawkings who are inherently gifted by dint of genetic advantage conferred by birth. After all, this child's parents are both doctors and that one has a mother who got into Harvard.

For me, there is no pupil I teach who doesn't have the potential to be remarkable. Some will have a head start encoded within their DNA which may make verbal or numerical processing easier and faster, while others will have physical attributes that confer advantages in sport or dance. No amount of environmental stimulus will help their peers to catch up. Arguably, this alone is no guarantee of success – academic, vocational or sporting.

How might those genes react when placed in a stimulating environment? Let's provide one and find out! The great majority of pupils within the normal distribution of a school population will benefit from a philosophy of teach to the top. It will make access to high-attainer provision more likely for more pupils. It will create conditions better suited to understanding the physical changes taking place in the brain structures of adolescents at different paces and ages across the school. It will also provide a safe space for students to acquire the emotional intelligence to take advantage of everything that the classroom offers through the modelling of adults and expert learners around them.

A colleague recently referred to this as 'coachability'. A coachable pupil won't shut off a challenge because it's too difficult, and the collaborative learning going on around her shared by expert learners will reinforce this ethos. A coachable teacher won't deny a whole class or year group the best feedback and revision strategies available to them simply because the latest data drop indicates that only a small cohort merit the time and effort. A coachable school won't impose subject ability setting so rigidly that a group of pupils climbing the scaffolding to higher attainment is frustrated that the framework vanishes when they look upwards and see that the next rung from the ladder is missing. A curriculum structure should flex and bend like an elegant bridge – the engineering accommodating the environment, not imposing itself upon it. None of this could happen, could it? Yes, it could. Yes, we can. Expert learners, the very paragons of coachability, can provide a design for life.

A new renaissance

Thinking about stretch and challenge in the twenty-first century took me to the fluid and exciting intellectual landscape of the Renaissance. I see present and future high attainers as new renaissance men and women, capable of connecting anything to everything and of seeing well beyond conventional academic boundaries. Subjects? Mere labels. Departments? Administrative conveniences. Schools? Uncomfortable pilgrim halts on the lifelong journey of learning.

Let's remind ourselves of how a few great Renaissance thinkers dispensed with conventional boundaries and embraced learning in its widest sense:

- Filippo Brunelleschi – mathematician, architect of the dome of Florence Cathedral, sculptor, artist, shipbuilder.

- Leonardo da Vinci – scientist, writer, anatomist, palaeontologist, artist, inventor.

- Christine de Pizan – the first professional woman writer in Europe, poet, biographer, courtier and authority on the art of government.

- Michelangelo – poet, architect, painter, sculptor.

- Giorgio Vasari – painter, architect, biographer, historian.

The term 'polymath' is often, quite rightly, used to describe the activities and achievements of these outstanding men and women. They regarded the pursuit and acquisition of knowledge as their lives' work and saw no physical, geographical or intellectual boundaries to what was possible. Their world view envisaged their role as straddling the temporal and the spiritual, the divine and the man-made. Nothing was impossible.

Our twenty-first century renaissance scholars will need similar ambition and vision. But as we saw in Chapter 2, visions of what should be possible in our lessons and schools are latent within the pupils we teach. If we give them the chance to tell us, and we really listen, as I tried to do when Russell Earnshaw asked my pupils about their ideal lesson, they will explain these dreams. These ideas deserve respect because they come from the future masters of the universe. Remarkable children look to the future with confidence.

However, there is a danger in spending too long dwelling on the Renaissance or inspirational individuals from the past: we come to see them as demi-gods, their achievements as incalculable and incomprehensible. Inventing prototype helicopters and tanks; building mathematically challenging structures, such as St Peter's Basilica in Rome and the Duomo in Florence, on a vast scale with rudimentary equipment; creating works of art breathtaking in their conception and execution; transcending the traditional divide between sculptor and artist; the list goes on. But they were not superheroes. Giorgio Vasari was a celebrated chronicler of the lives of the artists he knew and knew about, but he was all too aware of the human qualities and failings of the great people he described. They were heroes with feet of clay, not gods. If not of our time, they are still of our kind. This matters.

Twenty-first century renaissance scholars

I tell the parents of the Scholars at my school that their sons and daughters are excellent. They are the equals of their counterparts whose names proudly adorn the honours boards of their predecessors from the past 100 years. I have no real evidence for this, but I still believe it. The high-attaining students in your classroom right now can go on to emulate the achievements of past Renaissance men and women. They will be on a par with the cleverest children you've taught or known in your career. Kids were not cleverer in your classroom or school ten years ago, any more than they were in mine.

Below I've picked five modern equivalents of the Renaissance men and women listed earlier. They have all made a significant contribution to modern culture in a way that crosses boundaries. You will have your own list and will likely disagree with mine. Good! None of these people had exceptional educations, as far as I'm aware, but I'm sure they could all cite an inspirational teacher or mentor who helped them on their way.

- Germaine Greer – author, feminist, environmentalist, iconoclast and cultural critic.

- Stephen Hawking – world-leading theoretical physicist, cosmologist and writer.

- Jonathan Ive – industrial designer and creator of the iMac, iPod, iPhone and iPad.

- Elon Musk – entrepreneur, inventor and visionary for the Hyperloop railway, space travel pioneer and manufacturer of electric cars.

- Oprah Winfrey – TV host, publisher, businesswoman, philanthropist.

We are not judging these remarkable figures on the criteria of character or ethics. The test is for long-term influence on the world of tomorrow by dint of their actions and attitudes in response to the problems they have analysed. They and their ilk cross boundaries and challenge orthodoxies. They don't aim for the impossible but they make the unlikely happen. Renaissance thinking will do the same for my pupils and yours. Our high-attaining students can emulate and exceed what has been done in our lifetimes and in the past. More of them stand more chance of doing this if we help to get their education right now. Elon Musk will need astronauts – and remarkable expert learners, coachable to their core (such as Chris Hadfield and Tim Peake), are already inspiring the next generation of scientists and engineers in our schools.

OK, so my definition of remarkable is quite broad and loose, but I hope that it makes a fair point. I'd wager that every child coming into Year 7 already carries an interesting personal experience to share of setback, disappointment, failure, accident or illness to set alongside their achievements, successes and accomplishments. That makes them all remarkable in a very general sense, and all the more so when schools take into account the challenging family backgrounds of some young people. To have got to where they are now they have been eager and ready to learn *and* shown resilience and bouncebackability, and this is praiseworthy in its own right. As they settle into their new form or mentor group, their abilities have already been demonstrated and their capabilities are endless. But as they grow into their ever-so-slightly-too-big blazers and shoes, will they grow as learners or stay essentially the same size?

I hope that by using some of the approaches and strategies suggested in this book every single one of these students will leave our care at the end of their learning journeys having shown their abilities and improved them hugely. Some may be on a longer, lifelong journey and school is simply too early and too challenging for them, so they may have to wait and create opportunities to do their talents justice later in life.

Expert learners: from able to remarkable

Another group will complete their journey with us and fit within a narrower definition of remarkable – they will have become expert learners. I do not mean expert exam passers. They are torchbearers for learning, having perhaps been expert learners in our schools and colleges and having displayed attitudes to discovery and the pursuit of excellence from which the whole community has benefited. They will not, repeat not, always be the boy who is 'the best in his class' or the girl with the most GCSE passes at grade 9.

Some, like Asif and Yolanda, will start with the advantages of a high IQ, MiDYIS or similar test score, indicating high verbal and non-verbal reasoning processing power, which will make many learning challenges easier. But that does not make them geniuses who only have to turn up at an exam to pass with flying colours. Children underperform for many reasons and do not meet the statistical targets which even the largest and most robust data set predicts for them. Among these may be that they never become adept at acquiring the mindset and mentality of working hard or maintaining it. Many others, such as Anna and Tom, will start lower down the ability spectrum but will still become remarkable learners and students. The right environment and stimuli can make all the difference. Statistics and Chances Graphs offer predictions and estimations but not certainty and guarantees.

Getting the philosophy and context of more able education right will maximise the chances of more remarkability among more students, and that remarkability may take many forms, so what does it look like?

What have expert learners learned to do?

Students demonstrate that they have become expert learners in various ways. As Andy Tharby (2017b) says, 'It is important that high-achieving students come to see themselves as high-achieving students. The answer to the question "Who am I?" needs to be "Someone who is doing well at school, and wants to do even better".' In other words, they have become aware of the mysterious process of learning and how to decode it – they are self-aware, self-actualised learners.

- Expert learners drive us as teachers. If we want to know the limits for our more able pupils, let's push beyond them into the world of the remarkable. As Tom Sherrington (2017a) argues, 'I think teachers should consider the curriculum and plan activities based on the capabilities of the highest attainers as a total priority … teachers need to have the courage and confidence to challenge at the top end, relentlessly.'

- Expert learners take care of their own well-being and that of others. They show a compassion for their fellow students because the school curriculum has built in chances for them to do some local community service. The curriculum has integrated a sense of global awareness of climate change (geography), modern slavery (history) and linguistic diversity (modern foreign languages). Compassion is not an optional extra squeezed into a random PSHE lesson. Adults have led in curriculum mapping and construction and now remarkable students lead in showing the benefits of this connected thinking daily in the corridors and on the games field.

- Expert learners understand that learning can be like a rollercoaster – the unexpected should be expected. In any given week they will be in a struggle zone because they and their teachers recognise that the comfort zone is too boring and the impossible zone can be tackled in due course. Their resilience comes from walking the walk in lessons, not from hortatory corridor posters.

- Jim Smith, of 'Lazy Teacher' fame, calls pupils who can help others become unstuck when faced with a problem or challenge 'More Progress Coaches' (Smith 2012: 51). He observes that these aren't always the so-called experts but can also include others who would benefit from a wider range of strategies to unpick and resolve a problem.

- Expert learners love knowledge. They enjoy knowing stuff and sharing it. They also recognise that learning is a lifelong journey. They have already found topics and subjects which they love just for their own sake. Mr Miller's inspirational teaching may have helped them or sitting next to Mohammad in craft, design and technology for two years may have played a part, but when the crucial test is undertaken of taking away those foils, the passion for construction and design is still there. Remarkable learners also love to know things and to know what to do with what they know. They grasp that there is a lot more of the same out there in the big wide world beyond the school gates.

- Expert learners enjoy questioning in lessons, so they can lead others in formulating questions of their own for different purposes. Our society values oracy and an ability to speak fluently and confidently using a rich vocabulary which adults and children are not too scared or embarrassed to deploy. They are expert questioners because who wants to take everything for granted? 'How do we know this, Miss?' is a hugely powerful intervention. (Don't let that secret out, fellow teachers – best we keep that one to ourselves.)

- Expert learners are accomplished users of ICT but not because they are digital natives. Some will be, many won't – and in any case, there will be ICT ambassadors on hand to share their own expert learner knowledge about apps and programs. They understand that technology can provide an answer but rarely *the* answer; if it provides something that nothing else can then it is doing its job. Mark Anderson (2012) is an advocate of the Substitution, Augmentation, Modification, Redefinition (SAMR) Model for how to integrate technology into classroom practice. Using technology as a substitute for, or an improvement to, something we already do is all well and good, but modification is all about the redesign of a task and redefinition recasts it entirely. Expert learners don't need hard coding skills but they do need vision and an open mind.

- Working in pairs, groups or teams brings fresh challenges which expert learners are happy to accept as offering different ways to make them better learners. They understand the gains that collaborative learning can bring. They suspect, quite rightly, that the much vaunted qualities of leadership have been oversold. Collaborative learning needs team members to play different roles, such as facilitators, constructive critics, consultants and creators. Prop forwards in rugby who can kick forward, run, gather and get over the try line are like goal-scoring midfielders in football: priceless. Versatility is all, not ego-driven leadership.

- When offered advice or feedback on how to improve, expert learners respond actively and intelligently because they have practised their responses. Remarkable learners close the circle by continuing the dialogue internally, so that one task builds formatively onto another and feedback becomes a virtuous circle rather than a tick-box exercise. Expert learners gain from peer assessment and teacher assessment a sense of their own learning and where it might be heading. That will in turn prepare them for the next hair-raising rollercoaster bend or thrilling ascent.

- Expert learners understand that the right kind of revision will make efficient use of their time and will pay dividends for them. Who can't see the benefits of not wasting time? As cognitive science helps to provide evidence of what makes learning stick, they exploit this via Cornell note-taking, spaced learning and fun apps such as Socrative or Quizlet so that they stay motivated. Who knows, interleaved learning or some smart use of SQ3R may leave more time for Minecraft, Fortnite or the latest addictive game.

Profiling remarkability

These and many more attributes together build the profile of an expert learner. They have moved from able to remarkable. Anna and Tom can model a sequence of learning or revision in their heads before explaining it to Maya in their row or at their table. Having experienced some co-construction and seen the challenges of working within the tight curriculum of a limited number of lessons and the need for common whole-year assessments, for example, Asif and Yolanda have become their own curriculum designers and lesson planners. Learning outside the classroom holds no perils because that is where the remarkable student may have wanted to take the activity anyway – to a space within the school which is both more fitting and uplifting. Enrichment sessions and lunchtime and after-school sessions just throw down another gauntlet: let's get even more creative.

The games field sees everyone participating in every role and with an emphasis on enjoyment and taking part on equal terms, not rules and pain, emotional or physical. Onstage, they recognise the creative energies of everyone from the lighting crew to the lead actor. Remarkable learners can change roles like costumes. Everything connects to everything else. Drama, games and activities are so full of enrichment and learning that they really belong in every classroom. They are the epitome of the struggle zone because there is no hiding place, and the sense of shared responsibility and power is energising. I've had the privilege of directing school productions and I would say that it has been some of the most daunting but fulfilling work I have ever known. Drama gets to the inner core. It turns us inside out and takes us on an unforgettable learning journey of its own.

Expert learners are wasted if they are just used as tour guides on open evenings. They should be recognised in every mentor group and lesson, and not because they have completed the checklist of qualities listed above and are now politely biding their time until the next school visitor pops in. They are the living embodiment of the rollercoaster rider, inquisitive and not yet fully formed, enjoying the fact that they are still very much on the journey rather than representing the school's best efforts at the finished article.

Your expert learners are so good and so valuable that not only can they see what is next in the repertoire of knowledge and abilities they can acquire and practise, but they can also explain this to another pupil in their class, a cover teacher, a learning walk SLT member or a potential parent and their offspring. They may not be predicted to earn ten grade 9 GCSEs, but perhaps their learning journeys have been among the most exciting in the school – real rollercoasters. They may not have the sheer intelligence and raw processing power of some of their peers, but for a combination of all the right reasons that we are working so hard to instil in our schools, they are getting there. Surely, these remarkable young people are an essential part of any good school. They are the links in the great chain of remarkability which wraps around the school community to embrace pupils, parents, governors and teaching and support staff.

This is not an impossibly utopian picture. At the top of the previous section I carefully chose the words, 'What have remarkable students learned to do?' Not what were they born to do, or been bound to do since Year 7, or pushed by their parents to do. They have experienced an outstanding education because they have learned to do these remarkable things themselves. More could emulate them, if we help.

Some renaissance scholars are headed for Russell Group universities, if not Oxbridge or the prestigious Ivy League institutions, trailing scholarships and glittering prizes. We may hear of them in later years and dine out on stories of how we taught them everything they know and helped them on their way. These students are indeed remarkable and we should celebrate their achievements loud and long. Less comforting to think about is that our school system could readily allow more of these students to flourish. Ofsted has told us repeatedly and unequivocally that this is the case. More unsettling still is the idea that there may be dozens of such students sitting in front of us right now whose potential we are failing to unlock.

Daniel Willingham's *Why Don't Students Like School?* has a chapter entitled 'What's the Secret to Getting Students to Think Like Real Scientists, Mathematicians, and Historians?' (2009: ch. 6). At first sight, his rather bleak answer is that we can't. Novices can't become experts just by copying what experts do, whether that is reading a map, playing tennis or diagnosing an illness. Not only do experts have far more background knowledge to deploy but they also have the capacity to think in abstract terms – about the strategy of a tennis match or a chess game. Willingham argues that classroom students are not ready to create 'new knowledge' successfully, however adept they may be at understanding the concepts that others have created. He doesn't think that students can be experts.

Well, bowing low to Willingham's expertise in his field, I think there are enough exceptions and qualifications to these suggestions to bring them into question. I can't counter Willingham with research in behavioural psychology, but since his chapter contains anecdotal examples of lack of expertise then perhaps I may be allowed to offer some counter-examples which I think are emblematic of the experiences of many classroom teachers.

- Several years ago I attended a concert which included a premiere of an orchestral piece composed and conducted by a then 14-year-old pupil at my school. I would challenge anyone listening to this piece without prior knowledge to identify it as the work of a novice. Of course, technology is blurring the division – music notation software such as Sibelius brings composing possibilities into the classroom in ways once hard to imagine. However, according to Willingham (2009: 142), 'beginning students do not yet have the cognitive equipment in place to compose'. My student recently left school, aged 18, with seven A* grades – at A level.

- A Year 9 student at a local school has had an app accepted and published on the Apple Store.

- Our best sixth-form mathematicians are beyond the level of our best maths teachers, who then take on equally necessary ancillary roles in guidance and well-being.

233

- I have taught an A level history specification which actively requires students to think about why history is written and constructed in the way it is, not just how. Expert history students are not simply regurgitating dates and rote learning the causes of the American Civil War. They show metacognitive abilities which they use to marshal second-order concepts (e.g. continuity and change) in the construction of a persuasive evidence-based narrative of why one particular set of consequences, as opposed to another, occurred.

- Nationally, young people in many schools win poetry and short story competitions against adult competition.

To be fair to Daniel Willingham, few of our students can accumulate the decade or so of knowledge that expertise requires, although it is certainly possible in, for example, languages, maths and music by the sixth form. If he is taking aim at books which purport to offer the answer for how to hothouse children into scientists, mathematicians or musicians, then fair enough. But by modelling excellence, by creating a culture of practice and redrafting, by praising effort and establishing attainable success criteria, and by all the other steps which excellent teachers and supportive parents offer, pupils can produce outcomes which are remarkable, and which Willingham would find remarkable too. I know, because he is such a generous scholar, that he would celebrate them with the rest of us.

The great chain of remarkability

When I am asked about what helps more able students to become remarkable, my go-to response is to talk about making connections. Let's look at the first and most straightforward way of encouraging this in our classrooms.

High-attaining student Asif may, simplifying a lot, carry out a lab experiment proficiently as a practical and then write up a full and accurate report which accesses the top level of the mark scheme. The steady repetition of excellent work such as this will surely result in exam success.

Remarkable student Yolanda realises at some point during the set-up or the practical that mass spectroscopy in chemistry is essentially the same topic as mass spectroscopy in physics, but with some key differences. The former explores the results of the process of analysing the chemical make-up of a substance, whereas the latter studies the mechanics of the vacuum chamber, velocity selectors and so on.

Yolanda takes her experiment findings to her physics teacher, who gives her a *New Scientist* article where a practical application of similar work has just hit the news. Yolanda's report of this on Google Classroom interests Tom, who raises it in the recap session at the start of the next chemistry lesson. Mr Warner asks Yolanda and Tom to come to a catch-up session with Year 10 to help him explain the process with some pupils who find it hard to grasp. He catches Asif as the lab coats are being hung up and asks him if he would like to come along next time.

The great chain of remarkability is constructed from hundreds of similar interactions in a school. Asif and Tom are now forging individual links so capably that they are more than ready to look up and see how much more useful a chain is than a single link. Yolanda is busy chain-building around the science department and across year groups. As a collaborative learner, she will raise the sights of her class and perhaps prompt them to offer her new ways of forging links.

Below is a history 'Only Connect' template which I produced for my department. It will be copied and placed in every sixth-form folder and a simpler version will go to all other year groups. It isn't perfect, but it offers some thoughts and ideas about how to link one task to another in order to do something interesting with the knowledge that has been acquired. Transforming information from one format to another is, well, transformative. The benefits to memory, recall and understanding should be manifold.

The essence of this approach is to multiply the power of a single method by linking it to others.

Only Connect history stretch and challenge

Use the -ing multiplier to think of lots of different ways to connect one form of activity to another. The most important -ings are creating, thinking and imagining.

Reading	Ask your teachers to recommend an interesting book/approach relevant to your period.
	Use www.jstor.org. Use the library. Use www.lobworth.com. Use current book reviews (e.g. *History Today* magazine) and recommend books for us to buy. Use www.abebooks.co.uk and buy books for a penny. Then review, debate and blog about what

	you've read. *Connect reading to other activities on this list.* Reading is the single best way to enrich what you write – and your life.
Listening	Podcasts: *In Our Time* – one of the great cultural achievements of the last twenty years. Pick an episode and enjoy. *Connect*: review it/blog about it/share it in class.
	Critically assess Malcolm Gladwell's *Revisionist History* podcast (http://revisionisthistory.com). There are lots of others out there to sample, recommend, connect with, debate, review and blog about. *Connect listening to other activities on this list.* Which history podcasts should every sixth-form student know about?
Connecting	How do your two A level courses connect, if at all? How do your two courses and your coursework connect, if at all? How might they/should they connect? If you were designing a totally new A level course for future students, what would it look like?
Debating	Demand more history debating. The greatest US president? The most significant black civil rights leader? Make a podcast of the debate and ask someone else to review it or blog about it. Talk to a teacher about having a history-themed house debate. Consider the Historical Association's Great Debate too. *Connect debating to other activities on this list (e.g. blogging or podcasting).* There is evidence which correlates fluency in oral argument to capability in written argument, and vice versa.
Networking	Lower sixth: do you know the upper-sixth historians – their interests, passions and the universities they are applying to? Upper sixth: have you met the lower-sixth historians? Are there potential history Scholars we should know about?
	Do you know the reading interests of your teachers or other members of the department? Do other staff like history?! When former pupils come back, what is their experience of history at university? *Connect networking to debating.*
Blogging	We have had a history blog in the past – should it be revived? History is always in the news – that is how important it is. *Connect blogging to reading, reviewing, writing.*

Writing	Oxbridge and other university essay competitions are excellent practice. Go off-piste and select one from outside your syllabus. The department has plenty of expertise and resources to help you. *Connect writing to other activities on this list.*
Viewing	What history related films have come out recently that you could review? Should we be showing history films at lunchtime – if so, which ones and for which year groups? Is there a book of the film? *Connect viewing to reviewing to reading.*
Inviting	Nominate a historian for us to invite to speak at History Society. Why this person? What will they offer? *Connect inviting to networking to blogging.*
Playing	Do any students in your year have interests in traditional board games (e.g. Risk, Diplomacy) or electronic games (e.g. Assassin's Creed)? *Connect playing to blogging to podcasting.*
Attending	The Historical Association's Bristol branch has some fine, free talks lined up on a range of subjects from feminism to Henry VIII. Some of them involve walking tours of Bristol (https://www.history.org.uk/getinvolved/resource/9396/bristol-branch-programme). Attending a talk and then *writing/blogging/networking* about it adds another layer of challenge and interest.
Reviewing	Review a TV documentary or programme about the past. How successful was it in explaining the topic? Which year groups should view it? Who is it best suited for in a school scheme of work? *Connect reviewing to blogging or sharing.*
Sharing	How can you share a discussion about your favourite history topic with others? Is there a discussion forum (electronic) or lunchtime club? Can you share this passion with, for example, Year 8? *Connect sharing to networking.*
Podcasting	Make a podcast with your friends. You've just learned about the suffragettes in lessons – how do you feel about radical protest, then and now? Taking down the statue of Edward Colston?

	Everyone has views, so share yours. *Connect podcasting to debating.*
Modelling	You are the teacher. Can you construct a PowerPoint slide or similar which explains the current topic to your class? How would you model this with a starter, main and plenary? *Connect modelling to writing and listening.*
Designing	Bored with this year's work? Create your own course for your current year. What are the essentials in terms of content and skills? What are the desirables? What could you miss out and why? Share this with your teacher. *Connect designing to reading and debating, for example.*
Baking 'n' making	You've made a castle out of cake and a shanty town out of cardboard – what else could you make? Why would it help? Would this be fun with a younger year group? There are Playmobil animated videos on YouTube … *Connect making to playing and sharing.*
Filming	Filming is never easier than with a tablet computer. A monologue, a class debate, a play you've created … *Connect filming to making and playwriting.*
Playwriting	Scripted dramas are very powerful. Could you write a scene that would help to bring, for example, a rebellion or protest to life? *Connect playwriting to writing and sharing.*
Thought experimenting	Counterfactual history was all the rage a few years back. What if Nicholas II had clung on, or the Provisional Government had resisted strongly? What if Kennedy had served two full terms? *Connect thought experiments to reading and debating.*
Thinking	Last but not least: can you make your thinking visible? Leave a big margin in your next essay and use it to set out your thinking as you go. Or take a historical issue you know well and explain how your views have changed using this model: 'I used to think … because … Now I think … because … But now I need to know

> more about ... because ... ' *Connect thinking to inviting or writing, for example.*

From Lego to Minecraft: the renaissance school of the late twenty-first century

Schools are essentially blocks of Lego put together in what often seems like a random and ham-fisted fashion. No wonder the curriculum feels clunky and a poor fit. Was there ever a creator or 'blind watchmaker' who put these blocks next to each other, or did the school just evolve? Is this school fit for purpose in the 2020s? If some of your high-attaining students took the idea of designing their ideal lesson and spent a few hours designing their perfect school instead, what would it look like? Would the buildings and spaces work for the needs of students? I'm sure the exercise would produce some grand designs.

Markus 'Notch' Persson was a contender for my list of modern renaissance figures. He is at the heart of an extraordinary story. Minecraft is one of the most successful computer games ever – and I mean jaw-droppingly successful. At the time of writing it has sold over 154 million copies and has 100 million registered users around the world. Adults have given up their day jobs to earn a living from hits on their dedicated Minecraft YouTube channels. If your son or daughter has ever played Minecraft, you will have some inkling of the phenomenon it is. Addictive seems too inadequate a word. Many a parent or teacher, myself included, has suffered the frustration of trying to prise a child away from a mobile device, computer or TV screen in the face of tooth-and-nail resistance. 'Let me just finish this ... I'm just building ... I can't lose this world ... '

So why is Minecraft so successful? On the face of it, Minecraft should never have worked. The developers came from a small Swedish software publisher, not one of the industry giants. This is an ultra-competitive world where company development and advertising budgets are beyond huge. The market is notoriously difficult to break into. The game offers little by way of enticements. The graphics are almost comically clunky and boxy. The animals and humans look closer to Lego figures than anything else. Humanoid figures are threatened by bleating sheep. Yes, sheep! Many adults are surprised by the limited visual appeal of Minecraft compared to its sleek rivals. It's not a classic shoot 'em up or platform game. Aliens don't feature. There's no celebrity endorsement or cool pop soundtrack – indeed, the soundtrack seems to come from the BBC Home Service in the 1950s.

Yet Persson just needed a sandbox and word of mouth. When you first play the game, you are in a world with no rules and no one telling you what to do. There isn't a complicated start-up pack or a set of commands to remember. You pick up the controller and away you go. You are in Survival or Creative mode. In Survival, you need to build a shelter or you won't last the night-time. There are some 'creepers' and other mild threats. You can 'kill' but that's not what the game is about.

Instead, you build and you mine. You will probably start simple: a house with a chest, a furnace to keep warm and some simple furniture. You learn what is possible. Players construct amazing worlds which might feature palaces, mansions, deserts or enormous rollercoasters. It takes time, and no little skill, to manipulate the controller, but children manage it because the deliberate, purposeful practice helps them to improve. Perhaps they find the fine motor skills easier than clumsy adults, but that can't be the whole explanation. Minecraft motivates children like little else. So keen are they to learn that they rush to online gaming communities and create their own YouTube channels to view and share each other's creations, as my son did.

What does this teach us about our children?

Minecraft is a classic example of our children's remarkabilities. Unbeknown to most adults, they discovered and popularised a game that tapped into their imaginations and set them free of constraints. This was their world, not ours. Like a sandpit, they could build or knock down, keep or crush, without spending or requiring kit beyond the game itself and a console or playing device, which they had anyway. Lego shares these qualities. We can buy specialist Lego or Lego Technic models, some of which are vastly sophisticated and require complicated assembly. These appeal to parents and grandparents keen to boost their children's creativity. But many children are just as happy, and are arguably more stimulated, by a simple box of generic bricks which they can then turn into whatever they wish. If they don't like it, there is no loss in breaking up what they've made. My middle son built Lego football stadiums, gave the stands names and wrote signs and adverts on tiny slips of paper. He might not have liked a pre-constructed vision of a stadium in a box, even though it would have been much more authentic.

Open-world, no-limits, imagination-boosting activities work, and can be compulsively and maddeningly addictive. There is something about the quality of fascination with this type of activity which makes it stand out from a keenness to play most games. Whatever that elusive quality is, it isn't unique to Minecraft. As parents and teachers, many of us have experienced that living-in-the-moment thrill of realising that we have been so immersed in something we enjoy that time has flown by.

If we could capture that more often, we would be making first-rate provision for all our classes and having a lot of fun in the process. Increasingly, educators around the world are looking to Minecraft and similar games and thinking about how to tap into their potential. There is a Minecraft Education edition (https://education.minecraft.net) and clever teachers have wasted no time in setting up MinecraftEdu to share activities and possibilities. There's even Minecraft Lego now. Everything has connected.

Summary

Remarkable students are sitting in your classrooms today – potentially, every student staring back at you. It isn't one rule for some and another rule for others. We can apply this idea over time as well as across it. By this, I mean that there was no golden age when pupils radiated scholarship and respect, achieved outstanding results and exceeded their potential. What you and I have in front of us is as good as it has ever been.

Your renaissance children can achieve excellence. They can do this daily, inside the classroom and outside it. Give them the clunky Minecraft building blocks of knowledge and they will create ideal lessons, classrooms and schools to share with you, because you recognise their creativity and model the forging of connections for them. They are expert learners who regard themselves as coachable and open to new approaches. Perhaps the 'genius' of a Hillary Clinton or a Stephen Fry or any of the other renaissance men and women of our time, stems in part from just such habits of mind that connect everything to everything else in a great chain of remarkability.

The school surroundings may not be perfect but so it has often been with school buildings since the Renaissance, if not before. It is teachers who make the difference, not the buildings. Expert learners create the circumstances from the imperfect worlds around them. There may be disadvantage at home and in the surrounding area, but there should be none once they cross our thresholds. School communities recognise that renaissance scholars are made, not born. They are not perfect but they are on a remarkable journey with no limits.

Chapter 10

Towards a Manifesto
for Excellence

At the start of this book I offered five big ideas regarding provision for more able pupils:

1.   All students can and should become expert learners. There is no separate category labelled 'gifted and talented provision'.

2.   Teachers make a difference to the learning of high-attaining pupils: *adults teach, students learn, students lead*.

3.   Teaching to the top (and learning to the top) will make a difference because it will help to unlock the latent potential of every child in our classrooms.

4.   The learning journey for all our students is lifelong and is undertaken for its own sake – for the love of learning, not the passing of exams.

5.   Our expert learners will become remarkable students.

If these ideas sound optimistic or even idealistic, then I have tried to temper this with approaches rooted in experience and some strategies endorsed by research evidence in order to offer directions forward. To do nothing or continue with same old, same old is not an option. As discussed in the Introduction, two critical Ofsted reports in 2013 and 2015 found alarming evidence of sustained pupil underachievement in colleges and schools among pupils who might have been expected to progress from high Key Stage 2 outcomes to high GCSE scores. We stand condemned as a society for not tackling the advantage or excellence gap.

The excellence gap

The formidable Tim Dracup (2016) pointed out some years ago to all those who cared to read his forensic analysis of 'most able provision' some of the necessary steps to closing the excellence gap affecting thousands of pupils then and today. These included national evaluation of promising practice in developing new programmes designed to support disadvantaged students who are high attainers and a network of high-attainer 'hubs' to act as centres of excellence and to test EEF evaluations on the ground. Would that some of these ideas had been pursued.

In *Potential for Success*, Rebecca Montacute reports that high attainers make an 'average level of progress between Key Stage 2 and Key Stage 4', but those from disadvantaged backgrounds 'fall substantially behind' and record a negative Progress 8 score of -0.32 (2018: 3). That high attainers in primary schools don't make better than an average level of progress by the end of Year 11 is in itself a cause for concern, but the report also identifies a shocking gap of 20% between pupils from disadvantaged and non-disadvantaged backgrounds when measured by five or more GCSE passes at A*–A (between 52% and 72%). The situation is worse for pupils from disadvantaged backgrounds who are white than those who are black or Asian.

Among the recommendations that Montacute makes is for specific reporting of a school's provision for disadvantaged high-attaining pupils during Ofsted inspections, and also recording the access that schools offer to extra-curricular activities, enrichment and one-to-one support. These and some of the other measures she discusses could be implemented immediately and at no cost. In order for lower income families to gain access to enrichment, however, she recommends that a means-tested voucher system should be provided by the government or schools themselves. Likewise, she proposes that teachers with specialist knowledge and experience should be incentivised financially (and within their timetables) to teach in more disadvantaged schools.

Admirable as these ideas are, they will only attract support if funding can be found for them within MATs or schools or from government, and the fear is that even then this money would be taken from other areas of a very tight education budget, to the detriment to other students.

Potential for Success was published after much of this book had been written, and I am pleased that some of the approaches and strategies I have discussed find support within it – for example, structured mentoring programmes that point older students towards university applications and demystify access to higher education exist at my wife's school, mentioned on page 247. But none is more important than this recommendation:

> Due to the difficulties in identifying highly able students, wherever possible, interventions to benefit the highly able should be available to all students. All classes should have built-in stretching activities, and while certain extra-curricular activities may be particularly promoted to highly able students, where possible they should remain open for all students to attend. (Montacute 2018: 7)

An inclusive approach to provision for highly able pupils, those with high current attainment or the potential to achieve it, underpins all that I have tried to express in this book. The programmes we provide for high-attaining pupils, whatever we choose to call them, need to be flexible both in terms of how we identify appropriate pupils in the first place but also how we acknowledge that learning journeys are a rollercoaster for all pupils. Some may fall below a qualifying threshold for a gifted and talented programme, temporarily or long term, while others exceed it and are qualified to join. What will help in ensuring the integrity and flexibility of a high-attainer programme is having a cluster of staff who are trained and become experienced in this area of educational provision, rather than employing just one G&T coordinator. This will allow best practice to be learned and shared across and between schools, perhaps using the high-attainer networks I champion in this chapter, helping to ensure that pupil premium money is used effectively.

Montacute made one further recommendation relevant to this final chapter. This was to endorse the 2017 announcement of a Future Talent Fund, offering £18 million of government funding to trial projects looking at strategies to support disadvantaged high-attaining pupils – for example, enrichment activities, one-to-one tuition or examining whether evidence for broadening or deepening the curriculum might be effective. However, no sooner had bids for funding been invited than the scheme was cancelled, leaving the future of such interventions aimed at boosting social mobility uncertain.

The need for further research is obvious, however. We simply don't know if extra-curricular activities and enrichment offer an efficient and cost-effective way of closing the excellence gap. We don't have evidence-based conclusions about what works best and why. This makes it all the more imperative that we share what we do know, even if – and perhaps especially if – it challenges our assumptions.

Excellence for all

Why are we so scared of excellence? It would surely seem to the hypothetical visitor from Mars that in England we are terrified of aiming for the top. We will allow our very best universities to compete at this level internationally and permit a few Russell Group universities to come close in certain specialist areas such as engineering, but heaven forfend lest we champion excellence too loud and for too long. The very sight of the peaks might send us sliding down the scree-sided slopes of Mount Hubris. Politicians of every allegiance proclaim support for excellence in education; employers of businesses great and small bemoan the lack of it and draw unfavourable comparisons with alleged past golden ages of mathematical competence and literary fluency; no parent would consciously deny access to it on the part of their son or daughter. So why is first rate as rare as a blood moon?

Every year, educational reports are published offering evidence on the theme of the disproportionate lack of educational progress by the most socially and economically disadvantaged groups in society. For example, the Department for Education's *Educational Excellence Everywhere* (2016) highlighted once again that the needs of the highest attaining pupils have been neglected. Repeatedly, and depressingly, outcomes associated with the highest levels of academic attainment have been denied or made inaccessible to thousands of more able students because of where they live and their family circumstances. Schools alone cannot tackle such complex issues, and nor should they be expected to offer cure-alls for wider social ills. Yet they can and do offer hope, inspiration, aspiration and excellence amid very difficult circumstances. As Montacute (2018: 4) suggests, despite the 'substantial barriers' facing highly able pupils from disadvantaged backgrounds, 'what schools actually do for such students can be crucial for success'.

Excellence for all our children

My friend Inger O'Callaghan is the inspirational head at Glenfrome Primary School in Bristol. Her school is home to pupils speaking thirty different languages. Excellence is framed on every wall display, shared in every tweet and trackable on the laptops of every staff member in order to keep an eye on any pupil's progress. Quality first teaching is in the DNA of the school, as is patent to any visitor. High expectations of every pupil, including those who arrive speaking no or little English, is the norm. How is this achieved in daily practice?

As we would expect, teacher subject knowledge and a commitment to maintaining motivation and teamwork among staff are paramount. But this goes further and is tested regularly, because Glenfrome is linked to three other excellent inner city Bristol primary schools in the 4 Learning Partnership (www.4learningpartnership.co.uk). The heads of these schools hold each other to account with learning walks in one another's schools and with focused reviews of how pupil premium funding is being used, for example. 'Excellence for all our children' doesn't just appear on the 4 Learning Partnership website, it is put into practice with an annual Year 6 careers fair, a spelling bee and chess tournaments, all with the very active participation of the local community. Parental support for what the school does is paramount.

Strive for Five

Several miles away at Oasis Academy Brightstowe, where my wife teaches, staff likewise support children from deprived social and economic backgrounds with a package of measures tailored to offer educational excellence. The school mission statement is much more interesting than many: it aims for pupils to 'stand as equals in any circle for any opportunity'. This is put into effect with an unashamedly teach to the top philosophy which my wife labels as effectively the school's mantra. It is underpinned with support for any pupils who need it, whatever stage they are at.

'Strive for Five' identifies five areas of excellence which all teachers use to develop their practice: excellent knowledge, excellent instruction, excellent relationships and routines, excellent communication, and excellent progress and aspiration. This coherent approach informs 'book looks', learning walks, line manager discussions, data analysis and more. Beyond the classroom, the academy is providing experiences such as access to Future Quest (www.futurequest.org.uk), a local consortium led by the University of the West of England and funded by the Office for Students, which is working to encourage more young people into higher education. CPD is designed to engender a focus on developing learning and teaching using a coaching model which especially supports recently qualified teachers.

As we bang in the pitons and set the ropes, the ascents up the rock face of excellence can open to all. The climbers scaling the cliff must be the many, not the few. The excellence gap is a national scandal. Until we start collectively setting our eyes on the summit, supporting each other in selecting safe and efficient routes and literally teaching to the top (as some schools are doing already), it will continue to confine us to the foothills of academic and vocational achievement.

What is excellence anyway?

Excellence in education is elusive and ephemeral, inconstant and unattainable, chimerical and camouflaged. Intelligent young people surely deserve better. Why can't we have an attitude towards, and explanations and examples of, excellence that are, well, excellent and exemplary? Why can't a public body provide model answers and mark schemes rather than leaving us all to say that 'It all depends on … ' or 'Well, at the moment it means … '? If no one has the courage to do this at a national level, then perhaps we will have to do it ourselves in our own individual classrooms. David Didau (2015: 301) always says that no one knows our students like we do and no one has the right to come in and tell us that it might be better if we did this or tried that.

A toolkit of excellence

What we need is a grassroots excellence toolkit that is bespoke and unique to every school. This type of bottom-up, self-help approach is the antidote to scepticism about wholesale, radical reform in public education policy. You don't think it will ever happen, or even should happen? Fine, so start the revolution from your own bed and build your own toolkit of excellence.

Many years ago, I attended a brilliant INSET session led by the late Ian Coulson, then a history adviser in Kent. Ian magically produced a cantilevered toolbox in which he had collected what used to be termed 'realia'. I can't remember exactly what was in his toolbox but many history teachers, like me, have in their cupboards a piece of the Berlin Wall, badges, hats or dolls from Russia, a short length of fibre optic cable, a pottery shard, some Victorian lace, a gas mask – the list is endless. Ian suggested that we use these simple objects from daily life as hooks – wormholes into past lives and experiences. It was a micro version of Neil MacGregor's magnificent *A History of the World in 100 Objects* (2012): a lesson in how an artefact can trigger stories and how stories can unwrap imagination and pathways into worlds we have lost or not yet found. That is surely part of the magical purpose of learning with which we are entrusted.

Excellence led by government

Tim Dracup (2016) has charted the subtle and not-so-subtle shifts between the policies and practices of recent governments – and even within the policy of a single administration as education secretaries and schools ministers come and go. The picture he paints is largely one of inconsistency of definitions, changes in target and focus, and a lack of clarity in purpose. Should government education policy concern itself with gifted and talented provision at all and, if so, how? If not, what will the consequences be? These are not abstract and inconsequential questions, since a raft of funding and resources are at stake. In addition, spending for more able students is too often money taken from another education pot. If they try it, Tim will spot it.

There is a rational case for taking as much of the politics out of education as possible and handing over responsibility to an independent body. If Labour could do this in 1997 with the setting of interest rates by granting a power to the Bank of England once zealously guarded by the Chancellor of the Exchequer, and the Conservatives likewise in 2010 by establishing an Office for Budget Responsibility, then the precedents are set for wholesale ambitious public policy reform. 'Education, education, education', as New Labour's successful mantra from the 1997 election campaign had it, should become 'Evidence, evidence, evidence' for 2020.

I propose a new National Centre for Excellence in Schools with the statutory powers to, for example:

- Set up a single national exam board for England and Wales to ensure fair, uniform and excellent provision of specifications and examinations. How can it be appropriate for Anna to be entered for one examination with one board while her friend Pat in a neighbouring school tackles an 'easier' paper in the same subject from a notoriously 'easy' exam board?

- Break the corrupt bargain between exam boards and commercial publishers which allows an approved, logo-endorsed textbook to be issued for each popular course containing 'all you need to know', often written by a senior examiner. The effect is to reduce a potentially challenging and rich specification to a series of call-and-response questions – fostering the very worst kind of rote learning and teaching to the test.

- Abolish Ofqual, since it has singularly failed to oversee disparities and inequalities between exam boards and even within specifications offered by the same board. It is a self-referential quango, existing by and for itself. Excellence is not its watchword.

- Take overall responsibility for teacher training and endorse only those providers who are evidenced to be excellent. Teacher training is not a free market in services open to the lowest bidder. Education is not for sale.

- Offer independent assessment of Ofsted's role and activities. Ofsted, like Oxbridge, is a soft target for easy criticism. Instead of finding fault, we should acknowledge and build on its contribution to promoting excellence and tackling the attainment gap in schools. It cannot be accused of shrinking away from this challenge. Ofsted might therefore be part of the solution rather than the problem, and this deserves recognition. However, Ofsted too often substitutes judgement for accountability. Like it or not, schools need some measure by which they are held accountable to pupils, parents, teachers and local communities. But surely this was never intended to mean banners at school gates adorned with the Ofsted logo and proclaiming 'outstanding'? The rush to one-word descriptors for schools, their teachers, lessons and pupils is surely part of the problem we should be addressing, not a way forward for education in the twenty-first century.

The repurposing of Ofsted and the introduction of measures to make it fit for its role of supporting colleges and schools with professional, evidence-based insights and recommendations is needed urgently. Astonishingly, Ofsted recently admitted that it does not have evidence about the impact of its grading outcomes (outstanding, good, requires improvement, special measures) on schools and local communities. Research evidence about the efficacy of this very public process for learning and teaching could and should be immediate priorities for a new National Centre for Excellence in Schools. There is no credibility in an official body which marks its own work.

- Halt the further expansion of the academies programme and the growth of existing or new grammar schools unless and until independent verifiable evidence is provided for the excellence of the provision they offer. This includes closing the excellence or disadvantage gap. If we don't yet have the evidence, let's wait until we do.

- Set out some benchmarks and definitions of what 'excellent' looks like in vocational, technical and academic education which are backed up by research and common sense and are practical to administer.

- Commission literature reviews and research surveys from national policy-making bodies rather than relying on independent charities such as the EEF (excellent though its work is). Then follow the recommendations of such reports rather than shelving them.

In sum, radical change is needed if we are not to continue with a familiar catechism of complaints. If we are serious as a society about excellence for all and providing the conditions in which hundreds of thousands of our disadvantaged children move from able to remarkable, rather than merely the few already blessed ones, then the major public bodies charged with overseeing education need to be severely cut back and pruned, not merely deadheaded. The immediate results may look savage, but as any gardener will tell you, skilful wielding of the loppers and secateurs stimulates plant hormones that produce fresh, vigorous growth and future flowering.

If a teaching policy or practice is as comprehensively discussed and debated, with the evidence centre stage, as occurred with, for example, the ban on smoking in public places (based on the evidence of the harm caused by passive smoking to vulnerable groups in particular), then we have some hope of moving forward together. Surely, we cannot leave the education of millions of children to the whims of a particular education secretary with a singular vision that certain nineteenth-century novels should be taught in the nation's classrooms? If the funding of a government body is the issue, perhaps universities could be enlisted to pool their resources and expertise to offer the necessary guidance and leadership? What would be crucial is the independence of a National Centre for Excellence in Schools and its commitment to eroding the attainment gap caused by a lack of social and economic opportunity, not pupil ability.

The recent creation of researchEd (https://researched.org.uk) as a grassroots movement — avowedly international in outlook and with the exploration of evidence-led teaching and learning methods as its core purpose – should give inspiration to teachers from across the education world who want to inform their daily practice with methods and approaches that, statistically and evidentially, are likely to lead to improvements in response and outcome. Of course, some of this research has been initiated and developed by universities as part of PGCE or related courses, so there has never been an absence of educational experts willing to offer opinions and advice on what works and what doesn't. But the democratisation of the whole process, with the involvement of teachers and school leaders, has surely provided a new and important opportunity to base pedagogical practice on something more than hunch, hope and high-pressure sales methods from a myriad of competing suppliers of the latest educational must-have.

Naturally, the prospect of finding agreement on policy and approach from any given body or committee of experts on education is slender, but if this alone remains the main grounds for opposition to a National Centre for Excellence in Schools, then we might as well give up on all academic research per se as a waste of time and money. The National Health Service has the National Institute for Health and Care Excellence (NICE) to provide evidence-based guidance and advice to healthcare professionals and to develop quality standards for practitioners. Might this not be a useful parallel for those of us in education? If an independent body could come up with some framework documents offering definitions for such value-laden and contested terms as 'educational ability', 'attainment' and 'excellence', with the aim of applying these to public debate in the same way as happens in other key areas of public policy, it would be no bad start.

Let us at least agree where the goalposts go and how big the pitch is, even if we then send out teams with different strategies about how to win. So, we're looking to produce more software engineers to fill varying fields in entertainment, automotive engineering and cybercrime? That's going to take a lead time of a decade or more and will include setting benchmarks of excellence for the trainers and appraisers of the students coming through the system. A National Centre for Excellence in Schools will not only sow seeds for the future, but also earn its corn from the outset.

Excellence led by universities

The term *universitas* means 'the whole' or 'all turned into one', so any serious commitment by universities to excellence for all pupils and schools should continue the work of the proposed National Centre for Excellence in Schools. Universities should engage with it, apply it and refine it according to local context.

Universities are associated in the common mind with excellence, therefore they should arguably take a lead as part of their wider public responsibilities in shaping exemplary standards in schools and colleges. A university-based National Centre for Excellence in Schools would be a valuable addition to our educational landscape. Similarly, standards of public confidence in the quality of the degrees offered by universities need to be rock solid. How can the cheapening of top undergraduate degrees and a proliferation of income-generating master's qualifications of slender academic merit enrich a national drive for excellence? They cannot.

Any university worthy of the name should have a major commitment to more than just opening its doors to any local school. They should be financially supporting teacher research leads in schools by paying (teaching and learning responsibility) allowances. They should start in the areas of greatest social and economic deprivation. The universities of Oxford and Cambridge are excellent according to many international measures, but not by the crucially important measure of social diversity and inclusivity. Despite efforts to build outreach and wider access measures and programmes, Oxbridge remains a world of elite attainment beyond the reach of too many students from economically disadvantaged backgrounds. Likewise, the ethnic make-up of successful applicants consistently fails to meet the universities' internal targets, let alone the reasonable expectations of society as a whole. For these institutions to be considered excellent, we need to know what would be appropriate and realistic benchmarks for high-attaining students from minority ethnic backgrounds or areas of social deprivation. Should we apply nudge theory to Oxbridge, or will only radical measures such as quotas work?

However, while these institutions are an Aunt Sally, they are not always an appropriate one. As Oxford and Cambridge Universities sometimes gently point out, the reasons for non-application and low numbers of successful applicants are multi-causal. Sometimes these include perceptions of elitism and the impossibility of success generated within schools and colleges by the very teachers whose job it is to raise expectations until they can go no higher. This also needs action. Ironically, the financial resources of many Oxbridge colleges mean that accommodation and catering can be offered at subsidised rates, so attendance is often less expensive than at many other universities – if disadvantaged pupils and those from minority ethnic backgrounds could only get there in the first place.

Excellence led by schools

'Beacon schools' have been part of the educational framework in England for some time. Some have had public funding and support as a matter of national policy, while others have self-declared following the inspiration of a particular head or cluster of teachers. Either way, the outcomes produced have been impressive in terms of widening entry to excellence in locations which have not always had access to it. Increasingly, however, there has been a realisation that while a single floodlight can throw out good illumination, a series of well-positioned and complementary lights can do so much more to bring excellence out of the shadows. Networks or hubs of schools share resources and, arguably more importantly, collective intelligence and experience about what works and what doesn't, and insights about why this may be.

One such network is the Research Schools Network. There are currently twenty-two schools from Devon to Durham signed up to a commitment to use evidence to inform and improve practice within their schools and to act as hubs for their regions. How can schools share what they know about putting research into practice? The estimable Alex Quigley and his colleagues have shared good practice from Huntington School locally and nationally. Some networks are based on particular aspects of provision – such as London Gifted & Talented, led by Ian Warwick. For many years, Ian has been an inspirational figure in the movement to challenge preconceptions about provision for more able students and a generous provider of free resources via his website (http://londongt.org). The sheer breadth of his experience, derived from many years' teaching in challenging London schools, and a subsequent career advising many schools and bodies about what might work and why, merits the respect of all who attend his courses and read his publications.

So, successful templates already exist for high-attainment networks. Starting from scratch is unnecessary. These networks may be local, regional or national but a local membership is ideal. High attainment as a focus can be readily integrated within the strategy of an existing research hub. Alternatively, if a single focus is preferred to the multi-focus research model already outlined, then a specialist high-attainment network may be appropriate. What might such a network do?

- Compare Progress 8 data.

- Look at adding value in a pupil premium context.

- Share resources and expertise in preparing university/medicine/veterinary science/ Oxbridge applicants.

- Share resources or expertise around setting up a STEM cafe, joining an engineering education scheme, applying for Arkwright Engineering Scholarships or organising modern languages trips.

- Organise TeachMeets with an attainment/ability agenda.

- Endorse and put into a local and specific context key literature such as Rosenshine's 'Principles of Instruction' (2012).

- Share good practice in establishing and maintaining a staff journal club. We have one at my school led by the brilliant Paula Lobo where we look at and discuss several chapters from a prominent recent education book and consider its findings for our pupils (https://lobworth.com/journal-club).

Excellence led by teachers

Every teacher knows what excellence looks like in their subject. Every teacher knows how a good year assembly can be or how it could have become a memorable one. Every teacher knows how any 'OK' form period might have gone up a notch without huge effort. The best senior leaders I have worked with over many years have been committed to removing as many barriers and obstacles to those transitions as possible. Given all the restraints, funding issues, difficulties with absenteeism, poor student attitudes, behavioural problems and so on, there is still much that can be done to help the vast, overwhelming majority of teachers who want to share the best possible experiences with their students – not just the fair and routine experiences but the best attainable and the excellent. Make no mistake, every interaction matters. (Read John Tomsett's reflections on his experiences as a teacher and head in *This Much I Know About Love Over Fear* (2015) for more on this subject.)

Teacher subject knowledge is crucial to excellence. It underpins what is often, wrongly, seen as its antithesis – creativity. Teachers who know their onions command instant student and peer respect. Teachers with subject mastery can more adeptly model their explanations to suit all their learners. Teachers who know their stuff can do more with it, have fun with it and show their students how empowering knowledge can be. Putting it in crude terms, where a choice has to be made – as, for example, when setting up a new course or starting a new job – depth is better than breadth. Knowing a lot about a little has more chance of being inspiring, promoting deeper questioning and more excellent writing than a sketchy overview of a lot.

If academic excellence is the focus and the aim, pastoral care can't just take a back seat for a term. If tackling low-level disruption in class is necessary then allowing students to hand in work which is not the best they can achieve will undermine that ideal. If a critical mass of teachers within a staffroom are of the opinion that first rate is fine in theory and great to aspire to if anyone asks or checks up on it, but realistically just too much effort on a daily basis, the consequence will be that excellence won't be attained – not just by the high attainers who may push themselves further but by any student unlucky enough to be in that classroom in that year with that teacher.

A manifesto for excellence starts and potentially finishes at every teacher's classroom door. We cannot pass on this responsibility to our SLT or ALT and still less to national bodies. As a profession, we need to challenge our own squeamishness about scholarship – a term which Ofsted has recently restored from its politically correct periphery to the centre of its inspection regime. The way that a school views and treats its high-attaining pupils is now rightly seen as a touchstone of wider school performance, as it is with its lower attaining students. However, that doesn't necessarily mean that the 'middle third' is ignored. Every high expectation and every successful evidence-based intervention supports and improves their learning experiences too.

It's not a binary either/or with high-attaining students: giving them extra help (which we feel they don't really need anyway) doesn't necessarily mean neglecting others. Alternatively, ignoring them because they are bright and will cope anyway (although we feel guilty in doing so and know that even they can't do it alone), and concentrating instead on the grade 3/4 students for GCSE league table purposes and/or the 100% pass borderline doesn't work either. On the back of unconditional positive regard for students' potential and growth, a manifesto for excellence should offer the opportunity to allow apparent middling ability to blossom into definitively high attainment – which is why any self-respecting gifted and talented programme needs to remain open at every stage of a child's academic career.

Coaching for excellence

As I have stressed throughout this book, a model of delivery in schools which offers just one opportunity to have a go at something – to improve (or not) – and then to move on to the next busy thing is essentially flawed. Every method, technique, tip and idea has been rooted in the premise of repeat, practise, repeat, improve – not quite ad nauseam (I hope) but for sufficiently long such that the benefits of deliberate, purposeful practice kick in and produce the positive outcomes which improve motivation to continue the cycle. This is why coaching potentially offers so much more than classic, routine CPD days. Planning for the continuity and refinement of good practice means working in units of study and reflection – sequences not standalone, repetition not one-off.

INSET day = insanely numbing session of educational tedium day

The head offers a welcome back, introduces new staff, confidently rolls out the day's big theme by using an analogy from her holiday ('Birdwatching can tell us so much about how to improve our school, don't you think … ?'), cracks a bad joke, an iffy smile and hands over to …

Hard-pressed deputy 1, who has been tasked with leading staff through child protection, health and safety and behaviour management updates in a breathless half-hour-which-becomes-forty-three-minutes (you know because you've counted) before handing over to …

Hard-pressed deputy 2, whose turn it is to present their holiday PowerPoint on the designated big theme – Ready to Learn/growth mindset/knowledge organisers. Group work is a necessary antidote to all this chalk and talk, just as in a lesson, so you end up on a table with colleagues you barely recognise and with whom you would never go to the pub. Goodwill and weary decency see you scribbling on the mandatory sticky note or sugar paper about what 'gifted and talented' means to you or how you have devised effective strategies to deal with fidget spinners. 'Sorry guys, so many good ideas but just no time to share them all!' By coffee time it's all become a bit of a blur as you stagger to …

Friendly head of subject, who repairs the damage from the morning sessions by allowing you to swap more holiday tales and advice (which can't be minuted) about how to deal with 9E, with whom you've been landed this year. You fill in a feedback form on the day's CPD (it will be on the VLE if you are especially unlucky) with some 3s and 5s to prevent any comeback on your feedback, and then pitch in with relief to some lesson planning for 9E tomorrow. Meanwhile, the day's bright cheery focus has already disappeared from your working memory because so many other important things have crowded in and you've had no time and energy to reinforce and consolidate them.

CPD day = complete pedagogical disaster day

Contrariwise, coaching fosters a common purpose agreed between two partners. It then develops this with some clear explanation and modelling based on mutual observation and responses, and then builds further with deliberate and purposeful practice. Non-hierarchical, peer-to-peer coaching within a school or college or across a high-attainment network makes better use of precious time and resources and is much more cost-effective. Calling in an expert or consultant (who may not have been in a classroom with the likes of 9E for a decade) for a fat fee is unnecessary. Too much time is spent explaining context and circumstances to the expert, however much was promised about tailor-made advice to your institution, and too often there is little practical takeaway beyond the glossy binder and biro.

Schools offer their own best CPD on excellence – and if a school or a high-attainment network can't offer its own excellent training on excellence, who can? The answer is unlikely to come from the plethora of para-educational providers willing to sell solutions and subscriptions. Your school's own students will have starting points, not least because they really do want their own school to be better. Coaching for excellence starts in September and finishes the following August with A level and then GCSE results, which then kick-start the reflection process and the cycle continues. Not that this is the only success criterion, of course. The real benefits of a coaching model for schools come from the incremental changes to personal professional practice. These are all the more transformative because they have become deep-seated as a result of the cycle of practice and consolidation which characterises effective learning.

Coaching enables cumulative, small-scale improvements – sometimes labelled 'marginal gains' (from the world of competitive cycling) where tiny interventions scale up to medal-winning improvements (see Elder 2014). Building a culture of high attainment in a school is a journey several years in the making, but what could be more important or worthwhile? Coaching is no more the universal panacea than any other single action or response: it requires the training, commitment and motivation appropriate to any large, whole-school initiative, but there is ample evidence to suggest that schools which are serious about major attitudinal shifts in policy and practice include it as part of their strategy.

Those four to six hours spent doodling and playing bullshit bingo on the back row during an INSET day can be put to much better use. The day can be broken down into smaller, focused sessions of dialogue and practice in the form of live coaching which offers high impact and immediate opportunities to adapt habitual practices. As head of subject, I tried to move away from taking up too much valuable department meeting time for administration and heads-up announcements about what was already in the school diary. I realised that looking at exercise books together, asking a colleague to model how to use the new interactive whiteboard or discussing a learning and teaching method was a far better, if not always easier, use of colleagues' valuable time.

SLTs who find alternative ways to deliver vital information about the running of the school free up time for substantive improvements at a one-to-one level. Coaching for teacher excellence has much to commend it. It can support the school's drive for excellence by pinpointing the school-wide focus for learning and teaching and ensuring that all staff are working on areas of outstanding provision within that. Teacher excellence drives everything else.

Teacher excellence toolkits

You have six weeks with your Year 8 class. You can do anything you like with them in educational terms, consistent with your institution's policies on safeguarding and so on. The only criterion is that the work that this class produces must be by your definition excellent. The outcomes will be submitted to your high-attainment network and to the new National Centre for Excellence in Schools as part of their database of excellence. There will be no judgement or grading.

What will you choose to do, and why? How will you define, explain and model excellence to the class? What do they need to know before they can be super-creative? My guess is that no two teachers undertaking this exercise will approach and implement it in the same way. Instead, I envisage every class of students working with their teacher will produce an 'excellence toolkit' which might involve some of the methods outlined in this or similar books: reading some well-chosen material, reviewing and recapping, low-stakes quizzing so the knowledge sticks, a gallery critique of some poetry, peer feedback on the design or experiment, teacher-written comments, among a thousand different ways. The point is that it can be done, and if it is repeated, discussed, shared and refined it will be even better next time.

What does your excellence toolkit look like? What matters as much as the outcomes is the process we go through in thinking about what makes remarkable learning and teaching. How do we arrive at the best that can be envisaged and achieved by Year 8 in a limited time frame and with the resources available? How do we ensure that every child gets a chance to make their butterfly perfect, not just Austin?

Excellence led by parents

On the learning journeys that our pupils are undertaking, which I have argued should be lifelong and embarked on for their own sake, there will be setbacks and successes which I have characterised as a learning rollercoaster. Stretching the analogy perhaps a tad too far, it would be beneficial to ensure that more parents are on board. Pupils from disadvantaged backgrounds, in particular, will stand more chance of making and maintaining academic progress if they are supported by parents and local communities. Parents need to know about and share success to help create a virtuous circle or spiral of upward movement. As we saw in Chapter 8, initial research by the EEF (2018f) using text messages has been promising but much more needs to be done.

Excellence led by students

I have tried to outline some of the ways in which students can become expert learners and themselves lead others. *Teachers lead, students learn, students lead.* If we are serious about guiding students to become remarkable lifelong learners, then we cannot do it for them or to them. No amount of modelling or explanation will be sufficient, however high quality. The mainspring of change is Yolanda and Asif. In Chapter 2, I outlined what happened in my own school when a group of our Scholars were asked to outline their ideal lesson, which showed that students do know what excellence is and want it for themselves and their peers (despite protestations to the contrary sometimes), even if they disagree about how to attain or sustain it. No class will fail to respond intelligently to your question to them tomorrow to tell you what excellence looks like for their subject and age group. Likewise, if you set up student voice appropriately, they will offer honest suggestions about how to remove some of the barriers preventing more of them from getting closer to excellence. This peer culture is a hugely powerful force, and when harnessed appropriately and in the right circumstances it can lead to co-construction and similar methods which take the idea of a flipped classroom to a whole new level.

The evidence reviewed by Rob Coe (2016) is unambiguous about the need to judge effective teaching by the benchmark of student progress. 'She taught that electricity unit very well' is wish fulfilment. 'Her students could explain, design and build simple circuit boards by December, some of them very quickly' actually tells a senior leader something. Schools which take the temptingly simple route of providing more stretch and challenge for high-attaining or potentially high-attaining students through top-down interventions alone, ignoring the how and why of student progress, are unlikely to have a strong impact. For example, insisting on a 'spark question' or 'challenge box' on every PowerPoint (some schools do this) suggests gimmick and formula rather than offering students the chance to move a discussion along. Working in partnership, students and teachers can hit the struggle zone which will take them from their current knowledge and understanding to a new and unfamiliar place. Excellence will follow because it is this challenge which helps the class to retain the discussion in their collective and individual long-term memories. Cognitive scientists tell us that learning is defined as this very change in long-term memory. *Teachers lead, students follow, students lead.* This doesn't mean teacher leadership by writing the lesson objectives on the board for the fifth time that day.

When expert learners start to run an art club pretty much by themselves, or Year 12s coach younger pupils in basketball at lunchtime, or a cross-year group delegation talks to the school caterers about reducing plastic waste, a peer culture of pride is being fostered which demonstrates care about an institution and its values. The excellence is not about academic goals in themselves, but a peer culture which buys into and benefits from the shared aspirations of support staff, teaching staff and pupils. Creating a culture for academic excellence need not solely be about creating a culture of academic excellence.

Any manifesto for excellence led by students also benefits from seeing their school years as part of a lifelong learning journey. I taught Open University students for a number of years, mostly arts foundation courses. To describe my students as inspirational sounds patronising: juggling jobs, families and home lives, reading Marx and Mill in the evenings and then writing assignments to be posted to me for marking, attending summer school in what was probably a work holiday and then taking exams – that's uber-inspiration. I heard many stories of missed opportunities at school, of harsh teaching and of family circumstances curtailing education at 14 or 16, but those mature students still chose to give up their evenings and weekends to study *Wide Sargasso Sea* or utilitarianism with like-minded souls.

The Open University is one of the greatest success stories from twentieth-century education and its glories should be shouted from the rooftops. (I met my wife through the Open University so I have special reason to be grateful to it!) It embodies so many transformational ideas, of which two are especially relevant here. Firstly, that learning is valuable for its own sake. Why give up all that time and energy to study the Pre-Raphaelites and the Victorian music hall, as we did? There are dozens of vocational and business-related alternatives available, but Open University degrees are broad brush and not single subject-specific (or at least they were back then). The same could be said for Workers' Educational Association (WEA) classes, evening classes of many kinds and MOOCs.

Secondly, of course, the flourishing of MAs, residential study weekends and the like tells us what the Open University has always understood, which is that education is less like a bus ride into town and more like a round-the-world learning journey, lasting a long time and embracing many forms of transport and a few wrong turns. When our more able students see us in the classroom still learning, still finding out stuff and still going on courses, this idea is being modelled for them.

Student excellence toolkits

Our pupils love to know things because knowledge is power. If they know the common devices used by poets, they can comment more authoritatively on assonance and dissonance and relate this to what may be part of the poet's motivation and purpose or to help understand why she may have consciously broken the literary rules. Put together, the periodic table of elements, dates, facts, sums, words and places create citizens. If this all sounds rather Michael Gove, then so be it. Cultural capital is too important to be kicked around in a game of political football.

Interestingly, Ofsted's draft 2019 *School Inspection Handbook* states that as part of a judgement about the quality of education a school provides, inspectors will consider how well it equips pupils with knowledge and cultural capital, which is defined as: 'the essential knowledge that pupils need to be educated citizens, introducing them to the best that has been thought and said and helping to engender an appreciation of human creativity and achievement' (Ofsted 2019: 42). The phrase 'the best that has been thought and said' is pure Matthew Arnold, ironically an inspector of schools in mid-Victorian England.

In the Meccano kit of knowledge, the most valuable pieces are the universal nuts and bolts holding together any one of thousands of combinations of other pieces. They are the times tables, musical scales, key formulae – the basic chronology connecting everything. Nothing is possible without these building blocks. Students constructing their toolkits of excellence will learn to value these connectors, enabling links to be made between disparate pieces of knowledge and taking learning in new directions. Instead of pointing and sign language, verbs in a foreign language enable communication. Instead of random googling, an English dictionary, a thesaurus and a vocabulary list foster curiosity about the etymology of words and the richness of our language.

If teachers can have toolkits, why not students? I give my Scholars an A4 sketchbook at the start of the year and ask them to keep a journal of interesting experiences. This might be a review of a book they have read, a piece about an event they have attended or a visit they have made. Keeping a journal or learning diary, or just an informal record of what is interesting in the mind of a 12- or 13-year-old, is another little step on their learning journey. We learn things and remember them because we think about them. If my students do that for themselves, rather than having it done to them, my gut feeling is that they maximise the chances of the maximum number of these units tangling together into a double helix of excellence.

Summary

The story of provision for high-attaining children in England in recent years has not been an untroubled and fruitful tale with a happy ending. Ironically, we have set a poor example for these children by being unclear about our aims, divided in our approaches and inconsistent in our actions. As the adults in the room, we have failed to help sufficient numbers of pupils with the intelligence to succeed at the highest levels of education and to overcome the disadvantages they face, let alone those with the potential to succeed. It's no one's fault and it's everyone's fault.

A benchmark of excellence is a small step towards change. I am excellent, you are excellent, he/she/it is excellent: teaching to the top, supporting to the top and pushing beyond the top means that we and our students become excellent. Networks will help, nationally agreed benchmarks will help, nudging and reforming some of the established institutions and practices will help. The toolkit of knowledge, energy and love that you and I carry into the classroom tomorrow will help.

Conclusion

Expert learners are made, not born. You have the means in your school or college today to produce such learners in the thousands, not the tens. You can help to transform more able students into remarkable students because you already know what to do. The challenge ahead is to close the knowing–doing gap and to stop finding reasons and excuses not to do it. Anna, Tom, Maya, Asif and Yolanda are waiting.

So, how have our expert learners fared on their rollercoaster rides?

At the end of this stage of their lifelong experience of exploration, it may be unsurprising that Yolanda has built on her high prior attainment throughout secondary school and is aspiring to a place at Imperial College London to read engineering. The stimulus she received in maths and science from other developing expert learners, like Asif, has been a big help and taught her a lot about the value of collaborative learning, which an engineering degree will certainly foster.

Asif's own self-esteem as a learner took a knock as he realised that he could not just rely on pure processing power and 'natural ability' to tackle tougher problems. But he bounced back, secured good results and is now carefully considering his A level choices from a wide range of options.

As 'middle attainers' both Tom and Anna benefited hugely from some of the methods outlined in this book and are on their way to full-blown expert learner status. Tom may well take some of the debating skills he enjoyed acquiring in religious studies and apply for a law degree later on, perhaps at Liverpool or Manchester. Anna has been made aware by Dr Emma, a former pupil of the school, of open days at Cambridge and has just been to look around some colleges with a view to a possible natural sciences degree post A level.

Maya's difficult learning journey in English and her core subjects continued but she has now outlined her own alternative route into higher education via a local college. She has taken ownership of her own learning and has a detailed map in her head of a landscape of success.

Pen portraits of *your* school's expert learners might look better on your website and magazine adverts than the identikit security blanket adjectives which your marketing department may put out, such as 'compassionate' and 'enquiring' and 'independent'. There's a challenge.

Research evidence has provided you with a library of knowledge about what works in terms of effective questioning in the classroom, collaborative learning and feedback methods that stand most chance of being effective with your pupils tomorrow. Never has cognitive behavioural science been able to tell you more about the principles and practices at the heart of giving teachers and pupils the greatest chance of succeeding, from motivation to memory. The application of research in neuroscience to education is still in its early stages, but it is already starting to deliver findings with implications for your daily practice. A common core of sound pedagogy underpins much of what you do. Thanks to the generosity of spirit of so many educators and the desire to do the very best for the children in your care, you share resources, ideas, tips and cautionary tales via social media, conferences and TeachMeets as never before.

And yet. Thousands of children fail every year to make the progress they should in schools, particularly those already suffering economic and social disadvantage. Their potential is underestimated and their possible contributions overlooked in favour of their more confident and biddable peers. They deserve better, and what that means is more than just a little better. 'A little better' or 'The best we can do right now' won't cut it because it won't make enough of a difference. The benchmark must be excellence for all, rooted in unconditional positive regard for students, which should radiate from professionals committed to excellence in every conversation, interaction, assembly, form period, lesson and parents' evening.

As part of their professional obligation to high-attaining and potentially high-attaining students, all institutions should re-evaluate their curriculum and approach to attainment setting. No high-attainer programme has an iota of a chance of succeeding if it is nothing more than a bolt-on package comprising the occasional university visit or trip to the theatre. Wise curriculum planning frames the typical curriculum questions, such as 'Why should we study this unit?', within a broader outline, such as 'Why will studying this unit enable all students to become expert learners?' The same point holds for attainment setting. Are you satisfied that your current setting model fosters excellent learning in all sets, or only some of them? Your bottom set Year 9 English students deserve more than five years of low expectations, cover teachers and simple texts. 'It's not finished until it's excellent' applies not only to Year 9 English homework but to every aspect of school or college life, all the time.

The journey from able to remarkable is one from 'good enough' to excellence. How will you know if you are on this learning journey?

- If a coaching model is more likely to produce more engaging, effective and worthwhile CPD than your current INSET days, that's excellent.

- If asking your students what makes an ideal lesson in your school is likely to be challenging but fruitful and purposeful, that's excellent.

- If collaborative learning can show your colleagues and students an approach that works but they may not have considered, that's excellent.

- If your students develop a better knowledge of how they learn and revise and understand that their learning journey may resemble a rollercoaster ride, that's excellent.

- If your school or college is aware of the mental health issues attached to the pursuit of excellence, for both teachers and students, that's excellent.

- If *adults teach, students learn and students lead*, then you are helping them to move from able to remarkable.

Labels such as 'gifted and talented' are redolent with notions of genetic advantage. A stimulating school environment should enable every student to make maximum use of their genetic inheritance to become an expert learner. Expert learners have learned how to learn and have mental models of success which balance out the effort they need to put into a subject or activity with the rewards they will draw from it. Deliberate, focused practice becomes more than repetition but a means of learning in itself – one in which a row, table or class of students can join. They may not all start at the top but their intelligence helps them to get there. They take others with them on learning journeys which can be as unexpected and exciting as those of any astronaut.

Teachers who teach to the top model explanations and put a premium on knowing stuff because knowing stuff matters and is the bedrock for knowing what you can do with it. Knowledge is power in the excellent classroom, where expert learners model success to other learners via gallery critique and other methods so that learning is open, transparent and accessible. There is no limit to excellence set by a test or an exam board, not least because we do not yet have outside bodies capable of setting these necessary benchmarks. The dereliction of this fundamental duty is shameful, so we will just have to get on with it ourselves. Michael Marland (1975: 1) put it well many years ago:

> The more you look at schooling in practice, the more you study research and observation, and the more you consider the real problems of helping the young learn, the more you are forced to the simple conclusion that individual teachers are the most important factor. It is not the school organization, the syllabus, or the teaching method.

Rather, the level is set by you and your students working together to establish the best that this particular class is capable of, which no one but you and they will know – and they will know it better than you, so you need to involve them. Getting the approach to learning for high-attaining students right is the key: the strategies and methods set out in this book and in many others will help, but by themselves will be insufficient. Your approach is all, and you must be relentlessly and irrefutably challenging and optimistic.

Bibliography

Adams, Richard (2016) Older Teenagers 'Quicker to Improve Maths and Reasoning Skills', *The Guardian* (4 November). Available at: https://www.theguardian.com/society/2016/nov/04/older-teenagers-quicker-to-improve-maths-reasoning-skills-survey.

Alexander, Robin J. (2008) *Towards Dialogic Teaching: Rethinking Classroom Talk*, 4th edn. York: Dialogos.

Allison, Shaun and Tharby, Andy (2015) *Making Every Lesson Count: Six Principles to Support Great Teaching and Learning* (Carmarthen: Crown House Publishing).

Amass, Helen (2017) TES talks to ... Sarah-Jayne Blakemore, *TES* (17 March). Available at: https://www.tes.com/news/tes-talks-tosarah-jayne-blakemore.

Anderson, Mark (2012) Beginner's Guide to SAMR, *ICT Evangelist* (29 November). Available at: https://ictevangelist.com/beginners-guide-to-samr/.

Arnold, Matthew (2006 [1869]) *Culture and Anarchy* (New York: Oxford University Press).

Ashman, Greg (2018) An Interview with Dylan Wiliam (11 August). Available at: https://gregashman.wordpress.com/2018/08/11/an-interview-with-dylan-wiliam/.

Ausubel, David (1968) *Educational Psychology: A Cognitive View* (New York: Holt, Rinehart & Winston).

Bakhtin, Mikhail (1981) *The Dialogic Imagination: Four Essays*, ed. Michael Holquist, tr. Caryl Emerson and Michael Holquist (Austin, TX and London: University of Texas Press).

Ball, Philip (2018) The IQ Trap: How the Study of Genetics Could Transform Education, *New Statesman* (16 April). https://www.newstatesman.com/2018/04/iq-trap-how-study-genetics-could-transform-education

Banham, Dale and Hall, Russell (2016a) Active Learning at A Level: 'I Forget What I Was Taught, I Only Remember What I've Learnt', *Schools History Project* (9 February). Available at: http://www.schoolshistoryproject.co.uk/active-learning-at-a-level/.

Banham, Dale and Hall, Russell (2016b) Raising Attainment at GCSE and A Level: Using Recent Research to Inform Planning, *Schools History Project* (10 February). Available at: http://www.schoolshistoryproject.co.uk/raising-attainment-at-gcse-and-a-level/.

Beadle, Phil (2010) *How to Teach* (Carmarthen: Crown House Publishing).

Berger, Ron (2003) *An Ethic of Excellence: Building a Culture of Craftsmanship with Students* (Portsmouth, NH: Heinemann).

Berry, Jill (2018) Leadership and Well-being (27 May). Available at: https://jillberry102.blog/2018/05/27/leadership-and-well-being/.

Blakemore, Sarah-Jayne (2018) *Inventing Ourselves: The Secret Life of the Teenage Brain* (London: Doubleday).

Boaler, Jo, Wiliam, Dylan and Brown, Margaret (2000) Students' Experiences of Ability Grouping – Disaffection, Polarisation and the Construction of Failure, *British Educational Research Journal* 26(5): 631–648.

Buzan, Tony (1986) *Use Your Memory* (Harlow: BBC Books).

Cattell, Raymond B. (1971) *Abilities: Their Structure, Growth, and Action* (Boston, MA: Houghton Mifflin).

Christodoulou, Daisy (2016) Why Did Assessment for Learning Fail? [video] (23 June). Available at: https://www.youtube.com/watch?v=qLpAalDaqQY.

Christodoulou, Daisy (2017) *Making Good Progress? The Future of Assessment for Learning* (Oxford: Oxford University Press).

Coe, Robert (2013) Improving Education: A Triumph of Hope over Experience. Inaugural lecture, Durham University, 18 June. Available at: http://www.cem.org/attachments/publications/ImprovingEducation2013.pdf.

Coe, Robert (2016) What is Worth Reading for Teachers Interested in Research?, *Centre for Evaluation & Monitoring* (22 June). Available at: http://www.cem.org/blog/what-is-worth-reading-for-teachers-interested-in-research/.

Coe, Robert (2017) How Can Teachers Learn to be Better Teachers?, *Centre for Evaluation & Monitoring* (22 June). Available at: http://www.cem.org/blog/how-can-teachers-learn-to-be-better-teachers/.

Coe, Robert, Aloisi, Cesare, Higgins, Steve and Major, Lee Elliot (2014) *What Makes Great Teaching? Review of the Underpinning Research* (London: Sutton Trust). Available at: https://www.suttontrust.com/wp-content/uploads/2014/10/What-Makes-Great-Teaching-REPORT.pdf.

Counsell, Christine (2004) Looking Through a Josephine-Butler-Shaped Window: Focussing Pupils' Thinking on Historical Significance, *Teaching History* 114: 30–33.

Counsell, Christine (2018) Senior Curriculum Leadership 1: The Indirect Manifestation of Knowledge: (A) Curriculum As Narrative, *The Dignity of the Thing* (7 April). Available at: https://thedignityofthethingblog.wordpress.com/2018/04/07/senior-curriculum-leadership-1-the-indirect-manifestation-of-knowledge-a-curriculum-as-narrative/.

Cowley, Andrew (2019) *The Wellbeing Toolkit: Sustaining, Supporting and Enabling School Staff* (London: Bloomsbury).

Dawson, Ian (2015a) Enquiry: Developing Puzzling, Enjoyable, Effective Historical Investigations, *Primary History* 70 (summer): 8–14.

Dawson, Ian (2015b) Ian Coulson: In Memoriam, *Thinking History* (10 December). Available at: http://www.thinkinghistory.co.uk/diary/2015/12/ian-coulson-in-memoriam/.

de Pizan, Christine (2003 [1405]) *The Treasure of the City of Ladies,* tr. Sarah Lawson (New York: Penguin)

Department for Education (2016) *Educational Excellence Everywhere* (March). Available at: https://www.gov.uk/government/publications/educational-excellence-everywhere.

Didau, David (2013a) Deliberately Difficult – Why It's Better to Make Learning Harder, *Learning Spy* (10 June). Available at: https://learningspy.co.uk/featured/deliberately-difficult-focussing-on-learning-rather-than-progress-2/.

Didau, David (2013b) Improving Peer Feedback with Gallery Critique, *Learning Spy* (8 February). Available at: https://learningspy.co.uk/assessment/improving-peer-feedback-with-public-critique/.

Didau, David (2015) *What If Everything You Knew About Education Was Wrong?* (Carmarthen: Crown House Publishing).

Didau, David (2017) Why Feedback Fails, *Learning Spy* (10 January). Available at: https://learningspy.co.uk/assessment/why-feedback-fails/.

Didau, David (2019) *Making Kids Cleverer: A Manifesto for Closing the Advantage Gap* (Carmarthen: Crown House Publishing).

Dix, Paul (2017) *When the Adults Change, Everything Changes: Seismic Shifts in School Behaviour* (Carmarthen: Independent Thinking Press).

Dracup, Tim (2015) The Most Able Students: Has Ofsted Made Progress? *Gifted Phoenix* (4 March). Available at: https://giftedphoenix.wordpress.com/2015/03/08/the-most-able-students-has-ofsted-made-progress/.

Dracup, Tim (2016) Sir Michael on the Most Able, *Eponymous* (19 June). Available at: https://timdracup.wordpress.com/2016/06/19/sir-michael-on-the-most-able/.

Dracup, Tim (2017) Know Your Limits!, *Eponymous* (10 April). Available at: https://timdracup.wordpress.com/2017/04/10/know-your-limits/.

Dunlosky, John (2013) Strengthening the Student Toolbox: Study Strategies to Boost Learning, *American Educator* (fall): 12–21. Available at: https://www.aft.org/sites/default/files/periodicals/dunlosky.pdf.

Dweck, Carol (2012) *Mindset: How You Can Fulfil Your Potential* (London: Constable & Robinson).

Education Endowment Foundation (2018a) *Best Practice in Grouping Students. Intervention B: Mixed Attainment Grouping. Pilot Report and Executive Summary* (September). Available at: https://educationendowmentfoundation.org.uk/projects-and-evaluation/projects/best-practice-in-mixed-attainment-grouping/.

Education Endowment Foundation (2018b) *Metacognition and Self-Regulated Learning: Guidance Report*. Available at: https://educationendowmentfoundation.org.uk/evidence-summaries/teaching-learning-toolkit/meta-cognition-and-self-regulation/.

Education Endowment Foundation (2018c) *Philosophy for Children* (22 March). Available at: https://educationendowmentfoundation.org.uk/projects-and-evaluation/projects/philosophy-for-children/.

Education Endowment Foundation (2018d) Setting or Streaming (28 November). Available at: https://educationendowmentfoundation.org.uk/evidence-summaries/teaching-learning-toolkit/setting-or-streaming/#effectiveness.

Education Endowment Foundation (2018e) *Teaching and Learning Toolkit* (10 October). Available at: https://educationendowmentfoundation.org.uk/evidence-summaries/teaching-learning-toolkit/mastery-learning/.

Education Endowment Foundation (2018f) Texting Parents (19 November). Available at: https://educationendowmentfoundation.org.uk/projects-and-evaluation/projects/texting-parents/.

Einhard and Notker (1969) *Two Lives of Charlemagne*, ed. and tr. Lewis Thorpe (London: Penguin).

Elder, Zoë (2014) The Marginal Learning Gains Theory, *Innovate My School* (28 March). Available at: http://www.innovatemyschool.com/ideas/item/937-the-marginal-learning-gains-theory.html.

Ericsson, Anders and Pool, Robert (2016) *Peak: How All of Us Can Achieve Extraordinary Things* (London: Vintage Books).

Fawcett, David (2013) Creating a Culture of Critique, *My Learning Journey* (6 April). Available at: http://reflectionsofmyteaching.blogspot.com/2013/04/creating-culture-of-critique.html.

Fisher, Peter (2002) *Thinking Through History* (Cambridge: Chris Kington Publishing).

Fletcher-Wood, Harry (2016) Using Exit Tickets to Assess and Plan: 'The Tuning Fork of Teaching', *Improving Teaching* (24 April). Available at: https://improvingteaching.co.uk/2016/04/24/exit-tickets-assess-plan/.

Francis, Becky, Taylor, Becky, Hodgen, Jeremy, Tereshchenko, Antonina and Archer, Louise (2018) *Dos and Don'ts of Attainment Grouping* (London: UCL Institute of Education). Available at: https://www.ucl.ac.uk/ioe/sites/ioe/files/dos_and_donts_of_attainment_grouping_-_ucl_institute_of_education.pdf.

Gilbert, Ian (2018) *The Working Class: Poverty, Education and Alternative Voices* (Carmarthen: Independent Thinking Press).

Ginnis, Paul (2002) *The Teacher's Toolkit: Raise Classroom Achievement with Strategies for Every Learner* (Carmarthen: Crown House Publishing).

Gladwell, Malcolm (2009) *Outliers: The Story of Success* (London: Penguin).

Goddard, Vic (2014) *The Best Job in the World* (Carmarthen: Independent Thinking Press).

Hadfield, Chris (2013) *An Astronaut's Guide to Life on Earth* (London: Macmillan).

Haig, Douglas (2006) *War Diaries and Letters 1914–1918*, ed. Gary Sheffield and John Bourne (London: Weidenfeld & Nicolson).

Hall, Edward (forthcoming) Building a House of CARDS: The Practice Structures of Coaches in a Professional Rugby Union Academy. In *Sports Coaching: A Theoretical and Practical Guide* (London and New York: Routledge).

Hart, Peter (2009) *1918: A Very British Victory* (London: Phoenix Books).

Hart, Peter (2018) *The Last Battle: Endgame on the Western Front* (London: Profile Books).

Hattie, John (2009) *Visible Learning: A Synthesis of Over 800 Meta-Analyses Relating to Achievement* (Abingdon and New York: Routledge).

Hattie, John (2011) Visible Learning, Part 2: Effective Methods [video] (1 December). Available at: https://www.youtube.com/watch?v=3pD1DFTNQf4.

Hattie, John (2012a) Know Thy Impact, *Feedback for Learning* 70(1): 18–23.

Hattie, John (2012b) *Visible Learning for Teachers: Maximizing Impact on Learning* (Abingdon and New York: Routledge).

Hendrick, Carl and Macpherson, Robin (eds) (2017) *What Does This Look Like in the Classroom? Bridging the Gap between Research and Practice* (Woodbridge: John Catt Educational).

Holt, John (1967) *How Children Learn* (London: Penguin).

Jackson, Nina (2015) *Of Teaching, Learning and Sherbet Lemons* (Carmarthen: Independent Thinking Press).

Jones, Rachel (2015) *Teacher Geek: Because Life's Too Short for Worksheets* (Carmarthen: Crown House Publishing).

Kirby, Joe (2015) Marking is a Hornet, *Pragmatic Reform* (31 October). Available at https://pragmaticreform.wordpress.com/2015/10/31/marking-is-a-hornet/.

Kirschner, Paul, Sweller, John and Clark, Richard E. (2006) Why Minimal Guidance During Instruction Does Not Work: An Analysis of the Failure of Constructivist, Discovery, Problem-Based, Experiential, and Inquiry-Based Teaching, *Educational Psychologist* 41(2): 75–86.

Lemov, Doug (2010) *Teach Like a Champion: 49 Techniques That Put Students on the Path to College* (with DVD) (San Francisco, CA: Jossey-Bass).

Lemov, Doug, Woolway, Erica and Yezzi, Katie (2012) *Practice Perfect: 42 Rules for Getting Better at Getting Better* (San Francisco, CA: Jossey-Bass).

Lobo, Paula (2016) 'My Initial Concern is to Get a Hearing': Exploring What Makes an Effective History Essay Introduction, *Teaching History* 164 (September): 10–12.

Lohmann, Raychelle C. (2014) Top 10 Stress Busters for Teens, *Psychology Today* (19 November). Available at: https://www.psychologytoday.com/gb/blog/teen-angst/201411/top-10-stress-busters-teens.

MacDonald, Ian (1994) *Revolution in the Head: The Beatles' Records and the Sixties* (London: Fourth Estate).

McGill, Ross Morrison (2014) A 5-Point Plan for Teacher Wellbeing, *@TeacherToolkit* (3 July). Available at: https://www.teachertoolkit.co.uk/2014/07/03/5-point-plan-for-teacher-wellbeing/.

MacGregor, Neil (2012) *A History of the World in 100 Objects* (London: Penguin).

Marland, Michael (1975) *The Craft of the Classroom: A Survival Guide to Classroom Management in the Secondary School* (London: Heinemann Educational).

Massey, Robert (2014) Co-Construction: Students Building Lessons with You, *Distilling G and T Ideas* (9 February). Available at: https://rmasseygandt.wordpress.com/2014/02/09/co-construction-students-building-lessons-with-you/.

Miles, Barry (1998) *Paul McCartney: Many Years from Now* (London: Vintage).

Montacute, Rebecca (2018) *Potential for Success: Fulfilling the Promise of Highly Able Students in Secondary Schools* (London: Sutton Trust). Available at: https://www.suttontrust.com/research-paper/potential-for-success-schools-high-attainers.

Montacute, Rebecca and Cullinane, Carl (2018) *Access to Advantage: The Influence of Schools and Place on Admissions to Top Universities* (London: Sutton Trust). Available at: https://www.suttontrust.com/wp-content/uploads/2018/12/AccesstoAdvantage-2018.pdf.

Myatt, Mary (2017) Why We Should Stop Ability Setting in Schools, *Schools Week* (9 December). Available at: https://schoolsweek.co.uk/why-we-should-stop-ability-setting-in-schools/.

Newmark, Ben (2016) Verbal Feedback: Telling Them What to Do, *Learning History* (26 September). Available at: http://bennewmark.edublogs.org/2016/09/26/227/.

Nuthall, Graham (2007) *The Hidden Lives of Learners* (Wellington: New Zealand Council for Educational Research Press).

Ofsted (2013) *The Most Able Students: Are They Doing As Well As They Should in Our Non-Selective Secondary Schools?* (June). Ref: 130118. Available at: https://www.gov.uk/government/publications/are-the-most-able-students-doing-as-well-as-they-should-in-our-secondary-schools.

Ofsted (2015) *The Most Able Students: An Update on Progress Since June 2013* (March). Ref: 130034. Available at: https://www.gov.uk/government/publications/the-most-able-students-an-update-on-progress-since-june-2013.

Ofsted (2018) *School Inspection Handbook* (September). Ref: 150066. Available at: https://www.gov.uk/government/publications/school-inspection-handbook-from-september-2015.

Ofsted (2019) *School Inspection Handbook* (Draft). Available at: https://assets.publishing.service.gov.uk/government/uploads/system/uploads/attachment_data/file/772065/Schools_draft_handbook_180119.pdf.

Palminteri, Stefano, Kilford, Emma, Coricelli, Giorgio and Blakemore, Sarah-Jayne (2016) The Computational Development of Reinforcement Learning During Adolescence, *PLOS: Computational Biology* 12(6): e1004953. Available at: https://journals.plos.org/ploscompbiol/article?id=10.1371/journal.pcbi.1004953.

Parker, Walter C. (2006) Public Discourses in Schools: Purposes, Problems, Possibilities, *Educational Researcher* 35(8): 11–18.

Pavey, Sarah (2018) Library Lifelines. In Ian Gilbert (ed.), *The Working Class: Poverty, Education and Alternative Voices* (Carmarthen: Independent Thinking Press), pp. 135–137.

Pechmann, Cornelia and Reibling, Ellen Thomas (2000) Anti-Smoking Advertising Campaigns Targeting Youth: Case Studies from USA and Canada. *Tobacco Control* 9(2): ii18–ii31. Available at: https://tobaccocontrol.bmj.com/content/9/suppl_2/ii18.

Powley, Ruth (2013) G&T Teaching and Learning: Nurturing Scholastic Excellence, *Optimus Education* (10 October). Available at: https://my.optimus-education.com/people/ruth-powley.

Quigley, Alex (2012) Oral Formative Feedback: Top 10 Strategies, *The Confident Teacher* (3 November). Available at: https://www.theconfidentteacher.com/2012/11/oral-formative-feedback-top-ten-strategies/.

Quigley, Alex (2013) 'Disciplined Discussion' – As Easy As ABC, *The Confident Teacher* (26 December). Available at: https://www.theconfidentteacher.com/2013/12/disciplined-discussion-easy-abc/.

Quigley, Alex (2015) We Must Expect Magic from Every Student, *TES* (13 February). Available at: https://www.tes.com/news/we-must-expect-magic-every-student-0.

Quigley, Alex (2016) Going Beyond Gifted and Talented, *The Confident Teacher* (6 November). Available at: https://www.theconfidentteacher.com/2016/11/going-beyond-gifted-talented/.

Quigley, Alex (2016) *The Confident Teacher: Developing Successful Habits of Mind, Body and Pedagogy* (Abingdon and New York: Routledge).

Riley, Michael (2018) How the Process of Historical Enquiry Helps to Make School History More Accessible, *EUROCLIO* (24 October). Available at: https://euroclio.eu/resource/how-the-process-of-historical-enquiry-helps-to-make-school-history-more-accessible/.

Roberts, Hywel (2012) *Oops! Helping Children Learn Accidentally* (Carmarthen: Independent Thinking Press).

Robinson, Martin (2013) *Trivium 21c: Preparing Young People for the Future with Lessons from the Past* (Carmarthen: Independent Thinking Press).

Rowntree, Derek (1970) *Learn How to Study: A Guide for Students of All Ages* (London: Warner).

Rosenshine, Barak (2012) Principles of Instruction: Research-Based Strategies That All Teachers Should Know, *American Educator* (spring): 12–19, 39. Available at: https://www.aft.org/sites/default/files/periodicals/Rosenshine.pdf.

Ryan, Will (2018) Rotherham. In Ian Gilbert (ed.), *The Working Class: Poverty, Education and Alternative Voices* (Carmarthen: Independent Thinking Press), pp. 242–256.

Sabisky, Andrew (2015) Five Myths About Intelligence. In David Didau, *What If Everything You Knew About Education Was Wrong?* (Carmarthen: Crown House Publishing), pp. 395–415.

Sherrington, Tom (2012a) Gifted and Talented Provision: A Total Philosophy, *Teacherhead* (12 September). Available at: https://teacherhead.com/2012/09/12/gifted-and-talented-provision-a-total-philosophy/.

Sherrington, Tom (2012b) The 'Washing Hands' of Learning: Think Pair Share, *Teacherhead* (17 July). Available at: https://teacherhead.com/2012/07/17/the-washing-hands-of-learning-think-pair-share/.

Sherrington, Tom (2013) Planning for Co-construction with Year 9, *Teacherhead* (28 August). Available at: https://teacherhead.com/2013/08/28/planning-for-co-construction-with-year-9/.

Sherrington, Tom (2017a) Teaching to the Top: Attitudes and Strategies for Delivering Real Challenge, *Teacherhead* (28 May). Available at: https://teacherhead.com/2017/05/28/teaching-to-the-top-attitudes-and-strategies-for-delivering-real-challenge/.

Sherrington, Tom (2017b) *The Learning Rainforest: Great Teaching in Real Classrooms* (Woodbridge: John Catt Educational).

Sherrington, Tom (2019) *Rosenshine's Principles in Action* (Woodbridge: John Catt Educational).

Singer, Peter (2015 [1975]) *Animal Liberation* (London: Bodley Head).

Smith, Jim (2012) *Follow Me, I'm Right Behind You: Whole School Progress the LAZY Way* (Carmarthen: Independent Thinking Press).

Smithers, Alan and Robinson, Pamela (2012) *Educating the Highly Able* (London: Sutton Trust). Available at: https://www.suttontrust.com/wp-content/uploads/2012/07/Educating-the-Highly-Able-Report.pdf.

Snyder, Steve (2014) The Great Chain of Being, *Grand View University Faculty Pages*. Available at: http://faculty.grandview.edu/ssnyder/121/121%20great%20chain.htm.

Stephen, Martin and Warwick, Ian (2015) *Educating the More Able Student: What Works and Why* (London: SAGE).

Taylor, Becky (2019) The Evidence on Grouping by Attainment: Supporting More Equitable Practice in Schools, *UCL Institute of Education* (18 March). Available at: https://blogs.ucl.ac.uk/grouping-students/.

Thaler, Richard and Sunstein, Cass (2009) *Nudge: Improving Decisions About Health, Wealth and Happiness* (London: Penguin).

Tharby, Andy (2014a) Adventures with Gallery Critique, *Reflecting English* (27 March). Available at: https://reflectingenglish.wordpress.com/2014/03/27/adventures-with-gallery-critique/.

Tharby, Andy (2014b) Closed-Question Quizzing – Unfashionable Yet Effective, *Reflecting English* (9 November). Available at: https://reflectingenglish.wordpress.com/2014/11/09/closed-question-quizzing-unfashionable-yet-effective/.

Tharby, Andy (2016) Another Six Things – Stretching the High Starters, *Class Teaching* (17 May). Available at: https://classteaching.wordpress.com/2016/05/17/another-six-things-stretching-the-high-starters/.

Tharby, Andy (2017a) Content, Thinking and Shaping: Three Principles for Working with Brighter Students, *Reflecting English* (30 January). Available at: https://reflectingenglish.wordpress.com/2017/01/30/content-thinking-and-shaping-three-principles-for-working-with-brighter-students/.

Tharby, Andy (2017b) Creating a Culture for Academic Excellence, *Class Teaching* (11 May). Available at: https://classteaching.wordpress.com/2017/05/11/creating-a-culture-for-academic-excellence/.

Thorne, Sally (2018) *Becoming an Outstanding History Teacher* (Abingdon and New York: Routledge).

Tomsett, John (2015) *This Much I Know About Love Over Fear … Creating a Culture for Truly Great Teaching* (Carmarthen: Crown House Publishing).

Tomsett, John (2016) This Much I Know About … Unfettered Teaching (27 August). Available at: https://johntomsett.com/2016/08/27/this-much-i-know-about-unfettered-teaching/.

Tomsett, John (2017) This Much I Know About … Modelling Deliberate Writing to a Hall Full of More Than One Hundred Year 13 Students (14 February). Available at: https://johntomsett.com/2017/02/14/writing-q4-answers/.

Tricot, André and Sweller, John (2014) Domain-Specific Knowledge and Why Teaching Generic Skills Does Not Work, *Educational Psychology Review* 26(2): 265–283.

Wallace, Belle (2007) *Raising the Achievement of Able, Gifted and Talented Pupils within an Inclusive School Framework* (Oxford: National Association for Able Children in Education and London Gifted & Talented).

Wiliam, Dylan (2001) Reliability, Validity, and All That Jazz, *Education 3–13* 29(3): 17–21.

Wiliam, Dylan (2005) Measuring 'Intelligence': What Can We Learn and How Can We Move Forward? Paper presented at the annual meeting of the American Educational Research Association, Montreal, Canada, April.

Wiliam, Dylan (2009) Content Then Process [video]. Available at: https://www.youtube.com/watch?v=029fSeOaGio.

Wiliam, Dylan (2011) What is Assessment for Learning?, *Studies in Educational Evaluation* 37(1): 3–14.

Wiliam, Dylan (2014) The Formative Evaluation of Teacher Performance. Occasional Paper No. 137 (Melbourne, VIC: Centre for Strategic Education).

Wiliam, Dylan (2015) 10 Feedback Techniques That Make Students Think. Available at: https://www.dylanwiliamcenter.com/wp-content/uploads/2015/02/10-Feedback-Techniques.pdf.

Wiliam, Dylan (2016) *Leadership for Teacher Learning* (West Palm Beach, FL: Learning Sciences International).

Wiliam, Dylan (2018) *Creating the Schools Our Children Need: Why What We're Doing Now Won't Help Much (And What We Can Do Instead)* (West Palm Beach, FL: Learning Sciences International).

Wiliam, Dylan and Bartholomew, Hannah (2004) It's Not Which School but Which Set You're in That Matters: The Influence of Ability-Grouping Practices on Student Progress in Mathematics, *British Educational Research Journal* 30(2): 279–239. Available at: https://www.growthmindsetmaths.com/uploads/2/3/7/7/23776169/wiliam2001berapaper.pdf.

Wilshaw, Michael (2016) HMCI's Commentary: Most Able Pupils (June). Available at: https://www.gov.uk/government/speeches/hmcis-monthly-commentary-june-2016.

Willingham, Daniel (2009) *Why Don't Students Like School? A Cognitive Scientist Answers Questions About How the Mind Works and What It Means for the Classroom* (San Francisco, CA: Jossey-Bass).

Woollett, Katherine and Maguire, Eleanor A. (2011) Acquiring 'the Knowledge' of London's Layout Drives Structural Brain Changes, *Current Biology* 21 (24): 2109–2114.